Poetry & Translation

Poetry & Translation

The Art of the Impossible

Peter Robinson

LIVERPOOL UNIVERSITY PRESS

First published 2010 by
Liverpool University Press
4 Cambridge Street
Liverpool
L69 7ZU

British Library Cataloguing-in-Publication data

A British Library CIP record is available

ISBN 978-184631-218-2 cased

Typeset by Carnegie Book Production, Lancaster
Printed in Great Britain by the MPG Books Group, Bodmin and King's Lynn

For Ornella, Matilde and Giulia

Contents

Preface

When Ralph Pite and Deryn Rees-Jones invited me to write this book for their series, I was concluding a lengthy period of translating work, which resulted in the publication of *The Selected Poetry and Prose of Vittorio Sereni* (University of Chicago Press, 2006) and *The Greener Meadow: Selected Poems of Luciano Erba* (Princeton University Press, 2007). Both of these volumes were produced with the operative assumption that it was the aim in translating poetry to be faithfully accurate and to make translations that read well as poems in their own right. This dual aim was alluded to in the prefatory matter to both books and its implications were sketched in the Translator's Preface to the second. *Poetry & Translation: The Art of the Impossible* is ancillary to this work in attempting to lay bare (within the allotted space) interrelated ideas and principles about, critical responses to, and reflections on translating, that lie behind the apparently simple aim expressed and, to the best of my abilities, carried out in those collections of translated poetry — as they also were in *L'attaccapanni e altre poesie*, a collection of my own poems rendered into Italian in collaboration with my wife and published by Moretti & Vitali in 2004.

The first of these ideas is the all-but-universal assumption, most memorably voiced by Robert Frost, that poetry is what is lost in translation. One point of my subtitle is to underline that there is no point arguing against this near cliché in its own terms. Rather, I spend time exploring what those terms are, illustrating them in various versions and imitations, and examining the symbiotic relationship between this warranted assertion and exorbitant claims to creative freedoms made by some poets when rendering from other languages, claims dependent on the theory of loss for their methods' legitimacy. Yet to accept Frost's aphorism and go on translating, or to read translations, with their originals or alone, is to fall into inconsistency or accept a great gulf between theoretical preciseness and incoherent practice. One aim of this book has been not merely to explore aspects of this apparent paradox, but to dissolve it.

The Art of the Impossible aims to increase knowledge of, and thought about, the interactive processes of reading and writing poetry composed in mother tongues and in translation. Its seven brief chapters cannot pretend to exhaustive treatments or exemplifications of their subjects. Issues and topics are raised for discussion, not to close them down. Yet I have a case to make, and hope to frame it by keeping open the debate. To this end, the first chapter considers the importance for poets of reading translations from works whose originals they cannot access. Chapters 2 to 4 address the noted paradox that good translators of poetry are adepts at doing the impossible. The chapters 5 to 7 explore larger ramifications of poetry and translation in relation to world literature, the stubborn survival of the 'foreign', and the ethics of translating from the living and the dead.

This short book does not have the space to consider poetic influence where such levels of wholesale rewriting take place that local similarities between an original and a rendering of it in another language cannot be tracked. Nor is there space to explore translation between artistic media, or translated influence subsumed in autonomous work. Although this book offers a view of the translator-poet's tasks and roles, it does not begin to imagine that mine is the only view, or the best for all practitioners of this art. A variety of modes and styles are discussed for translating from languages which I have some knowledge of, and, since this is also part of the field for everyone, from languages I don't know. There are examples of critical appreciation devoted to translations, and competing translations, where I am familiar with the source language, as well as cases where I am reading the translation as a poem standing alone, because unable to respond to its original, while nevertheless remaining conscious of its necessary existence. I have not been able always to cite the originals of texts given here in translation. Original sources are, where possible, provided in notes.

A few brief sections of this book have appeared in different forms. Chapter 3 is a rewritten enlargement of an essay that appeared in *Agenda* vol. 42 nos. 3-4 (Spring 2007), composed while I was beginning to ponder what would go into this book. The issue addressed in the sixth chapter came to me while reviewing David Constantine's lectures, *The Living Language*, in *Poetry Ireland Review* 86, May 2006. The section on Vittorio Sereni's translation of Ezra Pound's 'Villanelle: The Psychological Hour' (long pondered in relation to a study of the original that appears in *Twentieth Century Poetry: Selves and Situations*) was first presented at a September 2004 conference on Poetry and Translation organized by Daniela Caselli and Daniela La Penna in London, and subsequently published in *Agenda* vol. 41 nos. 3-4, Autumn-Winter 2005.

Conversations with a number of my new colleagues at the University of Reading have been invaluable, and among them I would like to acknowledge the support and stimulus of talking to Simon Dentith,

Alison Donnell, Daniela La Penna, Andrew Nash, and Peter Stoneley. My knowledge of languages is nothing to boast about, and could be summed up by William Empson's line from his 'Aubade': 'The language problem but you have to try.' I am grateful to all those more linguistically gifted people who, whether now living or dead, have helped me over the years. Among them, I warmly thank Luciano and Mimia Erba, Franco Fortini, Christine Tweddle Garzón, Fumiko Horikawa, Nicole Ward Jouve, Marcus Perryman, John Pilling, Vittorio Sereni, Maria Teresa Chiari-Sereni, and my wife Ornella Trevisan.

Peter Robinson
30 June 2009

CHAPTER 1

On First Looking

I

When, between dawn and about nine o'clock one October morning in 1816, John Keats composed 'On First Looking into Chapman's Homer', he had parted from a night of poetic enthusiasm spent with his friend Charles Cowden Clarke in Clerkenwell. They had been looking into and reading out passages from a ca. 1614 edition of George Chapman's translation of the *Iliad* and *Odyssey*, which had been borrowed from Thomas Alsager (a friend of Leigh Hunt's) by Cowden Clarke: 'and to work we went, turning to some of the "famousest" passages, as we had scrappily known them in Pope's version'.[1] Cowden Clarke recalled the effect on Keats of lines from *Homer's Odysses* that describe the hero being washed on shore and, in particular, the phrase 'The sea had soakt his heart through' which produced 'one of his delighted stares':

> Then forth he came, his both knees faltring, both
> His strong hands hanging downe, and all with froth
> His cheeks and nosthrils flowing, voice and breath
> Spent to all use; and downe he sunke to Death.
> The sea had soakt his heart through: all his vaines
> His toiles had rackt t'a labouring woman's paines.
> Dead wearie was he.[2]

Cowden Clarke's word 'stares' may have been suggested not only by his friend's behaviour but also as analogous with the experience in the sonnet Keats sent to Clerkenwell in time for it to be read at a ten o'clock breakfast that following morning, the poem in which, in the famous confusion

---

[1] Charles and Mary Cowden Clarke, *Recollections of Writers* (London, 1878), pp. 128–30, cited in John Keats, *The Collected Poems*, ed. Miriam Allott (London: Longmans, 1970), p. 60.

[2] George Chapman, The Fifth Booke, ll. 608-14, *Chapman's Homer*, 2 vols., ed. Allardyce Nicoll (London: Routledge & Kegan Paul, 1957), ii, p. 102.

of conquistadors, stout Cortez 'stared at the Pacific'. Chapman's passage registered deeply with the poet, and four years later he wrote to Benjamin Haydon: 'At some future time I shall re borrow your Homer.'[3] 'The sea had soakt his heart through' lines may further have subliminally contributed to the sonnet Keats wrote when taking ship himself in the autumn of 1820, in which the compulsory 'breath' and 'death' rhyme is used, and the concluding phrase, also of five monosyllables, has the same two final words prefixed with a similarly sibilant verb — 'and down he sunke to Death' re-emerging as 'or else swoon to death.'[4]

Here, then, is a now classic instance of a young author finding his way to the composition of a poem that, in Leigh Hunt's words, 'announced the new poet taking possession',[5] a sonnet almost immediately published by Hunt in the *Examiner* on 1 December 1816. One of Keats's editors has described it as 'significant' that he 'and most of his contemporaries (though not Byron) should have favoured this translation and not the more recent one by Pope.'[6] It's only fair, though, not to overlook the role this other translator played in showing the two friends where in Chapman they should first explore — at 'some of the "famousest" passages, as we had scrappily known them in Pope's version' of *The Odyssey*:

> That moment, fainting as he touch'd the shore,
> He dropt his sinewy arms: his knees no more
> Perform'd their office, or his weight upheld:
> His swoln heart heav'd; his bloated body swell'd:
> From mouth and nose the briny torrent ran;
> And lost in lassitude lay all the man,
> Depriv'd of voice, of motion, and of breath;
> The soul scarce waking, in the arms of death.[7]

For Keats in 'On First Looking into Chapman's Homer' the issue is not so much the Homeric style, which he couldn't access in its original Greek, but the recovery of an Elizabethan vigour ('loud and bold') before the more familiarly civilized sounds of Augustan heroic couplets. It might even be thought that Pope's 'the arms of death' is makeshift, and that the inert syntactic parallel ('of breath ... of death') further weakens his close. An exploration of what contemporary poetry should then sound like was being conducted around competing translation styles. David Constantine notes that the sonnet Keats wrote in the early hours of the morning exemplifies the good a translation can do for 'a poet on the threshold of

---

[3] Maurice Buxton Forman (ed.), *The Letters of John Keats*, 4th edn. (London: Oxford University Press, 1952), p. 513.

[4] John Keats, *The Complete Poems*, ed. John Barnard, 3rd edn. (Harmondsworth: Penguin Books, 1988), p. 452.

[5] Leigh Hunt, *Lord Byron and Some of His Contemporaries* (London, 1828), p. 248.

[6] Elizabeth Cook (ed.), *John Keats* (Oxford: Oxford University Press, 1990), p. 563.

[7] Alexander Pope, book 5, ll. 580-87, in *The Odyssey of Homer*, ed. Maynard Mack (London: Methuen, 1967), p. 200.

coming fully into his gifts' and adds: 'Pope's version of Homer could not have done that. It needed the recovery of something by then already archaic ("rough-hewn doric", in Clarke's phrase) for the full novelty of the thing to be brought, with the shock of the foreign, into the present where it could live and work.'[8] This is doubtless true. Yet since both Pope and Chapman are translating Homer, it can't quite be the 'shock of the foreign' that is inspiring Keats, but a further vivid encounter with a pre-Augustan English version of 'the foreign' at a remove.

The surviving manuscript draft of 'On First Looking into Chapman's Homer' has variants from the published text, but comparison appears to show the poem coming 'as naturally as the Leaves to a tree', which Keats claimed he needed, or 'it had better not come at all':[9]

> Much have I travelled in the realms of gold,
>   And many goodly states and kingdoms seen;
>   Round many western islands have I been
> Which bards in fealty to Apollo hold.
> Oft of one wide expanse had I been told
>   That deep-browed Homer ruled as his demesne;
>   Yet did I never breathe its pure serene
> Till I heard Chapman speak out loud and bold:
> Then felt I like some watcher of the skies
>   When a new planet swims into his ken;
> Or like stout Cortez when with eagle eyes
>   He stared at the Pacific — and all his men
> Looked at each other with a wild surmise —
>   Silent, upon a peak in Darien.[10]

Though Helen Vendler writes that Keats 'describes the effect of reading Homer',[11] she quickly notes his not knowing Greek, momentarily appearing to overlook that it's Chapman who is heard to 'speak out loud and bold'. The sonnet evokes the experience of glimpsing something vast that, for the moment at least, he cannot go further towards. Explicating the simile at the close in which Cortez is there 'with all his men', Vendler generously adds: 'One makes literary discoveries not alone, but as a member of a trans-historical cultural company of writers, readers, and translators.'[12] Andrew Motion, who reproduces a manuscript copy of the poem in his biography, believes that the marks in the right margin indicating the rhyme scheme for an Italian octave were put there before he composed the poem: 'He was tired, and even though he had used the Petrarchan form during the summer, he reminded himself of the rhyme scheme by jotting it down

---

[8] David Constantine, 'Translation Is Good for You', *A Living Language: Newcastle/ Bloodaxe Poetry Lectures* (Tarset: Bloodaxe, 2004), p. 9.

[9] Keats, *Letters*, 27 February 1818.

[10] Keats, *The Complete Poems*, p. 72.

[11] Helen Vendler, *Coming of Age as a Poet: Milton, Keats, Eliot, Plath* (Cambridge, MA: Harvard University Press, 2003), p. 52.

[12] Ibid. p. 55.

in the right-hand margin.'[13] These lines, though, since they fit the varied vertical spacing of the handwritten lines, would appear to have been scratched in *after* the writing had been completed, and may not be in the same hand. Yet his observation is a reminder that the sonnet form in which Keats composed his poem is itself a translation from the Italian, as can be heard not only in the form's name, but in the names for its parts: the octave, volta, and sestet. Motion proposes that the poem, 'for all its wonderfully bold energy, succumbs to a moment of awkward translationese ("pure serene") which creates a sense of Keats standing apart from the main event.'[14] Thomas Hardy was closer when suggesting to Amy Lowell on 6 March 1925 that 'pure serene' was 'an unconscious memory of the line in Gray's Elegy ending, "purest ray serene"'.[15] Even if the sonnet betrays uncertainty of education and compositional skill, it was not a partly bungled act of *arrivisme* when Keats wrote the work for his friend, and by succumbing to the lure of poetic convention derived from Gray (but not translationese, since he is neither translating, nor working outside poetic codes of the time), the poet does not let his guard slip.[16]

Still, his poem *is* about 'standing apart from the main event' — the main event in the sestet's closing simile being the Pacific Ocean, or, reading the metaphor, the works of Homer and, through them, the realms of poetry. Keats's sonnet doesn't *betray* a sense that it is standing on the edge of something much larger; it is frankly and candidly *about* that feeling. It's a good poem on looking into a translation because it acknowledges both the further stretch of imagination required in reading translations, and the simultaneous and unavoidable sense of being excluded that this imaginative activity underlines. Robert Frost notes such exclusion as part of his stance against the translatability of poetry, which I consider in more detail in the next chapter. He writes: 'no translation of poetry will do: practically any book in any but your own language or languages is a closed book.'[17] Yet Frost's polemical position serves not only to underline the impossibility of translating poetry, but also its necessity. Keats was not much of a linguist, and in this he is closer to the norm of English language poets than, say, Vladimir Nabokov. This being the case, if poets such as Keats are to have a rumour or an echo of what may be contained in those closed books that Frost speaks of, then they will be entirely dependent on translators. It will make a significant cultural difference if the translator happens to be (and this may vary with the moment and its needs) a Chapman or a Pope.

[13] Andrew Motion, *Keats* (London: Faber & Faber, 1997), p. 109.

[14] Ibid. p. 112.

[15] Thomas Hardy, *The Collected Letters*, 7 vols., ed. Richard L. Purdy and Michael Millgate (Oxford: Oxford University Press, 1978-87), vi, p. 313.

[16] See my *Poetry, Poets, Readers: Making Things Happen* (Oxford: Oxford University Press, 2002), pp. 99-102.

[17] Robert Frost, 'Contribution to 25th Anniversary Bread Loaf Booklet' (1944), *The Collected Prose of Robert Frost*, ed. Mark Richardson (Cambridge, MA: Harvard University Press, 2008), p. 143.

Keats's sonnet has been deservedly annotated and discussed at length, but what I should like to underline is that the poem plainly addresses its extremely limited knowledge of Homer, the role rumour and repute play in the promptings of imagination, and, most of all, the activated contrast between speaking out and being silenced by awe. The relationship between a translation and an original is, in this light, aptly analogous to that between a young writer and a classic. This may be one reason why translations can so encourage poets: they often represent the encountering of an inspirational original that someone has chosen to translate with a craftsman-like effort to bring it to the reader. This craft-based art allows the poet-reader to envisage emulation within the dynamics of the impossible and awe-inspiring original through a plausibly achieved rendering of it. Frost's idea that 'there should always be a lingering unhappiness in reading translations'[18] can then serve the reading poet as the germ of an urge both to write poems, ones which will not produce such 'lingering unhappiness', and, if so inclined, to attempt translations of the same inspiring originals that might produce less of it.

If Keats had followed to the letter the closed-book attitude to poetry in translation that Frost was to champion, he could not have written his breakthrough early poem 'On First Looking into Chapman's Homer'. In the light of the discussion of impossibility in the following chapters, let me assert that the issue in discussing a translated poem cannot be *that* it diverges from its original, but *how* it diverges — and, in diverging, what relationships, kinds and qualities, it sustains, or downplays, in relations with its source text. These are relationships that can be explored if the reader has a reasonable degree of access to that source text, and, in the course of subsequent chapters, there will be instances of such relationships explored in detail. The subject of this introductory approach, though, is the role that may be played for poets by translations from languages that they themselves either cannot read, or cannot read sufficiently to manage without assistance. In the foreword to his *Adaptations*, Derek Mahon notes how some insist 'that the impersonation in English of poems from other tongues should be confined to those with a working knowledge of Greek or Russian, as the case may be — or indeed Spanish, Hebrew, Arabic, Ibo, Hindu or Chinese. (None of these last, unfortunately, are represented here).'[19] As Mahon's sentence both demonstrates and implies, the languages that poets are likely to be able to access will themselves tell a story of historical and cultural specificity. If Keats had gone to university he would probably have been able to read Greek, and might not have felt the need to consult Chapman's translation at all.

---

[18] Frost, 'Poetry and School' (1951), *The Collected Prose of Robert Frost*, p. 167.
[19] Derek Mahon, *Adaptations* (Oldcastle, Co. Meath: Gallery Books, 2006), p. 11.

II

Although Chapman introduced Keats to 'one wide expanse' that 'deep-browed Homer ruled as his demesne', the ancient Greek poet's territory (in this English rendering) had already been made relatively familiar to the young poet. When he first looked into Chapman's translation he had encountered the 'western islands' of Spenser and Shakespeare, contemporaries of Chapman who had prepared him for its Elizabethan energies. Part of what made it 'speak out loud and bold' was its relative familiarity, for in the original Greek it would not have spoken out at all. The impact of a translation requires, and derives from, such combinations of the unexpectedly surprising and the fairly familiar. A measure of discussion concerning translation argues over the relative values and roles for these aspects: the shock of the new, and the conceptual frames of the known. I turn now to relations between the strange and the recognizable in translations from languages where, like Keats with Homer, no attempt can be made to compare translation with original, and begin with William Empson's 'Chinese Ballad', a work whose source is also, in Frost's sense, a closed book both to its translator and to me.

The derivation of Empson's poem and its writing, in Peking probably during early 1952, have been noted by John Haffenden, who cites the poet-translator as saying: 'I burst into tears when I found it just fell into international ballad metre', and elsewhere of its 'falling straight into English ballad style'.[20] I assume his were tears of joy, for the poet also states that he was 'delighted' that this should happen. Empson tells us he was given an explanation of all the Chinese characters. In casting the sense as rhythm, he heard his lines as at first more approximately, then rigorously, shaping themselves into the eight syllables followed by the six of the ballad stanza, and found for it the even-numbered-line rhymes of an ABCA quatrain:

> Now he has seen the girl Hsiang-Hsiang,
> > Now back to the guerilla band;
> And she goes with him down the vale
> > And pauses at the strand.

We can hear this ambiguously beginning to happen in the first verse, because, although it may be scanned as a three-stress line, Empson's second 'Now back to the guerilla band' has eight syllables, matching his line 1. Is his stanza the tetrameter quatrain used to translate Horace, for some eighteenth-century hymns, and for Samuel Johnson's 'On the Death of Dr Robert Levett', or is it that of the literary ballad, brought to prominence with Wordsworth and Coleridge's *Lyrical Ballads*? Or is it a quatrain formed of three tetrameters followed by a trimeter? Empson's second verse approximates to this third possibility:

[20] William Empson, *The Complete Poems*, ed. John Haffenden (Harmondsworth: Allen Lane, 2000), p. 401.

The mud is yellow, deep, and thick,
    And their feet stick, where the stream turns.
'Make two models out of this,
    That clutches as it yearns.[21]

Here line 2 reverses its rhythmic impetus at a caesura strongly marked by the internal rhyme, which itself sticks the poem's feet in the thick mud, and by the matching spondees 'feet stick' and 'stream turns'. This eight-syllable second line, too, can be construed as having three stresses. Empson was at pains to note that the young couple part at this river, and the partisan is crossing where it turns because it is shallower at that point. What he doesn't say is that, aside from the formal allusions of its quatrain, he has established the timbre of his poem by means of two detectable auditory echoes. The first verse lightly recalls Dr Johnson's parody of Bishop Percy's *Hermit of Warkworth*: 'I put my hat upon my head / And walk'd into the Strand, / And there I met another man / Whose hat was in his hand.'[22] This 'Strand' comically locates the tones of a rural ballad at the heart of London. Empson returns the joke to its original context (in London's history as well, for the Strand runs beside the river Thames). Yet, by means of this allusion, Empson has introduced a gently distancing note into the first verse, a note that both alerts us to the pastoral simplicity of the situation, and detaches the poem from it by means of this literary self-consciousness. The translation is thus as if in invisible quotation marks, and the young woman's speech that concludes it becomes, as it were, a quoted quotation. Empson's tears might well have been from the joy of finding himself composing within the terms of the 'Proletarian Literature' chapter of his literary critical classic *Some Versions of Pastoral* (1935).[23]

The first line of his verse 2 sounds as if based on Frost's opening line to the final stanza of 'Stopping by Woods on a Snowy Evening'. For 'The woods are lovely, dark, and deep',[24] Empson (perhaps prompted by the near rhyme of 'woods' and 'mud', and the matching adjective 'deep') has 'The mud is yellow, deep, and thick', echoing its form, syntax, and even punctuation. While the echo in the first verse signals a range of ambivalences that Empson had laboured to reveal in his second book of criticism, the allusion in the second draws attention to the fateful situation in which this is happening. Frost's slowed line is the point in his poem where the lure of death is at its strongest, and the poem is drawn towards it, only to veer away into social responsibilities (related in the poem to the matter of keeping promises). Something similar is true of Empson's translation. The

---

[21] Ibid. p. 103.
[22] Samuel Johnson, *The Complete English Poems*, ed. J. D. Fleeman (Harmondsworth: Penguin Books, 1971), p. 128.
[23] Empson mentions the Border ballads and links them to both proletarian art and pastoral in *Some Versions of Pastoral* (London: Chatto & Windus, 1935), p. 6.
[24] Robert Frost, *Collected Poems, Prose, & Plays*, ed. Richard Poirier and Mark Richardson (New York: Library of America, 1995), p. 207.

young Chinese couple pause before parting at the river. He will go back to his 'guerilla band' to fight the Japanese (a point Empson makes in his note). Will he survive the coming danger of death? She has him go through an ancient ritual symbolically making them one flesh. He will return, and they will be able to have children.

At the end of the second verse, the young woman starts talking. Empson's translation has the interrupting structure of Wordsworth's 'The Sailor's Mother' in which, after a description bringing together the protagonists, her words complete the poem. Now unambiguous ballad stanzas alternate lines of eight and six, tetrameters followed by trimeters. 'Make two models out of this,' she says, 'That clutches as it yearns.'

> 'Make one of me and one of you,
>   And both shall be alive.
> Were there no magic in the dolls
>   The children would not thrive.
>
> 'When you have made them smash them back:
>   They yet shall live again.
> Again make dolls of you and me
>   But mix them grain by grain.
>
> 'So your flesh shall be part of mine
>   And part of mine be yours.
> Brother and sister we shall be
>   Whose unity endures.
>
> 'Always the sister doll will cry,
>   Made in these careful ways,
> Cry on and on, Come back to me,
>   Come back, in a few days.'[25]

Empson's translation also works like Tennyson's 'Marianna' or 'Ulysses', poems made from longer stories in which we are not told what the outcome of the pausing or departing situation will be. There appears to be a doubt, however, as to whether Empson knew the whole story from which his incident had been extracted. He may not have quite caught this implication when associating his work with another kind of poem that exercised both his creative and critical intelligence: 'I think, in this ballad, it is very fine metaphysical poetry at the end, when the clumsy little doll is to wait, through all eternity, just for a few days'.[26] So the translator brings his work into the ambit of John Donne's: 'A Valediction: forbidding Mourning':

> Our two souls therefore, which are one,
>   Though I must go, endure not yet
> A breach, but an expansion,
>   Like gold to aery thinness beat.

---

[25] Empson, *The Complete Poems*, p. 103.
[26] Ibid. p. 400.

If they be two, they are two so
   As stiff twin compasses are two,
Thy soul the fixed foot, makes no show
To move, but doth, if th'other do.[27]

Donne's title sounds like his poem will be about a death, even though the metaphor proves them united for eternity. The fear that the couple will never be reunited is fended off in Donne's poem of parting by the metaphysical conceit, in Empson's translation by the doll superstition. Donne was to return from his 1611 visit to France with Sir Robert Drury, and the Chinese lovers are reunited in their narrative poem. They don't wait for all eternity. Just as in *Measure for Measure* Marianna is rescued from the moated grange, and, conversely, in *Inferno* Canto XXVI Ulysses is drowned, so too in the narrative poem from which Empson's translation is an excerpt, we discover (thanks once more to Haffenden's notes) whether Hsiang-Hsiang's lover returns from the wars. Empson's editor summarizes the outcome of Li Chi's narrative poem *Wang Kuei and Li Hsiang-Hsiang*: 'After suffering years of oppression from Landlord Tsui, who mercilessly tortures Wang Kuei, the peasant lovers find common cause in their country's need to repel the Japanese invader; they reap their reward when the Red Army liberates the rural communities, whereupon Landlord Tsui is taken away for punishment.'[28] Though the propagandistic message of this is evident, 'their reward' presumably means that they can be reunited and have children.

Empson insisted that the translation was faithful to the meaning of the original, as here in a sentence from the Note he published in his *Collected Poems*: 'The translation is word for word, so far as I can know from simply being given the meanings of the characters; I added the bit about children, but I understand that is only like working a footnote into the text, because the term specifically means dolls for children.'[29] These must be the interpolated lines: 'Were there no magic in the dolls / The children would not thrive.' Empson's comments can only be approximate. There has also likely been some paraphrasing and condensing in his 'word for word'.[30] As his poem is a translation made by selecting a passage from a longer work, he is not translating the implications of the passage in context, as Haffenden also notes. This increases the literary quality of the piece (in the receiver culture's terms), by lessening the original's overt propaganda — something Empson need not have been consciously doing, since he may not have known the whole context.

[27] John Donne, *The Complete English Poems*, ed. A. J. Smith (Harmondsworth: Penguin Books, 1971), p. 84.

[28] William Empson, *The Complete Poems*, p. 401.

[29] Ibid. p. 400.

[30] For Empson on the need to condense when translating, see his letter to Chiyoko Hatakeyama cited in John Haffenden, *William Empson: Among the Mandarins* (Oxford: Oxford University Press, 2005), pp. 338–39 and 340–41. See also my 'C. Hatakeyama and W. E.' in *Versions of Empson*, ed. Matthew Bevis (Oxford: Oxford University Press, 2007), pp. 60–83.

The poet-translator notes that 'This bit was considered technically interesting because the theme had been used in classical style, first, I am told, by the Yuan poet Chao Meng-fu, and was now transposed or restored into popular style.'[31] 'Chinese Ballad', itself transposing and restoring, is a necessary mixture of the strange (Li Chi alluding to Chao Meng-fu) and the more familiar (Empson alluding to Donne, Johnson, and Frost). Translation has to be like this in order for it both to bring something over, and for it to be something that is brought over. Nor can the contribution to this translation of the British literary ballad tradition be underestimated. The extraordinarily moving close is produced by the repetitions of 'cry' and 'come back', helping create a sense of desperation or doubt, which is both confirmed by the closing rhyme, and magically contradicted, perhaps, by the emphatic spondaic pair 'few days' rhyming both with and against the standard iambic '-ful ways'. The poem's close freezes the situation in a state of perpetual yearning, yet with an underlined promise of permanent union.[32]

III

Empson's 'Chinese Ballad' hardly produces the disappointment that Frost states we should feel when reading a translation. It appears both a reasonably faithful attempt at the original, and a poem that is extraordinarily successful in its own right. The reasons for this success are not distinct from the traditional means that he adapts to his task, and these means, as referred to in the commentary above, also point to ways that English poetic techniques are intimate with translation: *spondees* and *iambs* are Greek names for quantitative measures adapted to the accentual patterns of spoken English; the tetrameter and trimeter lines of the ballad stanza are numbered using Greek and Latin prefixes; while the familiar word 'rhyme' has antecedents in French and Italian. 'Chinese Ballad' is another poem that many of us, including its translator, could never access in the original. Our exposure to it is entirely dependent upon the efforts of a poet-critic deploying both his creative skills and his knowledge of his own traditions to bring the poem to readers who do not have the language. It is one instance of a widely evident and increasing phenomenon in twentieth- and twenty-first-century poetry. Among the most admired and influential of poets in recent decades have been C. P. Cavafy, Rainer Maria Rilke, Osip Mandelstam, Fernando Pessoa, and Pablo Neruda. These are poets whose works can be found, at a remove, in competing translations, and, in at least three cases, poets writing in languages that have never been widely available as optional subjects in British schools.

[31] Empson, *The Complete Poems*, p. 400.
[32] See Christopher Ricks, 'William Empson: The Images and the Story', in *The Force of Poetry* (Oxford: Oxford University Press, 1984), pp. 241–43.

One backhanded compliment to such an interest in poetry from other cultures is its disavowal. In 1964 Ian Hamilton asked Philip Larkin: 'I wonder if you read much foreign poetry?' To which the poet replied: '*Foreign poetry? No!*'[33] Larkin might just be raising his eyebrows at Hamilton's faintly blimpish use of the word 'foreign' here, but more likely he's leaping on it to strike an attitude. This poet's lack of interest in poetry from other languages has never been wholly convincing. As early as 1955, in his *Times Literary Supplement* review of *The Less Deceived*, the distinguished poet-translator Michael Hamburger noted Larkin's debt to Baudelaire.[34] Publishing the 1943 poem '*Femmes Damnées*', Larkin admitted it showed he had 'read at least one "foreign poem"'. His 'at least' gives the game away, and Barbara Everett has both examined Larkin's debts to the French Symbolist poets, and defended his misleading reply to Hamilton.[35] Yet there is ample evidence of Larkin's resistance to the multiplied views of the world that an interest in languages will likely encourage:

> Foreigners' ideas of good English poems are dreadfully crude: Byron and Poe and so on. The Russians like Burns. But deep down I think foreign languages irrelevant. If that glass thing over there is a window, then it isn't a *Fenster* or a *fenêtre* or whatever. *Hautes Fenêtres*, my God! A writer can have only one language, if that language is going to mean anything to him.'[36]

Larkin's ideas about what people from other countries think about English poems is itself dreadfully crude, and his inclusion of Poe and Burns among English poems is confusing sides of the Atlantic, and both linguistically and nationally not quite precise either. Equally, not only does he give away the fact that he can translate the title of his 1974 collection *High Windows* into French (and could have done it into German too), he implies — without acknowledging it — the fact that the 'glass thing over there' isn't 'a window'. It is whatever it can be communicatively called in the world's array of spoken tongues.

Nevertheless, his final sentence felt true for him: 'A writer can have only one language, if that language is going to mean anything to him.' Larkin, in this respect, is close to the Frost who thought that 'there should always be a

---

[33] Ian Hamilton, 'Four Conversations', *London Magazine* vol. 4 no. 8, November 1964 and collected in Philip Larkin, *Further Requirements: Interviews, Broadcasts, Statements and Books Reviews* ed. Anthony Thwaite (London: Faber & Faber, 2001), p. 25.

[34] Michael Hamburger (anonymously), 'Poetic Moods', *Times Literary Supplement* no. 2807, 16 December 1955, p. 762.

[35] Cited in Andrew Motion, *Philip Larkin: A Writer's Life* (London: Faber & Faber, 1993), p. 73. See Barbara Everett, *Poets in Their Time: Essays on English Poetry from Donne to Larkin* (London: Faber & Faber, 1986), pp. 238–40. I discussed the matter at greater length in 'Philip Larkin: Here and There', *Review of English Literature* (Kyoto) vol. 59 (March 1990), pp. 3–8.

[36] Philip Larkin, 'An Interview with *Paris Review*', *Required Writing: Miscellaneous Pieces 1955–1982* (London: Faber & Faber, 1983), p. 69.

lingering unhappiness in reading translations'.[37] Now does the 'unhappiness' in reading a translated poem have to be an insignificant experience? Can it not access unexpectedly expressive felicities? Larkin's near contemporary, the poet and novelist Mairi MacInnes, has a poem called 'Reading Cavafy in Translation':

> He would never have liked me,
> A woman who's ample and hopeful and hardworking,
> Bothered by sentiment, neither stylish nor austere.
> Yet the loveless cadences of his translation
> Warm me like an old friend from the capital
> Met by chance on a provincial street.[38]

Like Keats's poem on looking into a translation of Homer, MacInnes's admits to not knowing the language from which her author has been translated. Her poem is also written, as an analogous act of homage, in the style of a Cavafy translation, such as the opening of his 'Finished': 'Deep in fear and in suspicions, / with troubled mind and frightened eyes, / we scheme away and fret at what to do'.[39] Arriving in Port Said on 16 May 1941, George Seferis couldn't help recalling his great predecessor: 'I think of Cavafy, as I inspect this low-lying land. His poetry is like that too; as prosaic as the endless plain before us. It has no rise and fall; it goes at a walking pace. I understand Cavafy better now'.[40]

Imitating translations of such a low-keyed address, MacInnes's lines often conclude in polysyllabic words with unrhymed and unstressed syllables: 'hardworking', 'translation', 'capital', and 'civilization'. Her poem too has its prosaic and loveless cadences, for the expression of an attraction towards, and blank acknowledgement of, what she calls his 'fortunate life':

> His observations are witty and precise.
> Like good stones in a jeweller's window
> They give out fire.
> They are the bounty of a fortunate life.
> I understood too that the original contains
> A familiar sadness about the civilization
> Falling away behind us, and a dry contempt
> For our inept love of the present,
> That flares sometimes, like beacons before Armada.[41]

Not only is the poem about reading a poet in translation, it reads as if

---

[37] Frost, 'Poetry and School' (1951), *The Collected Prose of Robert Frost*, p. 167.

[38] Mairi MacInnes, *The Girl I Left Behind Me: Poems of a Lifetime* (Nottingham: Shoestring Press, 2007), p. 34.

[39] C. P. Cavafy, *The Collected Poems*, trans. Evangelos Sachperoglou, Greek text ed. Anthony Hirst, introduction by Peter Mackridge (Oxford: Oxford University Press, 2007), p. 33.

[40] George Seferis, *A Levant Journal*, trans. Roderick Beaton (Jerusalem: Ibis Editions, 2007), p. 7.

[41] MacInnes, *The Girl I Left Behind Me*, p. 34.

it had been translated from another language. Its sense of loss in life is expressed in a language of loss that has been associated by many with poetry in translation. Elizabeth Bishop identified at the time of his death Dylan Thomas's gift 'for a kind of naked communication that makes a lot of poetry look like translation.'[42] This can be sensed in MacInnes's not using end-rhyme, in her seeming to summarize or paraphrase a set of feelings that are not enacted but referred to, and in the snatched-at similes, not metaphors, which don't themselves quite integrate with each other: the precious stones and the Armada beacons. Her poem concludes: 'A clever fellow, he'd be amused to see me mourn / The sky's slow clouding over / And my loss of the good to come.'[43] MacInnes's poem borrows the style of Cavafy so as lightly to mock her own mournfulness, with a refusal to compensate for it in a more buoyant, rhyming style that might appear a consolation in its textures for the sense of loss she outlines. Her method is to use the limitations of translationese as a means for catching a sense of diminishment in a life.

The disillusioned poetic devices produce their own coherently flattened emotion. MacInnes writes of how Cavafy's 'observations are witty and precise./ Like good stones in a jeweller's window / They give out fire.' In his 'Crise de vers', Stéphane Mallarmé deploys a similar image in his comment on the emergence of a new kind of poetry: 'The pure work of art implies the elocutionary disappearance of the poet who yields the initiative to words, set in motion by the clash of their inequalities; they illuminate each other with reciprocal lights like a virtual trail of fire on precious stones'.[44] Yet where Mallarmé's simile is about the 'fire' given out by collocated words, MacInnes's refers to the poet's 'observations' — as if contradicting the same poet's famous rebuke to Degas that poems are not made with ideas but words.[45] What this raises is the possibility that Cavafy's poetry may translate more than, say, Mallarmé's because it is a poetry of situation, observation, and reflection, one in which the 'poetry' is less in the words than it may be with a self-consciously 'pure' poet of the later nineteenth century. So Eugenio Montale, who translated Cavafy's most famous poem (known in English as 'Waiting for the Barbarians') into Italian as 'I barbari',[46] suggested that Cavafy was translatable by contrasting him with poets from the Symbolist tradition: 'Perhaps a comparison could be made with W. B. Yeats's Byzantium poems, but Yeats is a maestro of verse, a genius in the great European tradition that passes through Baudelaire, a poet entirely

---

[42] Elizabeth Bishop to Marianne Moore, 8 December 1953, *Poems, Prose, and Letters*, ed. Robert Giroux and Lloyd Schwartz (New York: Library of America, 2008), p. 793.

[43] MacInnes, *The Girl I Left Behind Me*, p. 34.

[44] Stéphane Mallarmé, 'Crise de vers', trans. Rosemary Lloyd, in *Mallarmé: The Poet and His Circle* (Ithaca and London: Cornell University Press, 1999), p. 232.

[45] See Paul Valéry, *Degas danse dessin* (Paris: Gallimard, 1938), p. 92.

[46] Eugenio Montale, *Tutte le poesie*, ed. Giorgio Zampa (Milan: Mondadori, 1984), pp. 773–74.

untranslatable; while Cavafy has limited relations with this tradition; and he is also translatable.'[47] Despite making this distinction, Montale also published 'Verso Bizanzio', his translation of Yeats's 'Sailing to Byzantium'.[48] In the following two chapters, I explore the idea that some poems may be more untranslatable than others by concentrating on attempts at poems of Rimbaud and Rilke, noting an unexpected alliance of pure poetry and national sentiment at the end of the nineteenth century.

Equally, it is unsurprising that Larkin, who exclaimed against reading poetry in translation, also made jokes about his dislike of travel to other countries: 'I wouldn't mind seeing China', he once said, 'if I could come back the same day.'[49] MacInnes, an English poet of Scots descent, wrote her 'Reading Cavafy in Translation' when permanently settled, through marriage, on the east coast of America. As in the emblematic case of Goethe's lyric 'Kennst du das Land?', which, in his novel *Wilhelm Meisters Lehrejahre*, pretends to be a work rendered from Italian, attachment to translation can be stimulated by the condition of exile, the feeling of being uprooted, which may produce a ubiquitous sense of loss. John Felstiner said of Paul Celan, a Rumanian-born poet living in Paris in 1962 and translating when his own vein had temporarily failed him: 'The exile of a German-speaker converged with a translator's inherent alienness.'[50] A less extreme, though similar, convergence of exclusions shows in the studied abstraction of MacInnes's poem, its seeming incapacity to evoke scenery or imagery for its state of affairs. The sunset at its close is not treated, not evoked, but referred to, once more, using the indirection of imagining Cavafy's views as a way of both disabling herself, and enabling the reduced thing that she feels she can do. The relation of Cavafy's own life and work to such a state of affairs is perhaps not quite as straight-forward as MacInnes's poem, for the sake of its contrasts, allows into play. The Alexandria where he lived wasn't, after all, either the capital of Egypt, or the capital of the diasporic Greek culture whose history he evoked. While playing the role of the cosmopolitan, as it might appear, he could be thought himself to be something of a provincial. His centrality, then, is itself the sign of a displacement.

IV

Cavafy may have been such an inspiration to poets, and in particular to poets in English, not least because he was himself both an anglophile and a

---

[47] Eugenio Montale, 'Un poeta alessandrino', *Il secondo mestiere: Prose 1920-1979*, 2 vols. ed. Giorgio Zampa (Milan: Mondadori, 1996), ii, p. 1805.

[48] Montale, *Tutte le poesie*, pp. 756–57.

[49] Philip Larkin, *Required Writing*, p. 55.

[50] John Felstiner, *Paul Celan: Poet, Survivor, Jew* (New Haven and London: Yale University Press, 1995), p. 203.

student of English poetry.[51] Cavafy's father's business brought the family to England, and the future poet lived in Liverpool and London for five years from 1872. English was one of the three languages he spoke fluently, and members of his family remained in Britain after his return to Alexandria in September 1877. His having been introduced to the English language, and to English poetry in the heyday of Robert Browning and the dramatic monologue (a significant influence on the non-lyrical strand in his oeuvre), may also have made him curiously available to us. This might be related more generally to his cosmopolitanism both of place and time, to his multilingualism, and to a life lived almost exclusively in seaports. What in translated poems is taken to be different, foreign, and difficult of access, can prove surprisingly familiar through, for instance, the international influences of nineteenth- and twentieth-century poetry in English.

E. M. Forster was among the first English-speaking writers to draw attention to Cavafy's importance. He did so by underlining the poet's strange familiarity and familiar strangeness. Forster noted, for instance, of Cavafy's conversation:

> It deals with the tricky behaviour of the Emperor Alexius Comnenus in 1096, or with olives, their possibilities and price, or with the fortunes of friends, or George Eliot, or the dialects of the interior of Asia Minor. It is delivered with equal ease in Greek, English, or French. And despite its intellectual richness and human outlook, despite the matured charity of its judgments, one feels that it too stands at a slight angle to the universe: it is the sentence of a poet.[52]

Standing 'at a slight angle to the universe' has come to symbolize Cavafy's art; but Forster's qualification underlines that standing 'at a slight angle to the universe' is characteristic of speaking 'the sentence of a poet.' Keith Douglas may have been recalling it when in 'Landscape with Figures 2' he evoked the dead men in Egyptian sands as 'at a queer angle to the scenery'.[53] It is a widely applicable phrase, though, characterizing with a geometrical metaphor both the uniqueness of outlook in a significant writer's work, and the implicit requirement to calibrate the 'slight angle' when either interpreting or translating that work. What is manifestly true of poets may be said of all writers and, less evidently, of all language speakers. Forster also notes that Cavafy's poems 'are all short poems, and unrhymed, so that there is some hope of conveying them in a verbal translation', and, after quoting some samples, he adds, 'Such a poem has, even in translation, a "distinguished" air. It is the work of an artist who is not interested in facile

---

[51] The same is true of the Portuguese poet Fernando Pessoa. See 'The Life and Times of Pessoa', *A Centenary Pessoa*, ed. Eugénio Lisboa and L. C. Taylor (Manchester: Carcanet Press, 1995), pp. 118–58, and Fernando Pessoa, *Selected Poems*, trans. Jonathan Griffin, 2nd ed. (Harmondsworth: Penguin Books, 1982).

[52] E. M. Forster, *Pharos and Pharillon* (Richmond, Surrey: Hogarth Press, 1923), p. 75.

[53] Keith Douglas, *The Complete Poems*, ed. Desmond Graham, 3rd edn. (Oxford: Oxford University Press, 1998), p. 110.

beauty. In the second example, though its subject matter is pathetic, Cavafy stands equally aloof.'[54] In 1951 Forster recalls being guided through a poem in the original, announcing that the 'first English translation of Cavafy was made by Cavafy':

> Cavafy is now saying with his usual gentleness, 'You could never understand my poetry, my dear Forster, never.' A poem is produced — 'The God Abandons Antony' — and I detect some coincidences between its Greek and public-school Greek. Cavafy is amazed. 'Oh, but this is good, my dear Forster, this is very good indeed,' and he raises his hand, takes over, and leads me through. It was not my knowledge that touched him but my desire to know and to receive. He had no idea then that he could be widely desired, even in the stumbling North. To be understood in Alexandria and tolerated in Athens was the extent of his ambition.[55]

What Forster evidently didn't know is that the first translations of Cavafy's poetry had been made into English by his brother John Cavafy, who was living in London at the time, a fact that suggests the poet had wanted at least to communicate with the English-speaking world in which he had been partly educated. Forster returns to the poet's similar differences, his different similarities, and, again, to Cavafy's conversation:

> Half humorously, half seriously, he once compared the Greeks and the English. The two peoples are almost exactly alike, he argued: quick-witted, resourceful, adventurous. 'But there is one unfortunate difference between us, one little difference. We Greeks have lost our capital — and the results are what you see. Pray, my dear Forster, oh pray, that you never lose your capital.'
>
> That was in 1918. British insolvency seemed impossible then. In 1951, when all things are possible, his words make one think — words of a very wise, very civilized man, words of a poet who has caught hold of something that cannot be taken away from him by bankruptcy, or even death.[56]

Rosemary Tonks observed in a 22 July 1963 interview with Peter Orr: 'in the case of Cavafy the whole poem is held together by the quality of the comment, almost, which is the comment of a delightfully wryly-humoured man who has seen every kind and turn of human circumstance.'[57] Such life experiences, she remarks with an emulative emphasis,[58] can provide examples for the extension of imaginative knowledge of the world — towards situations we may not have to experience, or ones that (however

---

[54] Forster, *Pharos and Pharillon*, pp. 76 and 79.
[55] E.M. Forster, 'The Complete Poetry of C.P. Cavafy', *Two Cheers for Democracy* (1951), Arbinger Edition, ed. Oliver Stallybrass (London: Edward Arnold, 1972), p. 233.
[56] Ibid. p. 237.
[57] Peter Orr (ed.), *The Poet Speaks: Interviews with Contemporary Poets* (New York: Barnes and Noble, 1966), pp. 258–59.
[58] See, for example, Rosemary Tonks, 'Story of a Hotel Room', *Notes on Cafés and Bedrooms* (London: Putnam, 1963), p. 24.

unexpectedly) we will. Cavafy's family had been effectively forced to return to Alexandria from England because of insolvency. Nor should we overlook the implication of Forster's own half-serious and half-humorous conclusion, for if we English have now lost our capital, then we really might be the same as the Greeks. The analogy between the Greeks and Romans and the British and Americans was being aired in the early 1950s. Oscar Wilde performs a similar sleight-of-mind, when writing in 'The Decay of Lying' that 'The actual people who live in Japan are not unlike the general run of English people; that is to say, they are extremely commonplace, and have nothing curious or extraordinary about them.'[59] Making possible cross-cultural communication is the capacity imaginatively to understand how differences can be variant forms of comparable human survival strategies. This is the serious import behind the jesting of both the Dublin-born and the Alexandrian Greek writer.

W. H. Auden's interest in Cavafy led him to some soul-searching about the nature of an influence drawn from a translated poem. Introducing the 1961 Cavafy versions by Rae Dalven, he resorted to an echo of Frost's aphorism about poetry and translation:

> C. P. Cavafy has remained an influence on my own writing; that is to say, I can think of poems which, if Cavafy were unknown to me, I should have written quite differently or perhaps not written at all. Yet I do not know a word of Modern Greek, so that my only access to Cavafy's poetry has been through English and French translations.
>
> This perplexes and a little disturbs me. Like everybody else, I think, who writes poetry, I have always believed the essential difference between prose and poetry to be that prose can be translated into another tongue but poetry cannot.
>
> But if it is possible to be poetically influenced by work which one can read only in translation, this belief must be qualified.[60]

In my chapter 3, I offer an argument for why Auden may be, speaking strictly, mistaken here about the translation of prose and poetry. Equally, that authentic poets can be usefully inspired by the inauthentic quasi-poetry which translations might be thought to manifest is far from impossible. Yet Auden's interest in the degree to which aspects of the poetic art may be more or less translatable is especially relevant to the case of Cavafy, a trilingual writer exercised by the translatability of his own poetry. Auden, on this occasion at least, comes to the conclusion that it is this poet's sensibility that can be translated:

> What, then, is it in Cavafy's poems that survives translation and excites? Something I can only call, most inadequately, a tone of

[59] Oscar Wilde, 'The Decay of Lying', *The Soul of Man under Socialism and Selected Critical Prose*, ed. Linda Dowling (Harmondsworth: Penguin Books, 2001), p. 187.
[60] W. H. Auden, 'C. P. Cavafy', *Forewords and Afterwords*, selected by Edward Mendelson (London: Faber & Faber, 1973), p. 333.

voice, a personal speech. I have read translations of Cavafy made
by many different hands, but every one of them was immediately
recognizable as a poem by Cavafy; nobody else could possibly have
written it. Reading any poem of his, I feel: 'This reveals a person with
a unique perspective on the world.'[61]

Despite its echo of Forster's 'slight angle to the universe', there is an inadequate
air to Auden's account of the matter, as if he were scraping around for an
explanation that will satisfy him. Such an inadequacy can perhaps be
sensed in the thought that any genuine poetry will have a unique tone of
voice and a unique perspective on the world. If this were the requirement,
then all poetry ought to be equally translatable.

In the course of the essay he does give a hint of one poem that 'I should
have written quite differently or perhaps not written at all' if it weren't
for his exposure to Cavafy when he notes that some of the Alexandrian's
poems 'are concerned with the history of Ancient Greece, one or two with
the fall of Rome'.[62] Auden had written a poem called 'The Fall of Rome',
among the best of his later short poems, in January 1947, and published it in
his 1951 collection, *Nones*, a decade before writing this introduction. Said to
have been inspired by its dedicatee, Cyril Connolly, who had dared Auden
to write a poem that would make him cry, it can also be read as a tribute to
Cavafy's vision of the ancient world:

> Private rites of magic send
> The temple prostitutes to sleep;
> All the literati keep
> An imaginary friend.
>
> Cerebrotic Cato may
> Extol the Ancient Disciplines,
> But the muscle-bound Marines
> Mutiny for food and pay.
>
> Caesar's double bed is warm
> As an unimportant clerk
> Writes *I DO NOT LIKE MY WORK*
> On a pink official form.[63]

There's a touch of both T. S. Eliot and Ezra Pound in this, as might be
demonstrated by citing the lexical heterogeneity of the quatrain poems of
the *Poems* 1919 volume, and from the 'translatorese' of the *Homage to Sextus
Propertius*.[64] Indeed, 'the classics in paraphrase'[65] is one of the characteristic

---

[61] Ibid. p. 335.
[62] Ibid. pp. 333 and 339.
[63] W. H. Auden, *Collected Poems*, ed. Edward Mendelson, 2nd edn. (New York: Vintage, 1991), pp. 332-33.
[64] See T. S. Eliot, *Collected Poems 1909-1962* (London: Faber & Faber, 1963), pp. 42-47, 51-52, 55-60; Ezra Pound, *Collected Shorter Poems* (London: Faber & Faber, 1968), pp. 207-30.
[65] Pound, 'Hugh Selwyn Mauberley', *Collected Shorter Poems*, p. 118.

voices of twentieth-century poetry. It manifests itself in stylized clashes of dictional registers. Of Cavafy's mode, Auden would write in his 1961 introduction:

> The most original aspect of his style, the mixture, both in his vocabulary and his syntax, of demotic and purist Greek, is untranslatable. In English there is nothing comparable to the rivalry between the demotic and purist, a rivalry that has excited high passions, both literary and political. We have only Standard English on the one side and regional dialects on the other, and it is impossible for a translator to reproduce this stylistic effect or for an English poet to profit from it.[66]

Auden's sense of the English language in 1961 is over-schematized. For the mixing of the purist and the demotic is what Auden manages to do in the stanzas above from 'The Fall of Rome', by taking the 'demotic' as the spoken and the 'purist' as the written, the scholarly, or literary. The shift from the latter to the former in the poem's final stanza, where the 'Herds of reindeer' travel over 'miles and miles' of moss 'Silently and very fast', instances the consequences of this fall for the future languages of Europe, by putting it in such focused yet colloquial terms.

Reviewing Derek Mahon's *Adaptations*, Martin Dodsworth praised 'the note of unhesitant clarity and of irony that refuses shame which', thanks to the versions by Philip Sherrard and Edmund Keeley, 'English readers are accustomed to think of as Cavafy's'.[67] Here is their version of his early poem 'Phonès' [Voices], probably written around 1889:

> Loved, idealized voices
> of those who have died, or of those
> lost for us like the dead.
>
> Sometimes they speak to us in dreams;
> sometimes deep in thought the mind hears them.
>
> And, with their sound, for a moment return
> sounds from our life's first poetry —
> like distant music fading away at night.[68]

Early in his writing life, Mahon composed a variation on Cavafy's same theme, redeploying a number of elements from his guide translation, compressing and condensing, while finding colloquially cadenced equivalent expressions for his adaptation:

> Definitive voices of the loved dead
> or the loved lost, as good as dead,

[66] Auden, 'C. P. Cavafy', *Forewords and Afterwords*, p. 335.
[67] Martin Dodsworth, 'The God of Details', *Agenda* vol. 43 no. 1 (Autumn 2007), p. 35.
[68] C. P. Cavafy, *Collected Poems*, trans. Edmund Keeley and Philip Sherrard (Princeton, NJ: Princeton University Press, 1975), p. 15.

> speak to us in our dreams
> or at odd moments.
>
> Listening, we hear again,
> like music at night,
> the original poetry of our lives.[69]

Mahon, as Dodsworth notes, 'abbreviates the Keeley/Sherrard version, brings the rhythms much closer to the spoken language, stressing the final syllable in every case but one, and changes the last two lines round, so that, instead of counterpointing "return" and "fading away", they bring to the fore an idea of life which is close to Mahon's own in his early poems.' It wouldn't be unfair to say that this compression achieves its own understated sense of loss by editing out the distance from which the voices have come, and the concluding emphasis that they will only be fleetingly heard. Cavafy's original is a nocturnal voice 'faraway, that fades.'[70]

Dodsworth then adds that 'this is not Cavafy entire — but then, not even Keeley and Sherrard can give us that. What it may be is Cavafy in essence, the original poetry of his life to which his poems seek to give us access.'[71] True, but the sense of music fading, of echo and loss, is in Cavafy's inspiring conception. Robert Liddell notes how the poem that Mahon reconfigures echoes Shelley's 'Music', Tennyson's 'Break, Break, Break', and Verlaine's 'Mon rêve familier'. The otherness of Cavafy's Greek is already allusively familiar. What's original to us is by no means necessarily what we originate.[72] Including echo and allusion, the 'original poetry of our lives', as here, might well be in translation. 'We are having trouble,' Lawrence Durrell wrote to George Seferis about a version of 'The King of Asine' made in collaboration with Bernard Spencer, 'translating you so that you don't sound like Eliot.'[73] To do justice to the original, back-translating the international influence, it might be necessary both to allow an echo of T. S. Eliot's 'The Journey of the Magi' and 'Marina' (both audible in 'The King of Asine' translation by Spencer, Valaoritis and Durrell)[74] to survive in the rendering, and yet to make multiply sure, as these translators do, that the influence is digested into a different texture and a distinct set of cultural locations and concerns. The translation of influence from the language into which the work is rendered points to such similarities and differences fairly at play in well-rendered poems.

---

[69] Derek Mahon, *Adaptations*, pp. 68–69.
[70] Cavafy, *The Collected Poems*, trans. Sachperoglou, p. 3.
[71] Dodsworth, 'The God of Details', p. 34.
[72] See Robert Liddell, *C. P. Cavafy* (London: Duckworth, 2000), p. 59.
[73] Durrell to Seferis, 29 March 1944, in Roderick Beaton, *George Seferis Waiting for the Angel: A Biography* (New Haven and London: Yale University Press, 2003), p. 229.
[74] See George Seferis, 'The King of Asini' [sic], trans. Lawrence Durrell, Bernard Spencer, and Nanos Valaoritis, *Personal Landscape* vol. 2 no. 3 (1944), pp. 9–10; and, revised, in George Seferis, *The King of Asine and Other Poems*, trans. Bernard Spencer, Nanos Valaoritis, and Lawrence Durrell (London: John Lehmann, 1948), pp. 71–73.

Mahon has also written a poem called 'Rage for Order' in which he articulates various personal predicaments within the coordinates of Cavafy's already formed authorial stance, his 'slight angle to the universe' effected by echoing those English Victorian and French decadent poets. Critics have discussed this in the light of Mahon's investment in the cult or image of the *poète maudit*.[75] 'Rage for Order' owes its title to the closing stanza of Wallace Stevens's 'The Idea of Order at Key West': 'Oh! Blessed rage for order, pale Ramon, / The maker's rage to order words of the sea'.[76] Mahon's poem makes no claim to such powers as are evoked in Stevens's manifesto-like incantation:

> Somewhere beyond
> The scorched gable end
> And the burnt-out
> Buses there is a poet indulging his
> Wretched rage for order —
>
> Or not as the case
> May be, for his
> Is a dying art,
> An eddy of semantic scruple
> In an unstructurable sea.[77]

Hugh Haughton has noted that this 'could represent any modern city in the throes of political violence', but also 'if we ignore the buses' it could be 'Cavafy's Alexandria.'[78] 'Rage for Order' is a latecomer poem in which a confident attitude to the matter of literary power is measured against a depressed sense of worldly chaos. 'A Dying Art' is the title of another of Mahon's early poems, aligning his own art with those of crafts and trades marginalized by modernity: '"That day would skin a fairy — /A dying art," she said.'[79] 'Rage for Order' associates the ambitions of a Stevens-like aesthetics with the historical expanse of Irish myth and folklore. Yet it is faced down by Mahon's sense of the deracinated contemporary, long detached from the communal role of the poet as, strangely enough, evoked by Wallace Stevens in his high claims for what poetry can do. Stevens's localism, his poems of that climate, required a detached stay-at-home internationalism, one including the idea that 'French and English constitute a single language' — though this did not prevent him from translating the

---

[75] Hugh Haughton, '"The Importance of Elsewhere": Mahon and Translation', *The Poetry of Derek Mahon*, ed. Elmer Kennedy-Andrews (Gerrards Cross: Colin Smyth, 2002), pp. 147–48.

[76] Wallace Stevens, *Collected Poetry and Prose*, ed. Frank Kermode and Joan Richardson (New York: Library of America, 1997), p. 106.

[77] Derek Mahon, *Collected Poems* (Oldcastle, Co. Meath: Gallery Press, 1999), p. 47.

[78] Hugh Haughton, *The Poetry of Derek Mahon* (Oxford: Oxford University Press, 2007), p. 80.

[79] Mahon, *Collected Poems*, p. 34.

one into the other.[80] Mahon ends by replacing the afflatus of Stevens's 'wretched' urge with some dry tones similar to those in Mairi MacInnes's 'Reading Cavafy in Translation'. 'Rage for Order' concludes:

> If he is silent
> It is the silence
> Of enforced humility,
> If anxious to be heard
> It is the anxiety of a last word
>
> When the drums start —
> For his is a dying art.
> Now watch me
> As I make history,
> Watch as I tear down
>
> To build up
> With a desperate love,
> Knowing it cannot be
> Long now till I have need of his
> Terminal ironies.[81]

This mockery of modernist poetry's grand ambitions to remake the world (echoes of the root and branch politics disfiguring Northern Ireland's culture at the time) is finessed by the turn to the defensiveness of those cosmopolitan ironies, the 'his' being in Mahon's poem that of the 'poet indulging' in verse 1, but also the world-weary wisdom of a defeated civilization in Cavafy's Alexandrian poetry. Translated poems, poems in translation, can be at their best when their themes are elegiac, disappointed, or fretted with loss. Poets will continue to read poetry in translation and find unexpected promptings there. In so doing, they counter the exceptionalism of those among their fellows, whether poets or critics, who prefer to argue that the native literature has it all, that translated poems are closed books, and that others' cultural fates will be spared us. Such poets, translating with help from languages that they may not be able to speak themselves, have the wit to suspect that it will not be 'Long now till' any of us, having lost, as it might be, our capital in 1951, have to borrow from the world of imaginative elsewheres in poetry for the 'Terminal ironies' of our own.

---

[80] Stevens, *Collected Poetry and Prose*, p. 914. For Stevens translating from the French of Joachim du Bellay and Jean Le Roy, see ibid. pp. 516-17 and 545-47.
[81] Mahon, *Collected Poems*, pp. 47-48.

CHAPTER 2

What Is Lost?

I

Robert Frost's is the most famous and widely diffused aphorism on translating, or not translating, poetry. He is reported to have said that 'poetry is what gets left out in translation'[1] according to one authority, or what gets 'lost' in translation, more usually. The remark appears in variant forms on a number of Internet sites, though it appears not to have a source in Frost's published prose writings.[2] The remark, quoted by Louis Untermeyer in 1964, is given as 'Poetry is what is lost in translation. It is also what is lost in interpretation' in *The Oxford Dictionary of Modern Quotations*.[3] Edmund Keeley, the translator of C. P. Cavafy, George Seferis, and other Modern Greek poets, paraphrases such 'dangerous generalizations' as: 'what constitutes poetry is exactly what is lost when poetry is translated into another language (ascribed to Robert Frost).' There is, he notes, 'a half truth' in this, but then adds: 'The other half truth' is the 'reverse image, equally valid, equally false.'[4] Thinking about it thus brushes off the problem, but only superficially, since a proposition can hardly be 'valid' and 'false' at the same time. In this chapter, I explore and illustrate the proposal that Frost's aphorism is, in its terms and implications, true and valid — and,

[1] Donald Davie, 'The Translatability of Poetry', *The Poet in the Imaginary Museum: Essays of Two Decades*, ed. Barry Alpert (Manchester: Carcanet Press, 1977), p. 153.

[2] Mark Richardson, editor of *The Collected Prose of Robert Frost*, reported by email on 13 March 2008: 'the oft-quoted quip ("Poetry is what is lost in translation") does not appear in the published prose, though RF did occasionally utter it (or forms of it) in public performances. He didn't say this in any essay he published, but he did say it.'

[3] No. 29 'Frost, Robert', *The Oxford Dictionary of Modern Quotations*, ed. Elizabeth Knowles Oxford: Oxford University Press, 2008), referenced online on 11 June 2009 at <http://www.oxfordreference.com/views/ENTRY.html?subview=Main&entry=t93.e659>.

[4] Edmund Keeley, 'Collaboration, Revision, and Other Less Forgivable Sins in Translation', John Biguenet and Rainer Schulte (ed.), *The Craft of Translation* (Chicago: University of Chicago Press, 1989), p. 54.

what's more, that it memorably captures (hence its familiarity) one of the inescapable conditions for those involved in poetry and translation.

Daniel Weissbort, a defender and promoter of poetry translating, adds to the chorus of those who reiterate Frost's aphorism, even as he deplores its being repeated: 'Robert Frost's quip that in the translation of poetry it is precisely the poetry that gets left out is routinely quoted, since it restates the widely held assumption that what defines poetry is that it *is* untranslatable.'[5] Frost's version of what constitutes poetry depended on 'sentence sounds' and 'the sound of sense'.[6] With a working theory dependent on the timbre of a language's inwardness with a native speaker, he would naturally consider 'the poetry' that inheres in this precise interplay to be untranslatable. Those specific effects of form, structure, and meaning cannot by definition be reconstituted using the materials of another set of interrelations from a different culture. As already noted, though, Frost did acknowledge that poems get translated, for example in his *Paris Review* interview, when he recalls meeting Ezra Pound 'through Frank Flint. The early Imagist and translator.'[7] There are published comments of his, too, which, while skeptical of translation, do acknowledge its existence — in 1944, for instance:

> One good thing to be said in defense of poetry is that it holds the imagination down to the rate of the speaking voice. Another is that it will convince almost anyone in the long run that no translation of poetry will do: practically any book in any but your own language or languages is a closed book.[8]

Seven years later, in 1951, he allows that there can be good translations, but not often: 'Another danger nowadays to sensitiveness is getting inured to translations. The rarity of a poem well brought over from one language into another should be a warning'; and he adds: 'For self assurance there should always be a lingering unhappiness in reading translations.'[9] Three years later in 'Message to the Poets of Japan', Frost cunningly wrote: 'I wish I could read in the original the Japanese poetry I have admired even

---

[5] Daniel Weissbort, 'Poetry', *The Oxford Guide to Literature in English Translation*, ed. Peter France (Oxford: Oxford University Press, 2000), p. 89.

[6] See Robert Frost, 'To John T. Bartett' (4 July 1913), *Collected Poems, Prose, & Plays*, ed. Richard Poirier and Mark Richardson (New York: Library of America, 1995), pp. 664–66.

[7] Frost, '*Paris Review* Interview', *Collected Poems, Prose, & Plays*, p. 874. F. S. Flint's works include *The Love Poems of Emile Verhaeren* and *The Mosella of Decimus Magnus Ausonius*, while *Otherworld: Cadences* (London: The Poetry Bookshop, 1920), pp. 62–66 contains, inter alia, translations from Albert Samain, José-Maria de Heredia, Emile Verhaeren, and Henri de Régnier.

[8] Robert Frost, 'Contribution to 25th Anniversary Bread Loaf Booklet' (1944), *The Collected Prose of Robert Frost*, ed. Mark Richardson (Cambridge, MA: Harvard University Press, 2008), p. 143.

[9] Frost, 'Poetry and School' (1951). Ibid. p. 167.

as it was in translation.'[10] When talking about 'Stopping by Woods on a Snowy Evening' on 30 June 1955 he said: 'I never read anything, in Latin, say, without a constant expectation of meaning that I'm either getting justified in or corrected. See. Confirmed in or Corrected. I've got that going on all the time or else I'd be a dead translator.'[11] Confirmed or corrected, he presumably acts like a *live* translator.

Yet once more Frost addresses the subject of poetry and translation when sending a message to the poets of Korea on 21 March 1957:

> Poetry and the other arts are for me what a country chiefly lives by. They mark national characters better than anything else. And they bring peoples together in spirit the more apparently that they separate them in language. The language barrier has so much to do with individuality and originality that we wouldn't want to see it removed. We must content ourselves with seeing it more or less got over by interpretation and translation. We must remember that one may be national without being poetical, but one can't be poetical without being national.[12]

While Frost appears to grant that translation can get over the language barrier, more or less, he returns immediately to what looks like safer territory for him — the highly ideological assertion in its Cold War context that to be poetical you need to be national. Poetry, according to Frost's definition, would also be what is lost in paraphrase, for if you can retain the poetry in a paraphrase, you can, similarly, paraphrase it in another language. These two concepts, that poetry is lost in translation and that it cannot be paraphrased, are both aspects of an essentialist definition of poetry, one that is linguistically essentialist, and under the interpretation that languages are national languages. For Frost, as he put it in a poem: 'good fences make good neighbors'[13] whether the fence is the tennis net which he thought free-verse writers preferred to do without, or the language barrier which he saw as having 'so much to do with individuality and originality' — or putting it thus in his address to the poets of Japan: 'An instinct told me long ago that I had to be national before I was international' and 'You may be more international than I am.'[14]

But did Frost say that it is 'poetry' that gets lost in translation, or 'the poetry'? He might grant, after all, that people can translate poems (and did variously acknowledge that such activities took place), but that what you get won't be poetry, because though you have produced texts that resemble poems, the poetry of the original has been lost, and so, however useful, they do not rise to being what he meant by poetry. This would, presumably,

[10] Frost, 'Message to the Poets of Japan'. Ibid. p. 175.
[11] Frost, 'On Taking Poetry', *Collected Poems, Prose, & Plays*, p. 822.
[12] Frost, 'Message to the Poets of Korea' (1957), *The Collected Prose of Robert Frost*, p. 182.
[13] Frost, 'Mending Wall', *Collected Poems, Prose, & Plays*, p. 40.
[14] Frost, 'Message to the Poets of Japan', *The Collected Prose of Robert Frost*, p. 182.

depend not on the accuracy of the translation, but the compositional skills of the translator as a poet in his or her own right. I imagine Frost would have accepted that Dr Johnson's 'The Vanity of Human Wishes' was a poem, but not, perhaps, a translation. Yet just as this line of thought appears to offer a lifeline to translations aspiring to the condition of poetry, I sense it slipping through my fingers. The aspirant translation could be poetry, but it wouldn't be so in its character *as a translation*. Its poetic quality would be something created entirely in the terms of the translating poet's skills as a composer of verse in the receiver language. Though poetry has been achieved, as it were, the contribution of translation as an activity has dropped out of the equation.

II

Thoughts such as this lie behind the justification for poetry being rendered from other languages which offers as its claim to our attention the argument that though not exactly in translation, and certainly not in exact translation, nevertheless readers are being offered an equivalent poem which bears a relation (of however remote a kind) to an original text. Words such as 'adaptation' and 'version' and 'imitation', as well as the preposition 'after', are used to suggest differently tenuous relationships between source text and rendering. Christopher Reid has published an entire collection, *For and After*, in which most of the poems are either dedicated to friends or derived from works in other languages, such as 'Au Cabaret-vert', which provides the sonnet template for 'At the Green Man', subtitled '*After Rimbaud*':

> For a week now, I'd been blistering my feet
> on the stony country roads. Then I came to Hemel Hempstead.
> At the Green Man, I asked for some French bread,
> butter, and ham with still a hint of its oven heat.[15]

Rimbaud spent some time in London, in Reading, and environs, so it's not impossible that something like this might have happened to him. A glance at Reid's acknowledged source, though, makes it clear that 'l'homme aux semelles de vent' had never crossed the Channel when he wrote his sonnet in October 1870: 'Depuis huit jours, j'avais déchiré mes bottines / Aux cailloux des chemins. J'entrais à Charleroi.'[16] Reid's self-evident strategy, as his mention of the English town, the common pub name, and reference to French bread underlines, is to make an anglicized Rimbaud-like poem.[17]

---

[15] Christopher Reid, *For and After* (London: Faber and Faber, 2003), p. 25.
[16] Arthur Rimbaud, 'Au Cabaret-vert', *Oeuvres complètes*, ed. Antoine Adam (Paris: Gallimard, 1972), pp. 32–33.
[17] For poets retaining Rimbaud's location name, see Ezra Pound, *The Translations of Ezra Pound*, ed. Hugh Kenner (London: Faber & Faber, 1953), p. 434, and Keith Douglas, 'Au Cabaret-Vert', *The Complete Poems*, ed. Desmond Graham (3rd edn., Oxford: Oxford University Press, 1998), p. 59.

When the original sixteen-year-old crosses the Belgian border and reaches Charleroi, he arrives '— *Au Cabaret-vert*: je demandai des tartines / De beurre et du jambon qui fût à moitié froid.' Rimbaud, it appears, was not himself translating exactly from life: the place was called *La Maison Verte*, and there may have been no ham.[18]

His ABAB quatrain becomes in English, thanks in part to the place name, one with an ABBA rhyme scheme. Though, like its original, Reid's sonnet rhymes, it isn't pedantically literal in the reproduction of the formal constraints. Yet, so far, this version closely adheres to the broad sense and occasion of the original, with the exception of those proper names. A reader might still wonder what kind of a person is speaking, especially when he asks for 'ham with still a hint of its oven heat'. A pernickety food buff who also likes going on strenuous country walks? Such qualms concerning the speaker's identity are increased in the second quatrain:

> Contentedly stretching my legs under the green-topped table,
> I'm studying the décor, when — wa-hey! up flies
> the bar girl with her voluminous tits and flashing eyes.
> (Getting past those defences shouldn't prove much trouble.)

Reid's verse condenses the following five lines of Rimbaud's sonnet:

> Bienheureux, j'allongeai les jambes sous la table
> Verte: je contemplai les sujets très naïfs
> De la tapisserie. — Et ce fut adorable,
> Quand la fille aux tétons énormes, aux yeux vifs,
>
> — Celle-là, ce n'est pas un baiser qui l'épeure! —

Rimbaud's attention to the naïf subjects on the wall hangings nuances his pleasure at the sight of the Flemish girl with the enormous breasts and vivid eyes (whose name, it appears, was Mia),[19] and who wouldn't be afraid of a kiss. The simplicity of the interior decoration and of the country girl, without affected primness or reserve, is topped off by the description of the food she places before him. The freshness of Rimbaud's poem, with the range of cultural implications it contains in the wake of France's defeat in the Franco-Prussian War, should not be underestimated either for its tacitly charitable politics, or the literary radicalism in its humble materials, its colloquial diction, alexandrines with informal enjambments and caesuras, or its inventive rhymes.

Reid is able to compact five lines into four because he has reduced the detail about the subjects on the tapestry to an unspecified interest in 'the décor'. The difficulty in imagining who exactly is speaking is aggravated by that suddenly exclamatory 'wa-hey!' This bit of ventriloquism doesn't

---

[18] For the place's name, see Charles Nicholl, *Someone Else: Arthur Rimbaud in Africa 1880-1891* (London: Jonathan Cape, 1997), p. 23, and for speculation about the food, see Graham Robb, *Rimbaud* (London: Picador, 2000), p. 58.

[19] Nicholl, *Someone Else*, p. 23.

sound like the English poet himself, and indeed the subtitle '*After Rimbaud*' has the additional function of minimizing a reader's tendency to identify the unnamed speaker of a lyric with the poet. But Reid's pernickety food fan has suddenly become a teenage libertine. The sense of his protagonist's detachment is produced by the clash of diction between that exclamation and the politely Latinate 'voluminous' for the girl's 'tétons énormes'. Reid's speaker, an Anglophone referring to 'French bread', doesn't think about whether the girl would be afraid of a kiss and what it might lead to, he imagines her having 'defences' to storm.

The girl in 'La Maline', Rimbaud's other sonnet inspired by this occasion, does teasingly invite a kiss. Not the type to be afraid of one in 'Au Cabaret-vert' and evidently independent minded, she can see the torn boots that this bedraggled and bohemian sixteen-year-old is wearing. She's laughing as she brings the food:

> Rieuse, m'apporta des tartines de beurre,
> Du jambon tiède, dans un plat colorié,
>
> Du jambon rose et blanc parfumé d'une gousse
> D'ail, — et m'emplit la chope immense, avec sa mousse
> Que dorait un rayon de soleil arriéré.

Rimbaud's sestet, rhyming EEFGGF, is composed by returning to the details of his food order, elaborating them with some colour and flavour, and staying with the girl who both brings the food and pours him out a large glass of foaming beer, presumably from a jug, the foam then touched with the last rays of the sun. His sonnet is subtitled 'cinq heures du soir', a detail which prefigures the importance of the day's walking, the relief of the rest for his legs, and the reassurance of human contact and plain, but good, country food. Is the description of the ham a metaphor for the girl's delicious body? In lines four and five he had moved from ordering 'du jambon' to stretching his 'jambes' under the table, so the association of 'ham' and 'hams' has, perhaps, been seeded into the poem. Yet the detail of the 'clove of garlic' also keeps the mind firmly on the food. The foam on the beer as she fills up the 'immense' glass may conceivably be a metaphor for a wet dream–like orgasm, but to spell it out (as Rimbaud doesn't) would disperse the wider import of his poem about a wholesome meal served to a teenage run-away by an ordinary girl in a poor hostelry at five one afternoon in the wake of the French defeat.

Since the speaker of Reid's rendering cannot be the sixteen-year-old Arthur Rimbaud, or his literary representative in 'Au Cabaret-vert', many of the original's contextual implications — not only implied by the poem itself, but its bearing the date of its occasion beneath the text, and thus its chronological place in the poet's oeuvre — have to be abandoned with Reid's version. 'At the Green Man' appears in a series of four adaptations from the Symbolists (the others being from Baudelaire, Mallarmé, and Valéry) with the generic title 'Smoking, Drinking, etc.', and his elaborations after Rimbaud take flight in the EFGEFG sestet:

> She smiles as she hands me a big Staffordshire dish
> of bread already buttered and home-baked ham,
> pink and white and keen to hail everyone
> with garlicky bonhomie. Plus, there's a bottle to replenish
> my long glass, which instantly heaves up oodles of foam
> in its haste to be blessed by a last-minute ray of the sun.

This is a skillful stanza, and one that doesn't suffer from jarring diction, as his second quatrain had. It's also closer to the original than is Ciaran Carson's Irish domestication, 'The Green Bar' ('I stretch my legs beneath the shamrock / Table. I admire the tacky '50s décor'), with its emphasis more on genial ingestion than the undercurrents of queasiness and ejaculation above:

> With hints of smoochy kisses and her gorgeous platter
> Of green gherkins, slabs of ham and bread and butter,
> Rosy, garlic-scented ham; and then she filled my beer mug
>
> With a bright smile, and turned herself into a ray
> Of sunshine, like an unexpected Lady Day.
> I guzzled it all into me. *Glug. Glug. Glug. Glug.*[20]

Carson's mock inept 'filled my beer mug / With a bright smile' allows him, in the spirit of the original, to be swigging the girl as well. His variation is published *en face* with Rimbaud's text to underline that he too is geographically and culturally translating. Reid's variant being set in England, though, and at a pub in the Home Counties, we can't expect the girl to be laughing as she puts the food on his table. Is she keeping her distance and being polite with that smile? Or is it more of a come-on? The speaker, we recall, isn't wearing scuffed-up boots: he's got blisters from his country rambles. There's a nice bit of Wedgwood pottery to appreciate, and then Reid smartly confuses the ham and the girl by keeping the referent of 'pink and white and keen to hail everyone / with garlicky bonhomie' ambiguously suspended between the food and the girl — though when we get to 'garlicky bonhomie' it seems more like the girl's breath than the ham's seasoning.

Reid's experiment in modernizing and anglicizing Rimbaud's poem is hampered at key points by its being a paraphrase-style translation. His subtitle '*After Rimbaud*' introduces the comparative condition of the text, even as it admits that a comparison will lead to the noticing of differences. In the case of 'At the Green Man' the details of the original occasion, even when selectively sampled in the rendering, produce an oddly implausible and more than faintly unreal situation with a speaker whose cultural identity and location are, now and then, puzzling. All translations display hybrid characteristics. The problems with the coherence of the speaker in Reid's poem are located at the point where Frost would have identified the

---

[20] Ciaran Carson, *The Alexandrine Plan* (Oldcastle, Co. Meath: Gallery Press, 1998), pp. 12-13.

'poetry' that 'gets lost in translation': namely in the significant counterpoint of a human voice and a metrical and formal pattern. Though Reid's is by no means an ignoble effort, the epicurean rewriting evidently intended, and one that excuses itself from pedantry about its paraphrasing of Rimbaud's sense by means of that preposition 'after', nevertheless, at the heart of the text are what seem hapless mismatches of situation, form, and speaking voice.

In a rich and varied culture (though one in which the difficulty of publishing poetry in translation should not be underestimated) it looks as if no one is going to want to say, or want me to say, that writers should be blackballed for translating in any of the innumerable 'free' ways currently practised. However, if the reader doesn't happen to enjoy the writing of the subsidiary text, or wincing moments in it, this work accrues to it neither the benefits of original composition as such, nor the multiplied interest that can occur in the case of a translation, for as Martin Dodsworth has noted:

> Reading translations of poetry which have been made by poets tests the reader because a double work of interpretation is required. You must try to understand both what the translator has done and what of the original is refracted through its new language. The reward, though, is also double, a double pleasure accruing when we feel we truly grasp the sense of the translation.[21]

Dodsworth makes the point that, reading translations, we inevitably exercise our judgment about the experience, the type of judgment depending on whether, for instance, we have access to the original or not. The version may be a fair example of the translator's own work, but its distances from its original, or lack of interest in the calibration of those distances, and indifference about the ontology of the original's voice, the cultural situation, or the impacting on the text of facts from that situation, could bring a reader to the point at which a free version will not provide enough to sustain the doubly rewarding attention that Dodsworth advocates.

A strategy for avoiding such difficulties when tracking a translated text to its source has been to assert that versions do not invite comparison with their originals. Don Paterson, in his provocatively aphoristic 'Fourteen Notes on the Version', appears to argue that such a detaching is the approach to adopt when reading translated poetry, and in this he lucidly sums up one entire strand in more than half a century of debate about the freedom poets claim in rendering poetry from other languages. 'A translation tries to remain true to the original words and their relations,' he writes:

> It glosses the original, but does not try to replace it. Versions, however, are trying to be poems in their own right; while they have the original to serve as a detailed ground-plan and elevation, they are trying to build themselves a robust home in a new country, in its

[21] Martin Dodsworth, 'The God of Details', *Agenda* vol. 43 no. 1 (Autumn 2007), p. 26.

vernacular architecture, with local words for its brick and local music for its mortar.[22]

Though Paterson doesn't spell it out, his contrast does appear to suggest that unlike translations, versions do aim to replace their originals — for you don't consult the architect's design to live in the house built from it. Paterson's analogy with architecture may be self-defeating, though, for a translation also uses local materials, and relies on the original as a 'detailed ground-plan and elevation'. Is the difference only that the translation invites reference to the original, while the version discourages it? There is evaluative implication in 'a robust home in a new country, in its vernacular architecture' — implying that to try and remain 'true to the original words and their relations' the translation will fail to provide a 'robust home' — though such homes were not a speciality of the poet Rilke, who wrote in 'Herbsttag' [Autumn Day]: 'Wer jetzt kein Haus hat, baut sich keines mehr' [Who has no house yet, will never build one].[23] Paterson's aphorism expresses an odd sense of relations between architect and builder, the latter leaving the ground plan and elevation behind, because he can't literally copy it, and improvising a thoroughly sound house out of the local materials. This builder would then make a point of effacing the design so that complaints by either architect, purchaser, or future inhabitants of the property have nothing upon which to base complaints about it not resembling the original project.

Paterson's justification for his theory of the version takes into implicit account Frost's remark on translation when it denigrates the mimetic efforts of translators. He notes technical errors derived from speed of composition in Rilke's *Die Sonette an Orpheus*. Versions, he continues,

> must have their own course, their own process, and have to make a virtue of their own human mistakes; they will have, in other words, their *own* pattern of error and felicity. Any attempt to replicate that of the original is perverse in the case of the error, doomed in the case of the felicity, and redundant in terms of the overall project.[24]

Because the translation of poetry is literally impossible, he suggests, there's no point even trying. The writer of a version is then justified in leaving the original behind when it comes to its flaws, in giving up when faced with its felicities, and sensibly dropping the architect's plan in order to take advantage of local materials. Paterson's use of the word 'replicate' is both crucial and fatal to his implicit argument, though, because once it's accepted he is right, and even translators cannot get exact matches, or replications, then the distinction he's articulating collapses. All translations are versions, and versions give an impression (at the very least)

[22] Don Paterson, *Orpheus: A Version of Rilke's* Die Sonette an Orpheus (London: Faber & Faber, 2006), p. 73.
[23] Rainer Maria Rilke, *Die Gedichte* (Frankfurt am Main: Insel Verlag, 1986), p. 344.
[24] Ibid. pp. 73–74.

of resembling their originals — originals that, in the case of the Rilke sonnets Paterson is adapting, are too familiar in the original German and in their multiple and varied renditions to be left behind. Paterson makes a formal nod in the direction of other types of translator in his Acknowledgements when writing: 'I am indebted to the many other translators of the Sonnets from whom I have freely and shamelessly adapted lines when theirs presented the better solution'.[25] His wording here implies that he is a translator too.

While not wishing to limit anyone's freedom to write and publish whatever they and their publishers think fit, one reason for agreeing to write and publish the present book is a longstanding unhappiness with this state of affairs, one in which Frost's edict is used to justify the opposite of what it appears to counsel. Liberties are supported with arguments that exclude the middle term in an account of translating which states that because exact reproduction of an original is impossible, poets should take advantage of this fact to spin off 'poems in their own right' that nevertheless retain odd relations with their sponsoring originals. The middle term or missing alternative, one which links these falsely contrasted methods by means of its innumerably different ways for attempting the impossible, is the practice of a faithfully imitative approximation. Creatively aware that what is being attempted is the rendering of a poem, such imitative activity includes the ambition that, faithfully approximating, the work ought to result — to the best of the poet-translator's abilities — in a poem.

III

Robert Lowell's volume, misleadingly called *Imitations* and first published in 1961, has come to seem a watershed. Danny Weissbort calls its introduction 'something of a benchmark for later discussions of poetry translation.'[26] As watersheds do, it divides the subsequent flow of texts and commentaries into rivers of imitators and of anti-imitators. In 'Rilke Where Art Thou?', Stephen Cohn begins by citing Lowell's conclusion: 'the excellence of a poet depends on the unique opportunities of his native language. I have been almost as free as the authors themselves in finding ways to make them ring right for me.'[27] One difficulty in discussing Lowell's work is his use of powerfully inaccurate phrasing. The 'excellence of a poet' does not 'depend on the unique opportunities of his native language', but on a poet's ability to access, activate, and deploy such opportunities — an ability that reflectively honest poets admit is not simply subject to their will. Since there is no limit to what those opportunities might be, and the language is

---

[25] Ibid. p. 85.
[26] Daniel Weissbort and Astradur Eysteinsson (eds.), *Translation — Theory and Practice: A Historical Reader* (Oxford: Oxford University Press, 2006), p. 352.
[27] Robert Lowell, Introduction, *Imitations* (Farrar, Straus & Giroux, 1961), p. xiii.

in a state of continual evolution, the poets can also discover opportunities. Dependence in this case is interactively complex.[28]

Beside Lowell's approximate formulation, Cohn places Richard Davenport Hines's being affronted 'by the high-handed re-writing or slipshod approximations to which several other translators have resorted', producing 'sentences that for all their flourishes are faithless, complacent, and false.'[29] Cohn wonders if there can be common ground between such opposed positions. Yet they are on the same ground. Lowell's 'almost as free' and Davenport Hines's 'faithless, complacent, and false' are united in their mutual confrontation, both implicitly mischaracterizing the situation of literary translation. While acknowledging such outcries again Lowell's stated position, Cohn admits that 'I can decide fairly swiftly that of these positions, each of which has its own integrity, I like Lowell's the best and feel most sympathy towards it'. But why succumb to the better of two, when there are other positions not even credited with existing? Cohn adds, 'To attempt to achieve a sensitive and responsible trot is something difficult enough, and well worthwhile, but this hasn't been my own intention.'[30] Here we can sense the waters rapidly dividing, for Lowell's 'almost as free' is tacitly contrasted with the 'sensitive and responsible' guide translation that follows the sense of the original.

Lowell's Introduction similarly notes that 'Most poetic translations come to grief and are less enjoyable than modest photographic prose translations, such as George Kay has offered in his *Penguin Book of Italian Verse*,' and, after canvassing various modes of going about the activity, he adds: 'I believe that poetic translation — I would call it an imitation — must be expert and inspired, and needs at least as much technique, luck and rightness of hand as an original poem.'[31] The continuing influence of this contrast shows in Paterson's use of the same analogy nearly forty years on: 'Literal translation can be useful in providing us with a black-and-white snapshot of the original, but a *version* — however subjectively — seeks to restore a light and colour and perspective.'[32] So the providers of literal renderings, sensitive and responsible, but modestly photographic, are conveniently contrasted with poets who aim or hope to be as 'expert and inspired' as the original writers. Lowell, though, does include a third category, one from which he hopes to exclude his own efforts, and which he describes as 'poetic translations' that 'come to grief and are less enjoyable'. Many things trouble me about this plotted terrain, and I briefly outline them before looking at Lowell's mixtures of truth and status assumption.

[28] See my 'Dependence in the Poetry of W. S. Graham', *Twentieth Century Poetry: Selves and Situations* (Oxford: Oxford University Press, 2005), pp. 69-98.

[29] Stephen Cohn, 'Rilke Where Art Thou?', *Agenda* vol. 42 nos. 2-3 (Spring 2007), p. 125.

[30] Ibid. p. 126.

[31] Lowell, *Imitations*, pp. xi, xii.

[32] Don Paterson, 'Afterword', *The Eye: A Version of Antonio Machado* (London: Faber & Faber, 1999), pp. 57-58.

He begins by claiming a degree of autonomy for his imitation texts, which were not published beside their originals *en face*. 'This book', he writes, 'is partly self-sufficient and separate from its sources, and should be first read as a sequence, one voice running through many personalities, contrasts and repetitions.'[33] Once again, 'partly self-sufficient and separate from its sources' is a powerfully assonantal chain which conceals a contradiction. His 'partly self-sufficient' does make a kind of sense. But does his 'partly ... separate'? Equally, if we imagine how this is supposed to be translated into the actual states of his texts, how are the partial self-sufficiency and separateness manifested? The relationships between the parts of the poem that depend on the originals and the parts that do not isn't promising for the aesthetic integrity of the imitations — a word Lowell took to catch the equivocal states of his texts, thought it might have implied an intention closely to shadow his sources, as we imitate those we admire in the hope of emulating them.

Lowell notes that 'I have tried to keep something equivalent to the fire and finish of my originals. This has forced me to do considerable re-writing.'[34] Once again, assonantal phrasemaking stands in for thought and reflection. Do his originals all display 'fire and finish'? Lowell's opening to 'Nostalgia', 'The sucking river was the child's salt tears',[35] if compared with Rimbaud's opening line from 'Mémoire' ('L'eau claire; comme le sel des larmes d'enfance'),[36] reveals that his pentameter, without caesura, has far more 'fire and finish' than does the French alexandrine, with its marked hesitation after 'claire' and before any main verb appears. Rimbaud follows this pause with a simile, a form of comparison that doesn't claim imaginative identity between the two terms, while Lowell converts it into a metaphor. His first line makes a far higher claim upon a reader's belief-suspension than Rimbaud's does, while the now eighteen-year-old French poet, launching his poem, deploys a tentative start, not a finish of any sort. Lowell's line comes to a stop at its end; Rimbaud's leads into a piece of associative syntax that only reaches a full stop after the first syllable of the seventh line. Taking Lowell's wish for his deed, though, this way of expressing his ambition invites the suspicion that he will be using strong-arm tactics where his originals had a subtler repertoire of approaches.

Lowell then admits that he has been forced 'to do considerable re-writing'. If this meant that he had worked to bring his English close to the originals by returning again and again to his drafts, then it would have meant one thing. On the basis of what his book contains, a reader may conclude it means he has rewritten the originals taking their words and meanings as a starting point upon which to finesse an expressive variation — but a variation expressive of what? Lowell's second paragraph is such a

[33] Lowell, *Imitations*, p. xi.
[34] Ibid.
[35] Lowell, 'Nostalgia', *Imitations*, p. 74.
[36] Rimbaud, 'Mémoire', *Oeuvres complètes*, p. 86.

muddle of thoughts attempting to answer such a question that it deserves to be looked at whole:

> Boris Pasternak has said that the usual reliable translator gets the literal meaning but misses the tone, and that in poetry tone is of course everything. I have been reckless with literal meaning, and laboured hard to get the tone. Most often this has been *a* tone, for *the* tone is something that will always more or less escape transference to another language and cultural moment. I have tried to write live English and to do what my authors might have done if they were writing their poems now and in America.[37]

His prose travels a long way in a few sentences from 'I have hoped somehow for a whole, to make a single volume, a small anthology of European poetry.' By the end of the passage, this has become European poetry as it might have been if the poets had been writing then and in America — a heterogeneous set of extraordinarily talented immigrants space- and time-transported to Kennedy's United States, all imitating the manner and tone of its prominent poet Robert Lowell. In a paragraph that moves from 'Boris Pasternak has said' to 'in America', Lowell's stance is, aside from everything else, a symptom of Cold War cultural politics. European poetry is to be saved from the Communist threat by being rendered into the style of the free world. The freedoms that Lowell claims may be thought, then, to oppose the restrictions upon what writers may be allowed to do, or not do, by Warsaw Pact states.

Yet another thing that the paragraph represents is the defensiveness of a collapsing stout party. Its circumstances can be traced in the 1961 exchange of letters between Lowell and Elizabeth Bishop, as well as in his reply to letters from T. S. Eliot leading up to the British publication of *Imitations*. Bishop had offered on 1 March 1961 'one or two things that bother me because they *look* like mistakes, whether or no. And though you have left yourself "free," I don't want to think of your being attacked for mistakes.'[38] Among the imitations that Bishop commented on in her draft letter (included in the mailing to the poet) was Lowell's version of 'Au Cabaret-vert':

> AT THE GREEN CABARET (one of my favorites, as I said in my other letter — in its innocent way, too) 'tartines' aren't tarts — they are the pieces of bread and butter served at French schools — 'I contemplated the very naïve subjects in the tapestry' — 'and it was adorable when' — You're [??] can *spike* it [??] — I suppose the 'Belgian pictures' is supposed

[37] Lowell, *Imitations*, p. xi.
[38] Elizabeth Bishop, *One Art: The Selected Letters*, ed. Robert Giroux (London: Chatto & Windus, 1994), p. 395. The materials (letters 229, 230, and 233 and a draft of one letter, appendix 1) relevant to this issue have been collected together in Thomas Travisano and Saskia Hamilton (eds.), *Words in the Air: The Complete Correspondence of Elizabeth Bishop and Robert Lowell* (New York: Farrar, Straus and Giroux, 2008), pp. 351-58, 366-68, 803-07.

> to tie in with the sonnet you've put as I I.? 'Pink and white ham
> flavored with a clove of garlic' — it surely would have been *baked in*
> the ham. (Even in a simple café I don't think the French would serve a
> clove of raw garlic) (~~cooking is more my line than yours!~~) — and 'filled
> up an immense stein for me, with its foam gilded by a ray of *late* sun.'
> The *late* seems important — the atmosphere of fatigue, late afternoon,
> and peacefulness. — 'behind' *looks* like a mistake, I'm afraid.[39]

In the 1 March letter itself Bishop notes that '(I did this once myself)' and
confines herself to a compressed comment on the missing '*late*' in the
last line, and the correction of 'tartines'. Aware as she wrote of the 'free
translation' sub-genre (into which the versions discussed above by Reid
and Carson evidently fall), Bishop identifies Lowell's imitation as evoking
Rimbaud in his time and place. His renderings are not geographically and
historically transposed, and, as a result, take upon themselves responsibility
for not mistranslating 'tartines / De beurre' or giving a wrong impression
about how the ham would have been served. In the published text, Lowell
has 'a large helping of tartines' in line 4, but 'brought me tarts and ham' in
line 11. He persists with, or even exaggerates, Bishop's culinary qualm with
'She stuck a clove of garlic in the ham' in line 12, but did revise the close in
accord with her suggestion by making it read: 'and slopped beer in my stein
— / foam gilded by a ray of the late sun.'[40]

On 27 June Lowell replied to Bishop that 'The whole is much more worth
dedicating to you now and I hope you'll be pleased'; while to Eliot three
days later he sends 'Many thanks for your two letters and the criticism. I
have taken most of it', adding that 'I am also taking the subtitle translation
away, and have written a short preface which clarifies what I am trying to
do.'[41] What the correspondence underlines, at least, is that Lowell's way of
approaching translation does not demonstrate what might be called the
creative writer's, rather than the academic linguist translator's, approach:
important poets who had themselves published, or were to publish, distinguished translations saw the matter differently even at the time. Eliot,
for instance, had returned to his translation of St.-John Perse's *Anabase*,
originally published in 1931, issuing a revised edition of his *Anabasis* (1959)
that included changes made by the French poet being translated.[42] The
elevation of Lowell's work to the status of example and model, to being a
watershed, may be thought a misfortune for poet-translators too.

In the paragraph above Lowell first tells us, courtesy of Pasternak, that
average translators get the literal meaning. I shall be devoting space, later,
to showing how this can never be the case. As if it followed logically, the

---

[39] Bishop and Lowell, *Words in the Air*, pp. 804–05.
[40] Lowell, *Imitations*, pp. 87–88. I have corrected the misprint, 'guilded' for 'gilded', in line 14.
[41] Robert Lowell, *The Letters of Robert Lowell*, ed. Saskia Hamilton (London: Faber & Faber, 2005), pp. 382 and 383–84.
[42] See T. S. Eliot, 'Note to Revised Edition' and 'Note to Third Edition', in St.-John Perse, *Anabasis*, trans. T. S. Eliot (London: Faber & Faber, 1959), pp. 13 and 15.

sentence continues by supposing that because they get the literal meaning, they miss the tone. This also prepares for Lowell's reversed assumption, or hope perhaps, that a translator could get the tone without the meaning. He informs us that 'in poetry tone is of course everything'. This is by no means true either, as Geoffrey Hill has attempted to demonstrate in his melodramatic, but at least better informed, contrast of pitch with tone.[43] Lowell then claims to have 'laboured hard to get the tone', only to admit truly, though not sufficiently clearly or thoroughly, that it can't be done, that it is another aspect of *'the Impossible'* referred to in my subtitle. Lowell writes that *'the* tone is something that will always more or less escape transference to another language and cultural moment.' Michael Hofmann has noticed the 'strangely self-annulling' character of the argument here, but maintains an allegiance to this side of the watershed by adding 'but I still think there's a germ of truth and interest and encouragement here.'[44] Its 'encouragement' can be demonstrated, for Lowell's 'self-annulling' argument highlights the self-authorizing performance of his prose.

But what claim is that 'more or less' in *'the* tone is something that will always more or less escape transference to another language and cultural moment' attempting to defend? Even such adjacent languages as English and French, or English and German, are sufficiently different in textures and tones, not to mention idiom and usage, for it to be literally impossible to reproduce the one in the other. This is why second language speakers, even very good ones, tend to sound slightly odd to the locals. Interpreters have to adopt forms of usage in the second language that produce, as equivalently as possible, the range of implication in the original utterance. As for Lowell's final assertion that he wants to write live English and to do what his authors might have done if they had been writing their poems then and in America, his idea encounters the problems noticed in the voice of 'At the Green Man'. There are other ways of thinking about the fictive ontological status of a translation. To my mind, the best of these would involve admitting that a translation cannot have the kind of cultural grounding that an original might demonstrate. A good translation is inevitably closer to Wordsworth's 'light that never was on sea or land'.[45] At least to place the translation as far beyond the reach of the appropriation that Lowell's Introduction haplessly displays would be a mark of respect towards the cultural and historical locations of the poet-translator's originals.

Most crucially, and disastrously, Lowell's admission that 'I have been almost as free as the authors themselves in finding ways to make them

[43] See Geoffrey Hill, 'Dividing Legacies', *Collected Critical Writings*, ed. Kenneth Hayes (Oxford: Oxford University Press, 2008), pp. 377-79.
[44] Durs Grünbein, *Ashes for Breakfast: Selected Poems*, trans. Michael Hofmann (London: Faber & Faber, 2005), p. xiv.
[45] William Wordsworth, 'Elegiac Stanzas', *Selected Poems*, ed. Damian Walford Davies (London: Everyman's Library, 1994), p. 329.

ring right for me' reveals a painful misunderstanding of what is involved in 'finding ways to make' a poem 'ring right' for anyone who reads it. Original authors, if they have any respect for their own materials and languages, are not at all 'free'.[46] The implicit contrast between poets who can write 'what they like' and translators who must modestly photograph their originals is false, because translators can never 'photograph' from one language to another, and original writers are involved in complex nets of responsibility to their inspiration, technique, language, materials, themes, oeuvres, and readers. They have greater ranges of potential for revision; but they also have no completed work of art to act as their guide. Their superficial freedom to change things around is curtailed by their obligation to find a form that rings right; the translator is reading a form that presumably rings right and must find an equivalent for that rightness in another language. Both poet and translator are working within constraints; they are not precisely the same, but they are related constraints. Lowell admits that poetic translators must be 'expert and inspired'; this is why, if he were being both of those things, he could not be 'almost as free' as his original authors. The expert and inspired only appear to be free within the complexes of responsibilities that are manifested by their expertise, one of which is to preserve the gift of their inspiration in the often laborious activity of transforming its promptings into a finished work.

Photography can also be practised as an art. A further problem with Lowell's argument is that the prose guide to the meaning of a poem, such as George Kay's, can never be a faithful rendering, because it lacks formal interest. Thus, while it may be sensitive and responsible at the level of paraphrase, it is neither responsible nor sensitive at the levels of rhythm, rhyme, enjambment, the matching of syntax to line or stanza, that's to say, at the complex technical levels where form shapes and comments on theme, and vice versa. Lowell's contrast between the expert poet translating as if he were writing a poem of his own, and the modest linguist providing a reliable crib for the inspired to use as a springboard, requires a false description of the work of both. The most lamentable consequence of this false division of labour is that it cuts the ground from under the feet of the person who aims to make a translation of a poem that is as faithful as possible both at the level of paraphrase and at that of formal expertise. Yet there is a further obstacle in the path of such a person, and that is the ingrained assumption to be met with on all sides that it is literally impossible to do both of these things at the same time. Languages are not homologous, and to attempt to render the sense is to lose the form, they argue, while to attempt to imitate the form inevitably loses the sense.

Alongside Lowell's statements of policy in his Introduction there is the example of his practice. His slippery defence of these imitations could be

---

[46] See my 'W. H. Auden Revises a Context', *In the Circumstances: About Poetry and Poets* (Oxford: Oxford University Press, 1992), pp. 24-29.

left to one side if his practice were overwhelmingly convincing.[47] Here is the penultimate quatrain of Rimbaud's 'Le bateau ivre', where, after eighty lines of excited poetry about the antics of the drunken boat derived from adventure literature and imaginative projection, the poet suddenly subdues his register and switches to the down-to-earth domestic situation of a child by a pond with a toy boat. I include the final line of the previous quatrain, to show the drop in pitch:

> Ô que ma quille éclate! Ô que j'aille à la mer!

> Si je desire une eau d'Europe, c'est la flache
> Noire et froide où vers le crepuscule embaumé
> Un enfant accroupi, plein de tristesse, lâche
> Un bateau frêle comme un papillon de mai.[48]

Sublime in its attuning of this sudden drop from the exalted to the sad, the passage frames and grounds the poem's adventurously restless imaginative ambitions within a condition of real entrapment that both offsets and legitimates them. Here is Lowell's handling of the transition:

> Oh that my keel might break, and I might drown!

> Shrunken and black against a twilight sky,
> our Europe has no water. Only a pond
> the cows have left, and a boy wades to launch
> his paper boat frail as a butterfly.[49]

An attentive reader would admit that Lowell manages an analogous drop in register, signalling it with 'Shrunken'; and though 'and I might drown!' is only a paraphrase of Rimbaud's sense, still, his exclamation steers quite close to its original. Rimbaud's picture of the child by the pond is vividly straightforward: he's crouching down, full of sadness, by dark and cold water towards a fragrant dusk, and he lets go his boat, a sailboat probably, because its sails can flap like a butterfly's wings. Though the water is cold and dark, the sky is scented, perhaps because it's spring and warm, and the boy is out at dusk because the weather is good enough (it's a May butterfly) to allow it. So, although the water is dark and cold and it's only a pond, no explanation is given for his sadness; but he is alone by the waterside, not in a gang, or with a brother or sister. The contrast with the previous lines of adventure and delirium suggests that launching the boat is a pathetic attempt to enact an imaginative escape, on the lines of Baudelaire's 'Le voyage', but with the trapped isolation of a poor provincial childhood in place.

My slight disappointment in reading Lowell's imitation is that, using

---

[47] For a discussion of Lowell's *Imitations* in relation to a speculative psychology of translating, see my 'Envy, Gratitude, and Translation', *In the Circumstances*, pp. 156–72.

[48] Arthur Rimbaud, 'Le bateau ivre', *Oeuvres complètes*, p. 69.

[49] Lowell, *Imitations*, p. 83.

whatever freedoms he may like to claim, he has still lost so much of this picture. Maybe 'cows have left' the 'flache' just before Rimbaud's poem takes place, but the French poet doesn't mention them; worst of all is the idea that the boy 'wades to launch' his boat. Now it could just be that he's in the water, though Rimbaud doesn't say he is, but in Lowell's version he's not crouching down to launch it. Also, 'launch' is the wrong word, even if it was suggested by its auditory similarity to the French: it's the wrong word because we are at the end of the poem and there is an act of renunciation going on at the metaphorical level of the entire imaginative flight. So Rimbaud writes that the boy let's the boat go, just as he is letting his poem go. This produces the sobering effect of making the entire poem appear to be the feverish workings of a trapped child's imagination. Lowell misses the 'full of sadness (or sorrow)' detail. He interprets and weakens the final simile by preempting it with his 'paper boat'. Rimbaud says that it's 'Un bateau'. Lowell's grammar is also slightly loose, so that for a moment you can think that it's the boy who is 'frail as a butterfly'. Weakest of all is the rewriting of the syntax at the beginning of the verse: 'our Europe has no water. Only a pond' is a disaster. It's true that there's a contrast between the freedom of an imagined America with its Red Indians in the opening lines, and he is presumably being reckless with meaning so as to render a tone for 'Si je désire', but why 'our' Europe? I dearly hope it isn't the free world's Europe as opposed to the eastern bloc's. It's hardly Lowell's, and Rimbaud doesn't claim it in that presumptuous fashion either. It rains in northern Europe, and there are rivers, and the North Sea, which lets into the Atlantic. I suppose it's wrong to take Lowell's line literally, for he has headed off such coarseness with 'our'; but since 'our' raises my hackles, the daft assertion that 'our Europe has no water', immediately contradicted by the introduction of the pond, reduces the vigorous Rimbaud's poem to near incoherence. In the balance sheet of any translation, for my taste the losses here far outweigh any gains from Lowell's determined phrase making. He could also have preserved a detail by translating 'papillon de mai' as 'May butterfly' and kept his rhyme on 'sky'.

IV

Among Lowell's most vociferous and distinguished opponents was Vladimir Nabokov, who asserted that to render the poems of others in Lowell's fashion was not merely morally wrong as regards the originals and their authors, but it was also a cruel disrespect of readers. After commenting on various errors and distortions in a Lowell version, Nabokov wrote:

> When I think that the American college student of today, so docile, so trustful, so eager to be led to any bright hell by an eccentric teacher, will mistake that adaption for a sample of Mandelshtam's thought ('the poet compares the sheep-skin sent him from abroad to the wolf hide he refuses to wear'), I cannot help feeling that despite the good

intentions of adapters something very like cruelty and deception is
the inevitable result of their misguided labours.[50]

Humbert Humbert, *Lolita*'s narrator and main protagonist, is working
in comparative literature throughout most of his narrative. Travesties of
French poetry are one of his ways of acknowledging his moral disorder,
as when, dreaming of Dolly Haze's daughter and granddaughter, he draws
a *double entendre* from the title of Victor Hugo's 1877 collection *L'art d'être
grand-père* by imagining a 'bizarre, tender, salivating Dr Humbert, practising
on supremely lovely Lolita the Third the art of being a granddad.'[51] Here
'something very like cruelty' is being contrasted with a respect for the
words and thought of another person, also vulnerable, because no longer
alive to contest the accuracy of the representation. In a letter replying
publicly to Lowell in *Encounter*, Nabokov wrote: 'I wish ... that he would stop
mutilating defenceless dead poets — Mandeshtam, Rimbaud, and others.'[52]
It should be acknowledged, though, that Mandelstam's widow 'greatly
liked' Lowell's adaptations of her husband's work, because 'everything is
unexpected' and, unlike what she calls 'rendering verse with great skill but
rather mechanically', translations such as his 'belong to literature' and 'are
quite free'.[53] I return to both the quick and the dead, and our duties towards
them, in my final chapter.

One problem associated with Nabokov's objections to the Lowell
approach is that his alternative mode produced, in the notorious instance
of Pushkin's *Eugene Onegin*, a text that could plausibly be described by
Lowell as 'a spoof at its readers, rival translators, Pushkin, and Nabokov
himself', in the statement he sent to Stephen Spender for *Encounter* in late
February 1966:

> I suppose every translator dreams of writing a version that will
> stand on its own feet, new, important, and yet relentlessly loyal to
> the original. In poetry this is almost impossible, and perhaps even in
> prose. Something very odd and catching has happened in Nabokov's
> *Onegin*, or so it seems to the reader with no Russian. Maybe a merely
> literal and literate prose reproduction rightly struck Nabokov as an
> appallingly commonplace assignment, and a stifling test for his zany
> genius. What he has written is a weirdly eccentric minor English
> poem, one that suggests that Pushkin's *Onegin* is not, as everyone
> claims, a national classic, but some wildly queer miscarriage, like
> Marvell's 'Appleton House,' a poem whose idiosyncratic freshness is

[50] Vladimir Nabokov, *Strong Opinions* (New York: Vintage, 1973), pp. 282–83.

[51] Vladimir Nabokov, *The Annotated Lolita*, ed. A. Appel Jr. (New York: Vintage, 1970),
p. 176.

[52] Vladimir Nabokov, *Selected Letters 1940–1977*, ed. Dimitri Nabokov and
M. J. Bruccoli (San Diego, New York, London: Harcourt Brace Jovanovich, 1989),
p. 387.

[53] Nadezhda Mandelstam to Robert Lowell, March 1967, cited from *Poets on Street
Corners*, ed. Olga Carlyle (1968), in Robert Lowell, *Collected Poems*, ed. Frank Bidart,
David Gewanter, and DeSales Harrison (London: Faber & Faber, 2003), p. 1156.

> so peculiar that it reduces the translator to a stutter of whimsicality and gristle. It's as though Nabokov swore to be faithful, and then felt that faithfulness would only bring him one of those coarse plaster busts of Homer, that doom of the usual conscientious translator.[54]

Leaving aside Lowell's dismissal of Andrew Marvell's most challengingly metamorphic poem, the polemical travesty of Nabokov's strong opinion about translation is a little more complex than this confrontation might suggest. In his three attempts to translate Pushkin's epic there is a 'shift to literalism', as it has been described, and Nabokov was himself perfectly capable of producing the fourteen-line rhymed stanzas in which the poem is written.[55] Nevertheless, the standoff between these two writers can be seen, emblematically, to represent extremes of the poetry and translation debate in the middle of the twentieth century, one that is still haunting our later day: powerful appropriation in the name of poetic freedom confronted by a dogmatic theory of devotion to the literal meaning of the original, in which the plague on both their houses is also suffered by third parties, the translated originals, caught between these mighty opposites. Poetry readers and other poets also suffer collateral damage, especially those many writers who take Lowell's example as permission to do as they please. Nor is it insignificant that his is a more toxic example than Nabokov's: few if any scholars or poets have followed, or are likely to follow, the example of his 'literal' version of Pushkin's poem, but Lowell's example has been taken as an invitation to 'legitimized' slapdash.

Despite the force of their confrontation, Lowell's and Nabokov's convictions about, and methods of, translation are parasitic upon each other. The freedoms that Lowell allows himself are provided with a sight-screen by the background notion of literal fidelity (in his case exemplified by George Kay's prose renderings), while Nabokov's later dislike of rhyming paraphrase and his ever more extreme notion of the literal meaning, the Cleopatra for which he would sacrifice everything, is dependent upon a vivid sense of what his choice requires him to eschew. Nabokov has poetic freedoms as the devilish temptation that gives virtue to his self-denyingly grotesque and footnoted literalism. In trying to refresh the discussion of how poems are translated, I put aside the idea that poetry is made by the exercise of unlimited creative freedom, as equally that there can be literal translations of a work of art. The immediate assumption might be that the last statement allows the translator a suddenly open field in which to operate. If there is no literal translation, there can be no meaningful sense of fidelity or accuracy; and so the imitators and version-makers can be given a free rein. *Not at all*: it is the fact that there can be no literal translation that allows there to be fidelity and accuracy, for these terms require that there is an acknowledged gap between the original and its translation. You can only be faithful to someone or some thing when you have acknowledged

---

[54] Lowell, *Letters*, pp. 466–67.
[55] See Weissbort and Eysteinsson (eds.), *Translation — Theory and Practice*, pp. 386–88.

both its integrity and the need for that to be cherished and protected. You can only make an accurate measurement or accurate picture of something if the means of measuring or picturing are evidently not the same as the object being measured or pictured. Fidelity and accuracy are matched to the acceptance of difference, while literal translation invites us to fantasize that such qualities can be dispensed with because we are aiming to achieve an exact reproduction. So-called literal translations manifest a series of translation choices founded upon granting importance to one aspect of the task to the manifestly evident, and therefore notionally 'modest', neglect of all others.

When Nabokov discusses the productions of the literalist, he describes the work of a writer who is inevitably making judgments, as here when comparing three methods of rendering the first four lines in Pushkin's poem:

> Now comes the literalist. He may toy with 'honorable' instead of 'honest' and waver between 'seriously' and 'not in jest'; he will replace 'rules' by the more evocative 'principles' and rearrange the order of the words to achieve some semblance of English construction and retain some vestige of Russian rhythm [56]

Exemplifying this approach would be the oddly prosaic verse-like writing that Nabokov himself produced to render Pushkin's epic:

> Another hindrance I foresee:
> saving the honor of my native land,
> undoubtedly I'll be obliged
> Tatiana's letter to translate.
> She knew Russian badly,
> did not read our reviews,
> and expressed herself with difficulty
> in her native tongue;
> hence wrote in French.
> What's to be done about it! I repeat again;
> as yet a lady's love
> has not expressed itself in Russian,
> as yet our proud tongue has
> to postal prose not got accustomed. [57]

The poetic inversions ('Tatiana's letter to translate') must be faithful to the Russian word order, to fit with Nabokov's theory, or they are stylistic ineptitudes. Some such case would have to be made for the odd word and phrase choices too. This translator is also interpreting and judging between words, and not only for 'literal meaning' — a notion that itself won't survive much thinking about, as we shall see. 'Principles' is more evocative than

[56] Foreword to Aleksandr Pushkin, *Eugene Onegin: A Novel in Verse*, trans. Vladimir Nabokov, vol. 1: *Introduction and Translation* (Princeton, NJ: Princeton University Press, rev. ed. 1975), p. viii.

[57] Ibid. 3.26, p. 162.

'rules' in Nabokov's comment on translating the opening lines of the poem, because of the backgrounds of usage that the two words have in the English language. But could not a translator also make decisions about rhyming and rhythm that sought to balance different aspects of what it means to be faithful to a poem in translating it? How can it be accurate to translate a poem that rhymes or is in a set metre without producing a translation that also renders, or at least structurally alludes to, this fact about the text being translated? Why keep the fourteen-line units but not the syllable count of their lines? What's more, it turns out that Nabokov's objection to rhymed paraphrase translations is that they allow the translator as would-be-poet to evade the challenges of rendering as accurately as possible the meaning of the text. Yet the meaning of a poem is inseparable from its structure. If you are going to translate the text as a poem at all, you will have to convey some sense of this too.

As for a rhyming paraphrase, there is perhaps nowhere better to go than Charles Johnston's version of the same stanza:

> I see another problem looming:
> to save the honour of our land
> I *must* translate — there's no presuming —
> the letter from Tatyana's hand:
> her Russian was as thin as vapour,
> she never read a Russian paper,
> our native speech had never sprung
> unhesitating from her tongue,
> she wrote in French ... what a confession!
> what can I do? as said above,
> until this day, a lady's love
> in Russian never found expression,
> till now our language — proud, God knows —
> has hardly mastered postal prose.[58]

Two things might be said about this: first, knowing no Russian and comparing it with Nabokov's version that prides itself on not betraying Pushkin's sense, it doesn't look as if Johnston strays far from the thematic content and implication of the verse; second, because he has written a rhyming stanza that has something of the Byronic *sprezzatura* that Pushkin himself was imitating, the creative intent of the original and of a poet's communicative impulse are more convincingly conveyed by Johnston's metrical rhyming lines than by the impure diction, archaic word order, and staggeringly prosaic free verse of the Nabokov version. What's more, if the word order is poetically arch ('a lady's love / in Russian never found expression'), the sustained rhythm of the stanza, the regularly occurring rhymes, and the fact that it is a rendering of a poem from the nineteenth century all mitigate the archness to near disappearance.

---

[58] Alexander Pushkin, *Eugene Onegin*, trans. Charles Johnston with an introduction by John Bayley (Harmondsworth: Penguin Books, 1979), 3. 26, p. 97.

Nabokov was perfectly capable of producing metrical rhymed translations, and, as I say, perfectly capable of reproducing the Pushkin stanza, as he showed in his poetic tribute to it, published as the first in a poem of two such verses in the *New Yorker* on 8 January 1955:

What is a translation? On a platter
A poet's pale and glaring head,
A parrot's screech, a monkey's chatter,
And profanation of the dead.
The parasites you were so hard on
Are pardoned if I have your pardon,
O Pushkin, for my stratagem.
I traveled down your secret stem,
And reached the root, and fed upon it;
Then in a language newly learned,
I grew another stalk and turned
Your stanza, patterned on a sonnet,
Into my honest roadside prose —
All thorn, but cousin to your rose.[59]

A further issue arises in the fact that Nabokov's version is both inimitable and, to my knowledge, un-imitated, whereas it is to Johnston's that we should go in search of the international transfer of poetic influence that generates new art — for it was his Pushkin that inspired Vikram Seth's *The Golden Gate*, a narrative poem set in San Francisco, and first published in 1986. This is what Seth does with an English version of the Pushkin stanza:

Reader, enough of this apology;
But spare me if I think it best,
Before I tether my monology,
To stake a stanza to suggest
You spend some unfilled day of leisure
By that original spring of pleasure:
Sweet-watered, fluent, clear, light, blithe
(This homage merely pays a tithe
Of what in joy and inspiration
It gave me once and does not cease
To give me) — Pushkin's masterpiece
In Johnston's luminous translation:
Eugene Onegin — like champagne
Its effervescence stirs my brain.[60]

Weissbort has implied that the vast majority of poetry translators, either in their practice or conviction, place themselves, or find themselves placed, within that dualistic structure, on one side or the other of that watershed, either the Lowell school, or, more rarely, Nabokov's. Yet paraphrasing as accurately as possible the sense of the original in rhymed stanzas that not

[59] Pushkin, *Eugene Onegin*, trans. Nabokov, p. 9.
[60] Vikram Seth, *The Golden Gate* (London: Faber & Faber, 1986), 5.5, p. 102.

only reproduce the rhyme scheme but also imitate the sound of a model for Pushkin's own poem, Charles Johnston's *Onegin* appears to be on neither side, or straddling both.

What may be mistaken about Nabokov's approach is that while he accepts that sacrifices will have to be made in making translations, he doesn't allow the sacrifices to be evenly distributed, negotiated, or complexly mitigated across the entire field of poetic composition. For him, the sacrifices have to be made in the field of sonic cohesion and formal significance. Once again, Lowell and Nabokov appear to be staring at each other from opposite sides of Frost's fence: the one claiming to be faithful to the poem by travestying the meaning, the other claiming to be faithful by travestying the form. The underlying assumption of these mighty opposites is that you can't do both at the same time. But, as Johnston's example may suggest, you can do far better than either of them polemically allow, if you adopt a different sense of what translating is and involves, and accept that if sacrifices are going to have to be made then they can be shared more equally across the falsely characterized form-and-meaning divide. This would enable us to approach a truer sense of how original poems are written, how they signify in the complex of their formal, syntactic, and semantic structures, and how translators who aim to translate poems as poems are obliged to perform across that spectrum too. I abandon the groundless freedoms of Lowell and the literalist debilitations of Nabokov, not only because both methods fail to deliver useful translations, but because both are partly implicitly and partly explicitly founded upon false understandings of poets' and translators' relations to their languages.

Elizabeth Bishop summarizes the theme of my book in a review of translations from Jules Laforgue by Wiliam Jay Smith:

> By now everyone knows how to review a book of translated poetry. First, one says it's impossible. Second, one implies that the translator is an ignoramus, or if that's going too far, that he has missed the plays on words; and then one carps about the inevitable mistakes. The first objection is still true: it is impossible to translate poetry, or perhaps only one aspect can be translated at a time, and each poem needs several translations.

If Bishop subscribes to the conviction that you can't do form and meaning at the same time here, she also admires the translator under review for 'an exceptionally good try' and thinks that 'his faithfulness to the French will impress most reviewers.' She cites an image from Jay Smith's introduction in which he too appears to admit the impossibility of the task: 'Translating poetry is like converging on a flame with a series of mirrors, mirrors of technique and understanding, until the flame is reflected in upon itself in a wholly new and foreign element. Such an operation is rarely, if ever, successful: the manipulation of the mirrors depends to such an extent on the sensibility and skill of the translator.' Bishop concludes: 'Besides being a pretty image, this is a true one, as anyone who has ever tried translating poetry will know. But surely, besides sensibility and skill, it depends (about 50 percent, I'd say) on luck: the possibilities of the second language's vocabulary.'[61] Composing poets, as much as translators, working in their own linguistic idioms are, as Bishop makes clear here, hardly free. They listen to the language forming, and respond to shapes found by developing upon them, and by adjusting backwards, in either case with a responsibility to what has been produced and to what can grow out of it.

The composition of original works does not strictly mean finding ways of saying what you want to say, but of finding what the poem can say for you in the process of working on it. This equally depends, to borrow Bishop's calculation, at least fifty percent on the vocabulary of the language in which the work is being composed. The freedom of the poet to say things is constrained by the creative attention to the work that is emerging in the language. The poet-translator rendering another's text is constrained in ways that are similar and analogous to those of the composing poet. It is often asserted that formal constraints can be of great help in focusing the poet's compositional work. There seems no reason in principle why this should not also be true of the translating poet. Lowell and Nabokov represent two extremes, sharing the same ground in their opposition to each other. Between both, in a reformulation that takes us away from such zero sum territory, lies the space in which poetry is translated — losses, gains, luck, or lack of it, and all. So it is to the relationship between poetry's being 'impossible to translate' and each poem's needing 'several translations' that I now turn in a chapter about the English afterlife of Rainer Maria Rilke's verse.

[61] Elizabeth Bishop, 'The Manipulation of Mirrors', *Poems, Prose, and Letters*, ed. Robert Giroux and Lloyd Schwartz (New York: Library of America, 2008), p. 696.

CHAPTER 3

Thou Art Translated

I

'Bless thee, Bottom, bless thee. Thou art translated',[1] exclaims Peter Quince
in *A Midsummer Night's Dream*. In the well-known scene, Bottom the
Weaver, his head metamorphosed to that of an ass, encounters his fellow
players. Here the word 'translated' might equally need translating into
'transformed'.[2] Charles Nicholl translates a 1586 use of the word from the
fashion trade reporting a payment for 'translating [altering] & mending of
an attyre for the hed'.[3] Translators can do no other than alter, but unlike
this headgear transformation and that of Bottom's head, the translation of
a poem or other verbal artifact will be an inexact copy whose relation to
its original more resembles that of a variation to its theme. Shakespeare's
use of the word is expressive of the shocking discrepancies that can be
felt when encountering such translating. For poetry to be translated, in
the sense implied by this chapter's title, is for it to be altered into a form
that is comically unsuitable, improper even, and enjoyed by those such
as Titania under delusive influences. Yet in Shakespeare's play the dangers
of humiliation are for the most part averted, the transformations are only
in play, and Bottom's features are restored. Among the ambiguities and
ironies of the famous phrase that I take for a title to this chapter are the
thought that poetry can be translated, but what readers will get is an ass's
head. Yet for Bottom the dream was true, and a tribute to art's equivocally
metamorphic powers. *A Midsummer Night's Dream* is a comedy, and its
dramatist artfully keeps open the ways its ironies will play.

It isn't difficult, then, to see why people say that poetry cannot be
translated, and why poets who feel nevertheless drawn to impersonate

---

[1] William Shakespeare, *A Midsummer Night's Dream*: 3. i. 112.

[2] This is the translation given in the Arden and Cambridge editions of the play.

[3] Charles Nicholl, *The Lodger: Shakespeare on Silver Street* (Harmondsworth: Penguin
Books, 2008), p. 142.

poems in English should be inclined not to call their resulting texts translations. I would like to dissolve this apparent contradiction between pre-theoretical or under-theorized assumptions about language and evident practice. However, the contradiction will not disappear by asserting that because it is translated, poetry must be translatable. We saw Lowell note, in support of those that assume poetry cannot be translated, that 'Most poetic translations come to grief',[4] something which can be illustrated from his own publications. To dissolve the contradiction it is first necessary to accept that those who claim poetry cannot be translated are, according to their justifiable assumptions, correct, but that what they say about poetry is variously true for all human language use.

Rainer Maria Rilke, one target of Don Paterson's considerable altering powers, is among the most translated of modern poets. Joseph Brodsky noted in his essay 'Ninety Years After' that 'in the past three decades translating Rilke has become practically a fad'.[5] The second of Rilke's untitled sonnets to Orpheus becomes a poem Paterson calls 'Girl':

> Almost a girl ... Who suddenly took wing
> above that wedding of the voice and lyre,
> who blazed below the veils of her own Spring
> and made herself a bed inside my ear.
>
> And slept in me. And all things were her sleep.[6]

Paterson describes his aim as to build a local habitation from Rilke's original, seeming to leave it behind by deploying vernacular styles and materials. Yet the most immediate feature of this famous poem's opening five lines is the unusual character of both what the voice says and how it is speaking. The lines are about a girl who dies, and the poet internalizes her death, finding her in him at springtime. The sonnet has an extreme condensation of theme, and unusual speech — the girl making a bed in his ear being perhaps the strangest. Despite the talk of a robust home in a vernacular architecture, it's rare, if not unknown, for a poet writing in English to speak like this. Who's voicing these observations? In his own works Paterson doesn't tend to strike such notes. 'The Ferryman's Arms' begins not uncharacteristically: 'About to sit down with my half-pint of Guinness / I was magnetized by a remote phosphorescence'.[7] What has got into *him*? If we go to Rilke's original in search of a possible answer, we find that despite his claims ('This is not a translation, but a version')[8] the oddity of speech in the rendering is a derivative, and a close one, of the German poet's lines. The passage about the girl making a bed in his ear is almost exactly rendered: 'und machte

---

[4] Robert Lowell, Introduction, *Imitations* (Farrar, Straus & Giroux, 1961), p. xi.

[5] Joseph Brodsky, 'Ninety Years After', *On Grief and Reason: Essays* (London: Hamish Hamilton, 1996), p. 382.

[6] Don Paterson, *Orpheus: A Version of Rilke's* Die Sonette an Orpheus (London: Faber & Faber, 2006), p. 4.

[7] Don Paterson, *Nil Nil* (London: Faber & Faber, 1993), p. 1.

[8] Paterson, *Orpheus*, p. 73.

sich ein Bett in meinem Ohr./ Und schlief in mir. Und alles war ihr Schlaf'[9] ('and made herself a bed in my ear./And slept in me. And all things were her sleep.') Not only does Paterson approximate to the original's simple and direct language, by neatly turning his English he gets a syntactical ordering, and a rhythm, as close as possible to Rilke's. 'Girl' as a whole is a good and faithfully close translation. It might be contrasted with many a poem such as Eiléan Ní Chuilleanáin's 'After Leopardi's Storm' — where both the title and comparison with the original reveal an almost autonomous poem, one wittily playing with the 'After' preposition too, for its original is called 'La quiete dopo la tempesta' [The Quiet after the Storm].[10]

Asking who is speaking in a translation is not an empty question. Aside from the critical issue of how the speech is to be understood, it raises a qualm about how these versions of Rilke are presented. On its title page the book is attributed to Don Paterson. It's called *Orpheus*, as if it were about the Greek musician and poet-figure, while in a subtitle that doesn't appear either on the jacket or, conventionally enough, on the half-title page, it is described as 'A version of Rilke's *Die Sonette an Orpheus*'. The front jacket flap translates that original title as *Sonnets to Orpheus*, so that's cleared up. Why isn't the book described as by Rainer Maria Rilke, with the title rendered as it is on the jacket blurb, and with 'translated by Don Paterson' as the acknowledgement of his role in the performance? Aside from spoiling the separation of types in his distinction between a translation and a version, it would prevent the selling point outlined on the blurb: 'Paterson's translation', it inconsistently notes, 'is an act of intense and sustained attention, which has in turn yielded new poems of striking authority, independence and lyric grace.' Not wanting to contest the phrase about Paterson's act in rendering these poems, I would ask if the 'authority, independence and lyric grace' don't in combination make claims for Paterson that might be shared between him and the author of the original sonnets. It's the word 'independence' which does the damage, a word that the lines about the girl making herself a bed in the poet's ear don't much support.

The 'striking authority' of Paterson's version derives much of its directness and force from the authority of the German poet. Translations have an ontological ambiguity that needs to be understood and addressed by anyone doing any form of rendering from another language or source text. The works produced are, and have to be read as, the sound of one voice in effect pretending to be another's, what Matthew Mead has called 'the ventriloquist's-dummy aspect of translation'.[11] Paterson performs 'an act of

---

[9] Rainer Maria Rilke, *Die Sonette an Orpheus*, I. 2, in *Die Gedichte* (Frankfurt am Main: Insel Verlag, 1986), p. 675.

[10] See Eiléan Ní Chuilleanáin, *Selected Poems*, ed. Peter Fallon (Oldcastle, Co. Meath: Gallery Press and London: Faber & Faber, 2008), p. 110, and Giacomo Leopardi, *Canti*, ed. John Humphreys Whitfield, rev. ed. (Manchester: Manchester University Press, 1978), pp. 103–04.

[11] Matthew Mead, Introduction, Ruth and Matthew Mead, *Word for Word: Selected Translations from German Poets* (London: Anvil Press, 2009), p. 12.

sustained attention', but in vocalizing the original the poet-translator will also be acting out an echo of the original's acts:

> Und fast ein Mädchen wars und ging hervor
> aus diesem einigen Glück von Sang und Leier
> und glänzte klar durch ihre Frühlingsschleier
> und machte sich ein Bett in meinem Ohr.
>
> Und schlief in mir. Und alles war ihr Schlaf.[12]

Compared with Paterson's version, these lines from the untitled second poem in the first part of *Die Sonette an Orpheus* tend to support the proposition that poetry is translatable, even as Paterson's ideas about the art, and ways of presenting his work, make him appear on the Lowell side of the debate. His practice vindicates him, which makes it the more disappointing that his accompanying justification misleadingly makes an autonomous status claim for the versioning poet. Translators not known as poets may be implicitly denigrated by such claims. My subtitle proposes that translators are artists too, even if not often granted such a title.[13]

'While we may find J. B. Leishman's rhymed version of the Sonnets uncomfortably aureate,' Paterson suggests, 'we can hardly say that Wyatt's interpretations of Petrarch have dated; we recognize that the master he was serving was English lyric, not Petrarch.'[14] Brodsky's defence of Leishman's Rilke succinctly states a counter-argument: 'the translator's surrender of his ego to the reader's comfort; that's how a poem ceases to be foreign.'[15] The New Testament source of Paterson's wording ('No man can serve two masters')[16] prevents him from reflecting that Wyatt might have been serving the two masters of both English lyric and an awareness of Petrarch's poetry in the British Isles. He is usually accredited with being among the first to introduce the Italian poet into the country's poetic culture. The Bible's sentence also requires Wyatt to be serving a master that he was himself helping to invent as he rendered the Italian into his English lyric. Poetry in the vernacular is an evolving interpersonal phenomenon to which Wyatt was himself contributing. As Seamus Heaney implied in his 'Singing School',[17] the 'English lyric' can be a cruel taskmaster of an abstraction. It may help to consider both language and poetry not as a compound persecutory platonic entity that the individual writer must serve, but as

---

12 Rilke, *Die Gedichte*, pp. 675–76.
13 See Lawrence Venuti, *The Translator's Invisibility: A History of Translation*, 2nd edn. (London: Routledge, 2008), chapter 1.
14 Paterson, *Orpheus*, p. 74. For Leishmann's translations of the sonnet, see Rainer Maria Rilke, *Sonnets to Orpheus*, trans. J. B. Leishman (London: Hogarth Press, 1936), p. 39.
15 Brodsky, 'Ninety Years After', p. 382.
16 Matthew 6: 24. This verse asserts that 'Ye cannot serve God and mammon'; it is elsewhere recommended that ye 'Render to Caesar the things that are Caesar's and to God the things that are God's' (Mark 12: 17).
17 See Seamus Heaney, *North* (London: Faber & Faber, 1975), p. 65.

areas of multiply overlapping activities to which many people variously contribute. When Wyatt encountered Petrarch's poetry during his visit to Italy in 1527, he was acting as an ambassador, not of English lyric, but with money from Henry VIII. We are serving more than one master every day of our lives, even if those masters are no more than our desires and our prudential calculations. There's no reason why in writing we shouldn't be under similarly conflicting demands and feel the psychological need to balance responsibilities.

What's more, in making a translation it isn't possible to distinguish between serving the language culture by writing in a fresh idiom, and serving that culture by importing a way of thinking, a formal structure, or a memorable conjunction of metaphors. Translating Petrarch wouldn't have been an occasion to serve the interests of an emerging English lyric if it hadn't also been a matter of bringing over into the language culture a new way of seriously taking your emotions personally through the vicissitudes of a life — as in *Canzoniere* 132, which has a claim to being the single most influential European lyric ever written or translated, and especially its sestet's paradoxical close:

> E s'io 'l consento, a gran torto mi doglio.
> Fra sì contrari vènti in frale barca
> mi trovo in alto mar senza governo,
>
> sì lieve di saver, d'error sì carca
> ch'i' medesmo non so quell ch'io mi voglio,
> e tremo a mezza state, ardendo il verno.

In 2002 Anthony Mortimer published a translation of Petrarch's original, composed in the mid-fourteenth century, making it into a rhymed English sonnet whose sestet reads:

> And if I do consent, wrongly I grieve.
> By such cross winds my fragile bark is blown
> I drift unsteered upon the open seas,
>
> in wisdom light, with error so weighed down
> that I myself know not the thing I crave,
> and burn in winter, and in summer freeze.[18]

Translators cannot be serving the English lyric merely by making sure that their vernacular is in order. They have to be bringing over something irreducibly valuable to themselves, and their readers, from the other language culture's way of thinking, in this case the paradoxical metaphors for love which have been so successfully adapted that they have become a common currency: 'Allas, what is this wondre maladie? / For hete of cold, for cold of hete, I dye' by Chaucer (ca. 1383), or 'I waue in doubt what helpe I shall require, / In Sommer freeze, in winter burn like fire' by Thomas

---

[18] Francesco Petrarch, *Selected Poems*, trans. Anthony Mortimer (Harmondsworth: Penguin Books, 2002), p. 69.

Watson (1582), or 'Which way in this distraction shall I turn, / That freeze in Summer, and in Winter burn?' by Philip Ayres (1712).[19] This much-translated heat and cold paradox has so taken root in Anglophone poetic culture, that it can insinuate a deeper hinterland of affective tenderness than appears to be expressed — as in the closing lines of 'Here Lies a Lady' by John Crowe Ransom: 'In love and great honor we bade God rest her soul / After six little spaces of chill, and six of burning.'[20]

Paterson supposed 'we can hardly say that Wyatt's interpretations of Petrarch have dated'; yet perhaps 'dated' is a judgment that peculiarly suits translations as relatively recent as Leishman's Rilke, because their language is near enough to seem not quite up to date. It might make less sense to say that Arthur Golding's translation of Ovid's *Metamorphoses* is written in a dated English than to acknowledge it to be written in a language that once very much was, but is now no longer, colloquially current. Being 'dated', in this sense, means confined in a transitory state between 'up to date' and 'of the past'. In that latter clear category a translation such as Golding's is well positioned for revival, as Ezra Pound shows in his *ABC of Reading*.[21] That Shakespeare is believed to have read Golding's Ovid with some attention might equally suggest how this translator served the English language whether that was the master he had half an eye on or not, as Jonathan Bate has noted: 'If Shakespeare and his contemporaries owed their intimacy with Ovidian rhetoric to the grammar schools, their easy familiarity with Ovidian narrative was as much due to Golding.'[22] To place a quotation from Golding's version of the story of Tereus, Philomel, and Procne from *Metamorphoses* Book 6 next to its retelling by Ted Hughes in *Tales from Ovid* is to hear the contrast between a vivid English that is no longer current, and an inert near-contemporary talk that though perhaps not yet past its sell-by date has the stamp of an already past moment upon it. This is the instant at the end of the tale when the rapist king is transformed into a hoopoe:

> And he through sorrow and desire of vengeance waxing wight, ⎫
> Became a Bird upon whose top a tuft of feathers light   ⎬
> In likeness of a Helmets crest doth trimly stand upright.   ⎭
> In stead of his long sword, his bill shootes out a passing space:
> A Lapwing named is this Bird, all armed seems his face.[23]

Here is the same moment in Ted Hughes's version:

> No longer caring what happened —
> He too was suddenly flying.
> On his head and shoulders a crest of feathers,

---

[19] See Thomas P. Roche Jr. (ed.), *Petrarch in English* (Harmondsworth: Penguin Books, 2005), pp. 82, 128, and 165.

[20] John Crowe Ransom, *Selected Poems*, 3rd edn. (New York: Knopf, 1991), p. 140.

[21] See Ezra Pound, *ABC of Reading* (London: Faber & Faber, 1961), pp. 124–31.

[22] Jonathan Bate, *Shakespeare and Ovid* (Oxford: Oxford University Press, 1993), p. 29.

[23] W. H. D. Rouse (ed.), *Shakespeare's Ovid, Being Arthur Golding's Translation of the Metamorphoses* (London: Centaur Press, 1961), p. 135.

> Instead of a sword a long curved beak —
> Like a warrior transfigured
> With battle-frenzy dashing into battle.[24]

And here is an attempt by two poets much younger than Hughes to render the same passage in rhyming couplets, somewhat as Golding had done:

> Tereus too, lent wings by his grief and his thirst
> For revenge, turns into a bird with a Mohican crest
> And a long beak, but no sword. So now you know what
> The hoopoe always looks so angry about.[25]

Though Bate observes that 'Ezra Pound exaggerates typically' when he claims that Golding's Ovid 'is "the most beautiful book in the language"',[26] it would be possible to prefer his version, however old hat, to these more contemporary writers'. Though none of these versions are close to the Latin, all three are translating Ovid, and all bring over that moment of metamorphosis. Yet it would be possible to aver that the word choices in Hughes's stanza or the couplets of Wheatley and Quinn are not rhythmically distinctive enough to suggest that they were either calibrated to linguistic choices in the original, or sufficiently vivid and direct to rival Golding. Is the ambiguous 'dashing' quite the word to describe such a warrior in attack mode? Might not the anachronistic comparison to a 'Mohican' haircut already risk the need for a fashion note? Does Hughes's simile ('Like a warrior transfigured / With battle-frenzy dashing into battle') help envisage the metamorphosis, or tend to hinder it by clinging with its simile to an image of the figure from which King Tereus has been transformed? While 'dashing' or 'Mohican' may have a tang of period flavour already sounding slightly dated, I can't say the same for Golding's choices. Too much time has passed: they're not dated; they're old.

But still, can translations be said inevitably to date, in ways that original poems do not? This must be the implication of arguing thus of Wyatt's Petrarch versions: because the poet wrote them in service of the English lyric, and not in the subservient service of Petrarch, or knowledge of Italian poetry, the versions rise to being poems in themselves, which then makes them available for the real-poetry-doesn't-date claim. Among the problems with this formula is that it places works that are worth translating, because they have stood the test of time, against translations of those works (some of which may stand that test and many of which may not). Yet missing here are all the millions of published poems in native languages that have not stood the test, and are not thought worth the bother of translating. On such

---

[24] Ted Hughes, *Tales from Ovid: Twenty-Four Passages from the* Metamorphoses (London: Faber & Faber, 1997), p. 245.

[25] David Wheatley and Justin Quinn, 'Tereus, Procne, Philomela', *After Ovid: New Metamorphoses*, ed. Michael Hofmann and James Lasdun (London: Faber & Faber, 1994), p. 168.

[26] Bate, *Shakespeare and Ovid*, p. 29, citing Pound, *ABC of Reading*, p. 127.

a level playing field, I would imagine far more original work has 'dated' than have translations. But Paterson seems to imply that translations *inevitably* date. Is this fair? 'Bless thee, Bottom, bless thee. Thou art translated' is a strikingly old-fashioned way of addressing a colleague. Written in one style of a period in the history of the culture and language, it cannot avoid being in such a style ... and time passes. Even when the writer is a Shakespeare, this does not mean that his work didn't at one time seem dated, or that, so to speak, it dated. In this respect, there is, once again, no clear distinction to observe between a poem and a translation. There can be no such distinction between a translation and a version, because all translations are versions, and though the reverse need not always be exactly the case, the kinds of version I am concerned with are renderings with a poetic licence claim attached. There are also a great many poems making no claims to be translations that are nevertheless shaded with translated elements, as for example Lowell's poem from 'The Lesson' which the poet acknowledges 'picks up a phrase or two from Rafael Alberti', though it borrows rather more.[27] Whether a text is a version or a translation has no necessary bearing on its potential longevity.

What may be meant when we say a text has not dated is that it still has value and relevance for us. This is, I would suggest, independent of when it was written, by whom, or as a translation or not. It depends on contemporary readers' relations with particular texts, and these relations are not easy to predict, nor do they stay the same from one period to another. It is possible for literary texts to un-date, one of the most widely noted examples being John Donne's poetry; the recent renewal of interest in writing by women such as Sylvia Townsend Warner also underlines this. Ezra Pound's *Cathay* is rather less dated, in this respect, than innumerable oeuvres of poetry that contain little or no translational matter, doubtless written with the intention of serving English lyric. The reason for this is not because Pound was serving poetry in calculatedly cavalier fashion, as he was in *A Homage to Sextus Propertius*. In *Cathay*, Pound's translational choices cover the gamut of reasons: ignorance of the language, careful editing for the target audience, period ideas of the culture from which he is translating, the finessing of memorable speech. He was presenting translations of his poets for the Anglophone poetry audience of his day. They have not dated because, in ways for which many reasons can be and have been adduced, they are felt still to be worth reading; but they are also and simultaneously already dated in that they exemplify early twentieth-century literary *chinoiserie*. Translation styles also shadow, and often foreshadow, the styles of periods whose prominent works are claimed not to have dated. Early translations of Petrarch might be a case in point.

---

[27] Robert Lowell, Note to *For the Union Dead* (1965), *Collected Poems*, ed. Frank Bidart et al. (London: Faber & Faber, 2003), p. 319.

II

Reviewing a translation of aphorisms by Karl Kraus, Michael Wood noted that

> The ideal aphorism has a gap in it, a sort of leak which its very tidiness enhances. Wittgenstein writes: 'The philosopher treats a question; like a disease.' Erich Heller calls the punctuation here the most profound semi-colon in literature. I'm not sure what the competition is, but it's clear that the standard translation ('The philosopher's treatment of a question is like the treatment of an illness') loses all the interesting disturbance of the German syntax.

Wood also expresses support for 'the refreshing view that translation is an opportunity rather than an impossibility'.[28] His implication seems to be that all translation can be, or has been, thought of as impossible, something the reviewer is tired of hearing reiterated. But I'm wearier of hearing that everything except poetry can be translated. It's an idea expressed in an aphorism of Kraus's, not translated in the book under review: 'One can translate an editorial but not a poem. For one can go across the border naked but not without one's skin; for, unlike clothes, one cannot get a new skin.'[29] This metaphorically expresses the truth in Frost's 'Poetry is what gets lost in translation' by implying that a native language composition in verse would be as detachable without loss from its linguistic textures as would our skin.

And who better to support the claim made by that anti-modernist settler native, Frost, who wrote that 'I had as soon write free verse as play tennis with the net down',[30] than Marjorie Perloff, apologist for an unfaltering American avant-garde modernism? Perloff has expressed her commitment to the assumption that Wittgenstein believed 'Philosophy can only be done as poetry' and has also, not exactly consistently, dismissed the idea that Wittgenstein's writings might be untranslatable in the way that she believes poetry to be:

> In formulating his aphoristic propositions, Wittgenstein is not interested in the subtleties of figurative language but, on the contrary, in the difficulty of determining the *denotative* meanings of ordinary words and phrases placed in particular syntactic constructions. Hence, although, as in the case of any philosophical discourse, there are more or less adequate translations — translations that render as fully as possible the author's *intended* meaning — Wittgenstein's

---

[28] Michael Wood, 'Start Thinking', *London Review of Books* vol. 24 no. 5, 7 March 2002, p. 11.

[29] Karl Kraus, *Half-Truths and One & One-and-a-Half Truths: Selected Aphorisms*, ed. and trans. Harry Zohn (Manchester: Carcanet Press, 1986), p. 67.

[30] Robert Frost, 'Poetry and School' (1951), *The Collected Prose of Robert Frost* ed. Mark Richardson (Cambridge, MA: Harvard University Press, 2008), p. 168.

propositions are by no means *untranslatable* in the sense that the *Duino Elegies* or Lowell's 'Skunk Hour' are untranslatable.[31]

This is not true of Wittgenstein's remark about rhyme published in *Culture and Value*: 'Der Reim von >Rast< mit >Hast< ist ein Zufall. Aber ein glücklicher Zufall, & Du kannst diesen glücklichen Zufall entdecken.' Peter Winch is obliged to render this by picking another rhyme in English where two words with fairly contrastive meanings have similar sounds: 'It is an accident that "last" rhymes with "fast". But a lucky accident, & you can discover this lucky accident.' He scrupulously points out that in German the contrast of sound and meaning is more pronounced, for 'Rast' is 'rest' and 'Hast' is 'haste'.[32] Wittgenstein's remark pays tribute to a poet's luck and powers of discovery, for Goethe's motto read: 'Ohne Hast aber ohne Rast' [Without haste but without rest]. In a chapter starting from Wood's review of Karl Kraus in translation, one entitled 'Wittgenstein's Semi-Colon', Stephen Mulhall argues that 'the philosophical value of the thought will be internally related to its literary form — will depend on the extent to which it finds words which hit on the correct nuance.'[33] If so, its translator must attempt an approximation of this literary form and correct nuance, so as to approximate to the thought. This is a task, strictly speaking, no less impossible than translating 'Skunk Hour'. There is, moreover, a line of thought in the philosophical exploration of truth, one skeptical about the guarantee that the expression of a truth in one language can be translated into another without risk of a non-truth's expression. The philosopher Donald Davidson, for example, has observed that 'If one knows how to translate a language L into one's own language it does not follow that one can automatically produce a truth definition. Translation relates languages to one another', he adds, while truth 'relates a language to the world.'[34]

Perloff's pronouncements rest on the old-time new critical separation between connotation and denotation, one hard to credit since in practice the two cannot be distinguished. So-called connotations are meanings triggered by so-called denotation, while such denotation cannot banish connotative implication even when expected to signify like algebra. Perloff assumes acceptance of her convenient notion that poetry is untranslatable.

---

[31] Marjorie Perloff, '"But isn't *the same* at least the same?" Wittgenstein on Translation', *Differentials: Poetry, Poetics, Pedagogy* (Tuscaloosa: University of Alabama Press, 2004), p. 63.

[32] Ludwig Wittgenstein, *Culture and Value: A Selection from the Posthumous Remains*, rev. 2nd edn., ed. G. H. von Wright et al., trans. Peter Winch (Oxford: Blackwell, 1998), pp. 93, 93e.

[33] Stephen Mulhall, *Wittgenstein's Private Language: Grammar, Nonsense, and Imagination in* Philosophical Investigations, §§ 243–315 (Oxford: Oxford University Press, 2007), p. 91.

[34] Donald Davidson, 'Epistemology and Truth', *Subjective, Intersubjective, Objective* (Oxford: Oxford University Press, 2001), p. 179. See also 'how we can talk in one language about the truth of sentences in other languages', Donald Davidson, *Truth and Predication* (Cambridge, MA: Harvard University Press, 2005), p. 30n.

Yet if she means that the words of one language cannot be reproduced without loss by the words of another language, a banality, then it is true of all writing. Equally, if translation were, like politics, an art of the possible, then poetry is translatable like everything else. What is produced is not the same, but then it never is with any translation. If you think the losses are worse with poetry than with the propositions of, say, *Philosophical Investigations*, could this be because you are reading Wittgenstein inattentively? Which rendition of Wittgenstein's German aphorism cited above about philosophers and diseases better conveys the author's meaning — Michael Wood's with its semi-colon, or the usual rendition with its simile, its balanced repetition of the word 'treatment', and no syntactic 'leak'? Wood and Heller seem to say that the author's meaning is part and parcel of the syntactic structure of the writing and its punctuation. If so, we approach the sensible point of accepting that the author's meaning is no more and no less than what can be understood from the composed words. In these terms, another level playing field worth rolling, nothing is translatable, if by translation is meant replication (to recall Paterson's word), the transfer from one language into another of exactly the original's significance in all its phonic, syntactic, and semantic specificity. It's not the 'poetic' that cannot be translated, fully or partially, it's the whole of the original's language itself.

Kraus's aphorisms are difficult to translate because, like poetry, they depend upon play between the meanings of words in the original language. It would be surprising if this were not also the case with Wittgenstein's aphoristic propositions. Let's take the most famous: 'Wovon man nicht sprechen kann, darüber muss man schweigen.'[35] The English language has no natural equivalent for the German 'man'. Its disappearance means the loss of the internal rhyme that forms the sonic backbone of the sentence (man ... kann ... man). English is far less inflected than German, so there can be no echo in the final syllable of the two verbs 'sprechen' and 'schweigen'. The time-honoured and author-aided C. K. Ogden translation can't find equivalently parallel verbs: 'Whereof one cannot speak, thereof one must be silent.'[36] A drawback of this nobly memorable version is that it sounds like early twentieth-century advice for a polite person about when to talk and when to hold one's tongue. What's more, as poetry so often is, the sentence has two ways of being construed, depending on how that 'muss' is understood. With Wittgenstein's sentence, problems don't only arise from the fact that the German 'man' can't simply be transposed into English; they remain, unresolved, in the translated ambiguity of 'muss' in 'must', either logical or moral compulsions driving the 'muss' in 'muss man schweigen'. This is a case of indeterminacy that resembles an Empsonian type of poetic ambiguity. In the first, it is tautological and banal: it follows

[35] Ludwig Wittgenstein, *Tractatus Logico-Philosophicus* (1922), trans. C. K. Ogden (London: Routledge, 1995), p. 188.
[36] Ibid. p. 89.

that you have to be silent upon those things about which you are incapable of speech; in the other, it is an ethical injunction yoked to a fact believed to have been demonstrated: you ought to remain silent upon those things about which you are unable to speak (however much you can blather about them). The former articulates a literal impossibility; the latter counsels an end to talking nonsense. To dispense with the moral interpretation, as Wittgenstein may or may not have supposed his readers ought to do, we will perform a translation-like interpretive clarification of the sentence.

Davidson has also argued, in 'A Nice Derangement of Epitaphs', that communication between language speakers requires acts of instant disambiguation and interpretation that he calls 'passing theories'.[37] 'Bottom ... Thou art translated': but so too are we all when being heard, as can be noted in the ass others may make of our words. Allowing that Wittgenstein consciously or subliminally intended both interpretations of 'muss', the complex sense of the aphorism becomes: because the tautological reading is demonstrated, the moral injunction can be asserted with force. Wittgenstein's final remark on philosophy (as he is believed to have thought when completing the *Tractatus Logico-Philosophicus*) is a poetic wedding together, by means of the play on the word 'muss', of a tautological fact and a profoundly believed-in value. Yet since the first sense cannot be unambiguously cleared (in Wittgenstein's own sentence), what is said to follow from it cannot be unassailably true. Wittgenstein's later philosophy awaits attention in the ambiguous final remark of his earlier.

One reason why it would be better to recognize that, strictly speaking, absolutely nothing is translatable is that this fact places poetry on the same footing as other language use. Poetry is not a special case of language; it is the ordinary case of language, but one where the inevitable losses and gains of translation — which are always issues, and always important — are more or less universally recognized as indispensably important. The Perloff argument is that if you are translating anything except poetry, then it's fine to translate the Italian 'cane' into the English 'dog', but in a poem (where perhaps it rhymes with 'pane' [bread]) you can't have the rhyme and the meaning, so you have to choose, or find a different pair of rhyme-words. Yet this is what translators will variously do. Among my aims is to show how the way we talk about translating poetry could be brought into better relation both with the nature of language difference, and with the practical facts of translation, including poetry translation. The isomorphism of concepts and sounds in different languages, highlighted by the problem of translating rhyme, is present in any translation. We have seen how in the work of a philosopher it can be crucial. Consider the case of a piece of advertising that relies on a pun, or of the challenge set for a simultaneous translator or interpreter when a politician makes a joke to amuse some visiting dignitaries. Poetry has been privileged with being a special case,

[37] Donald Davidson, 'A Nice Derangement of Epitaphs', *Truth, Language, and History* (Oxford: Oxford University Press, 2005), pp. 99–104.

removing it from life and relieving us of the the need to consider its language issues as they impact outside poetry and, equally, of difficulties in thinking about such issues as they impact upon poetry.

Jonathan McVity, a translator of Karl Kraus, offers the refreshing idea that difficulties are prompts to faithfully equivalent invention.[38] Something similar may be said for the translation of poetry. Many poets acknowledge that constraints can be the forcing house of creation: the name for the Provencal poets, the troubadours, is cognate with the French verb 'trouver', to find. This name derives from their use of highly complex rhyme schemes, and formal dispositions (such as the sestina), by which they paint themselves into corners from which they escape by creative innovation.[39] Nor are such strategies to be associated only with poets from distant eras, as can be seen from the methods used by Raymond Roussel (1877-1933), or by the Oulipo group (founded in 1960 by Raymond Queneau and François Le Lionnais), who adopt taxingly arbitrary devices to spur invention. A translator is inevitably confronted with such apparently arbitrary, and certainly unpredictable, discrepancies between linguistic forms and possibilities: these too can be the engines of creativity, if not conveniently avoided or escaped under the covers of those tacit allies, literal impossibility and poetic licence.

III

So not only has Frost aphoristically captured a widely assumed view of whether poetry can be translated or not, he has recruited unexpected allies to his version of the argument, among them Marjorie Perloff: 'We usually think of the "poetic" as that which cannot fully translate, that which is uniquely embedded in its particular language', she observes in her essay about Wittgenstein on translation, adding that 'The poetry of Rainer Marie Rilke is a case in point.'[40] She then turns to William H. Gass's *Reading Rilke: Reflections on the Problems of Translation*, a fascinating exploration of one writer's obsession with an author in another language. Gass compares and contrasts the efforts of many translators as they attempt to render the character and detail of Rilke's poetry. He begins his section entitled 'Ein Gott Vermags' [A God Does It] by considering the first sentence of the *Duineser Elegien* ('Wer, wenn ich schriee, hörte mich denn aus der Engel / Ordnungen?') in versions by fifteen translators including Gass himself. Perloff concludes that not only is his version of the line 'no better', but the characteristics of German when contrasted with English usage intensified

[38] Karl Kraus, *Dicta and Contradicta*, trans. Jonathan McVity (Urbana and Chicago: Illinois University Press, 2001), pp. 154-60.
[39] See *Lark in the Morning: The Verses of the Troubadours* ed. Robert Kehew, trans. Ezra Pound, W. D. Snodgrass, and Robert Kehew (Chicago: University of Chicago Press, 2005).
[40] Marjorie Perloff, *Differentials: Poetry, Poetics, Pedagogy*, p. 60.

by Rilke's unique art 'create a dense sonic network that is inevitably lost in translation.'[41]

What she says is incontestably true: and 'inevitably lost' means that for her translations of poetry must, without exception and inescapably, at least partially fail. So when the pastoral-traditionalist Frost and the postmodern-futurist Perloff agree that the 'poetry is what gets lost in translation', it may be that a truth is being used defensively to simplify a more complex situation. Because the 'poetic' as Perloff puts it, or 'poetry' as Frost does, won't exactly reproduce in another language, can it not be translated? Their truism conceals the likelihood that the word 'translate' is taking a vacation in Wittgenstein's sense ('For philosophical problems arise when language *goes on holiday*').[42] Poet-translators can take the strict impossibility as part of the normal circumstances in which renderings are made from one language to another. The Italian poet Giorgio Caproni, writing about his translations from the French of René Char, notes: 'I say imitation because I'm aware that a perfect restitution remains forever, in as much as we're dealing with translated poetry, a chimera, not least because of the inevitable usury that the words, like money, suffer in the exchange'.[43] The word 'imitation' is also used in the title of Thomas à Kempis's volume *The Imitation of Christ*. We needn't assume that Lowell's loose approximations constitute the only application for the word. In translating Char's *Feuillets d'Hypnos*, Vittorio Sereni as much as states that he is imitating their historically occasioned cultural stance during the years 1943-1944, when Char had the code name of Captain Alexandre in the French Resistance.[44]

Yet if 'translate' doesn't mean 'perfectly reproduce' or, to recall Paterson's word, 'replicate' its original, then could the poetry or the poetic prove as more or less translatable as anything else? Looking again at the first sentence of the *Duineser Elegien*, could we come to a conclusion other than Perloff's? Gass does make distinctions between translations that are closer to the sense of the German, and some which are so far away as to risk being called 'mistakes' (though we shouldn't forget that one defining characteristic of a translation would be that it rises to containing mistaken renderings from another language). Yet looking over the samples that Gass cites, I'm struck by the amount of language that they share, the number of approximate synonyms that they deploy, and the near agreement they demonstrate about how that first question in Rilke's poem might be rendered. The translations have a large overlap of shared vocabulary: eleven of them begin 'Who'; fourteen include 'if'; all of them have 'angels'

[41] Ibid. p. 61.
[42] Ludwig Wittgenstein, *Philosophical Investigations* 3rd edn., trans. G. E. M. Anscombe (Oxford: Blackwell, 2001), p. 16e.
[43] From René Char, *Poesa e prosa*, ed. Giorgio Caproni (Milan: Feltrinelli, 1962), in Vittorio Sereni, 'Prefazione', René Char, *Fogli d'Ipnos 1943-1944*, trans. Vittorio Sereni (Turin: Einaudi, 1968), p. 6.
[44] See my 'Envy, Gratitude, and Translation', *In the Circumstances: About Poetry and Poets* (Oxford: Oxford University Press, 1992), pp. 151-52.

or 'angelic'. 'Ordnungen' gives pause, but five of them have 'orders', two others have 'order', and three others have 'hierarchies' or 'hierarchy'.[45] We might then conclude not that the line is untranslatable, but that the various failures of the translated versions perfectly to match the German, with their fair degree of agreement about the approximate sense, shape, and point of the line in the poem being translated, reveal that there is a high measure of consonance about what the line means and how it could be rendered in English. Perloff, a native German speaker, can make subtle and telling discriminations between the different word choices of the various translators, as can Gass. Some versions of the line are closer and more faithful than others. Yet because *everything* in the strict sense clung to by Frost and reiterated in slightly different terms by Perloff is impossible to translate, this opens the way for the practical activities of approximating translation that go on all the time. Of the efforts that Gass cites, most fall within the parameters of the plausible, and they each require interpretation as translations.

Yet Gass is in substantial agreement with Frost and Perloff: 'find an English song for these words, these phrases, from "Die Spanische Trilogie,"' he urges; and, after a quotation spree including, with line-breaks suppressed, his 'favorite, ... *wie ein Meteor in seiner Schwere nur die Summe Flugs zusammennimmt*', he adds: 'You don't have to know German. Just look at it: *zusammennimmt*. A god can't do it.'[46] T. S. Eliot's strange gods would include the one referred to in Rilke's phrase from the third of *Die Sonette an Orpheus*, 'Ein Gott vermags' — A god does it. Eliot seems to support the 'lost in translation' faction when he remarks in 'Rudyard Kipling' that 'the music of verse is inseparable from the meanings and associations of words'.[47] Perloff reminds us that the original's fusion of auditory shape and significance cannot be exactly reproduced ('zusammennimmt' is rendered as 'concentrates' by Michael Hamburger and 'gathers within' by Stephen Mitchell).[48] Not that most translators will have wanted to reproduce it, mind you, because the noises would sound bizarre in English.[49] The sonic structure of the translation must function entirely within the coordinates of the target language, even when it is able, by chance or good fortune, to borrow a strain of verbal music from the original. But a god wouldn't need

---

[45] William H. Gass, *Reading Rilke: Reflections on the Problems of Translation* (New York: Basic Books, 1999), pp. 56–57.

[46] Ibid. p. 72.

[47] T. S. Eliot, 'Rudyard Kipling', *On Poetry and Poets* (London: Faber & Faber, 1957), p. 238.

[48] Michael Hamburger (trans.), *An Unofficial Rilke: Poems 1912-1926* (London: Anvil Press, 1981), p. 33, and Stephen Mitchell (trans.), *The Selected Poetry of Rainer Maria Rilke* (London: Picador, 1982), p. 119.

[49] But see Ron Padgett, *Quelques Poemes / Some Translations / Some Bombs* (New York, 1963), in which he composes English lines that try to mimic as closely as possible the sound of poems by Pierre Reverdy, which he manages by ignoring the sense of the original French, and in doing so reaches towards the extreme opposite end of the scale from translations that preserve sense but not sound.

to do it, being, perhaps, linguistically all-knowing, while a living person might and, with luck and patience, may find equivalent resources in the contours of the receiver language.

Perloff's and Gass's instances of what cannot be fully conveyed are supported by observations on both the differences between German and English, and details of Rilke's poetic techniques. If the former is the problem, then all translation across this language barrier — whether of poetry or prose — must face similar losses. Yet for Perloff '*poetry* is that which deals with the connotative and tropical power of words and the rhythmic and sonic quality of phrases and sentences, whereas *philosophy* ... involves the conceptual and abstract language of making meaningful propositions.'[50] These latter, she asserts, are translatable without significant loss; and by quoting English, German, and French versions of a Wittgenstein remark from *Philosophical Investigations* she illustrates to her satisfaction that the differences of formulation and texture from language to language are incidental. This point is not consistent with her discussion in *Wittgenstein's Ladder* where she takes Elizabeth Anscombe's translation to task for distorting the philosopher's sense, and offers alternative renderings.[51] She may believe that Anscombe simply fails to achieve the denotative transparency Perloff takes to be the mark of translation in this field, but the examples read as debates about the rendering of nuance and implication. By contrast, Lawrence Venuti takes up Anscombe's Wittgenstein to exemplify the contribution of the translator to the appreciation and fame of the philosopher — alighting on precisely the 'language *goes on holiday*' remark as one of his telling instances.[52]

Perloff's distinction between denotative and connotative is the exaggeration of an emphasis to the point of a falsehood. R. G. Collingwood, in 'Philosophy as a Branch of Literature', even as he defends a distinction between philosophy and poetry, one that Wittgenstein aphoristically challenged, allows that philosophers should borrow from the poet's means:

> the philosophical writer ... must never use metaphors or imagery in such a way that they attract to themselves the attention due to his thought; if he does that, he is writing not prose but, whether well or ill, poetry; but he must avoid this not by rejecting all use of metaphors and imagery, but by using them, poetic things themselves, in the domestication of prose: using them just so far as to reveal thought, and no further.[53]

50 Perloff, *Differentials*, p. 64.
51 Marjorie Perloff, *Wittgenstein's Ladder: Poetic Language and the Strangeness of the Ordinary* (Chicago: University of Chicago Press, 1996), pp. 75, 186.
52 Lawrence Venuti, *The Scandals of Translation: Towards an Ethics of Difference* (London: Routledge, 1998), pp. 107-14.
53 R. G. Collingwood, *An Essay on Philosophical Method*, pp. 209-14, cited in Bernard Williams, 'An Essay on Collingwood', *The Sense of the Past: Essays in the History of Philosophy*, ed. Miles Burneyat (Princeton, NJ and Oxford: Princeton University Press, 2006), p. 343.

My point is not that philosophers are wrong to give priority to the revelation of thought, but that if they should do this, or cannot avoid doing it, by using metaphors and imagery, then the supposed impossibility of translating poetry also applies to their words. Frost himself asserted: 'Poetry is simply made of metaphor. So also is philosophy — and science, too, for that matter, if it will take the soft impeachment from a friend.'[54] Philosophy has persuasive tropes and connotations, rhythms and sounds.[55] Most poetry contains meaningful propositions, ones like 'The woods are lovely, dark, and deep'.[56] Perloff's assertion underestimates the art of a prose translator conveying both matter and style.[57] Though Lichtenberg and Nietzsche each wrote aphoristically, and the later admired the former, their writings are not similar. *Le style c'est l'homme même*, and to translate their ideas so that they sounded the same would be not to translate them. R. J. Hollingdale, who has memorably rendered both, makes his Nietzsche sound compulsively authoritative, while his Lichtenberg jots down pennyworths for his own amusement and interest. Writers revising know that there are, strictly, no synonyms: to change the words to make a sentence flow better is to change, however minimally, what it says. In 'Translation — For and Against' it was finding Nietzsche translated while browsing at a Paris bookstall that prompted Walter Benjamin to note: 'There is no world of thought which is not a world of language'; for 'the horizon and the world around the translated text had itself been substituted, had become French.'[58] Translated terms (such as 'amour' for 'Liebe') aren't synonymous either.

Critics or poets fall back on the distinction Perloff describes as 'perhaps so obvious ... we don't usually take it into account', namely, that in poetry the figuratively musical, the 'connotative and tropical', the 'rhythmic and sonic' is essential, while in other texts (including Wittgenstein's philosophy) it's 'the *denotative* meanings' that are rendered. Nevertheless, clarity too has its auditory component, and technical translators are experts at adapting figuratively to set their texts effectively in different linguistic marketplaces.[59] Paterson also evokes Perloff's hoary verbal division of labour:

[54] Frost, 'The Constant Symbol' (1946), *Collected Prose*, p. 147.

[55] On the allusively metaphorical density of J. L. Austin's philosophical style, see Geoffrey Hill, 'Our Word Is Our Bond', *Collected Critical Writings*, ed. Kenneth Hayes (Oxford: Oxford University Press, 2008), pp. 146–69, and Christopher Ricks, 'Austin's Swink', *Essays in Appreciation* (Oxford: Oxford University Press, 1996), pp. 260–61.

[56] Robert Frost, *Collected Poems, Prose, & Plays*, ed. Richard Poirier and Mark Richardson (New York: Library of America, 1995), p. 207.

[57] On translating the style of prose fiction, see Tim Parks, *Translating Style: The English Modernists and their Italian Translations* (London: Cassell, 1998).

[58] Walter Benjamin, 'Translation — For and Against', *Selected Writings* vol. 3: *1935-1938*, ed. Howard Eiland and Michael W. Jennings, trans. Edmund Jephcott, Howard Eiland, et al. (Cambridge, MA, and London: Harvard University Press, 2002), p. 249.

[59] For Parks's account of how technical translations have to be interpretive if they are to function properly, see *Translating Style*, pp. 1–8.

'since science uses language in a purely denotative way, linguisticians [*sic*] understandably tend to throw their weight behind that theory. Poetry is just as interested in what words connote, however, and the overlap between their connotative haloes, their common *feel*, is often strongly manifest in shared features of their sounds.'[60] Paterson again reaches for a religious term to characterize metaphorically the features of his activity. But words don't have haloes; they have uses. The notion of a word's connotations derives from its flexibility of employment. Since speakers and writers nuance the implications of a word in ways that cannot be given clear or absolute limits, by placing it with other words to effect expressive alliterations, ironic reversals, or modulations of sense, the impression is given of a glow of possible effects surrounding the word. Rather, in every case of a word in use its so-called connotations are being used to so-called denote something. 'You're fired!' expresses both the fact that you have lost your job and the style of management by which you have lost it. Its emotional effect on you is likely to be one communicative intention in the utterance. The boss of a company who resorts to this expression may call upon a Shakespearean usage without being aware of it: 'Yet this shall I ne'er know, but live in doubt, / Till my bad angel fire my good one out.'[61] When scientists and philosophers try to write with what Bernard Williams calls 'precision by total mind control' they have to use words, and their 'ambiguity-free' statements, expressed in words with saintly 'haloes' and all, will still have to be understood by readers capable of interpreting and resisting the sorts of 'mind control' to which they are being subjected. There can be no communication without autonomous interpretation.

More troublingly, Michael Hamburger suggests, in his introduction to *An Unofficial Rilke*, that the poet's fluency with the 'poetic' features of a text helped precipitate the central crisis and dilemma of his creative life: 'Rilke's virtuosity of feeling encountered too little resistance from the hard real quiddity of things — and people'. 'This', Hamburger adds, 'was Rilke's peculiar danger — a facility most conspicuous in his multiple rhyming, alliteration, assonance — all of them linking devices that suggest semantic, as well as sonic, affinities'. Commenting on his 'dynamization and neologization of verbs and their prepositions', Hamburger typifies 'his use of "ausgefühlt" in a letter of 1914 — "felt through", by analogy with "worked through" or "thought through". This "feeling through" the most diverse material was Rilke's speciality and strength as a poet, his weakness and inadequacy as a man.'[62] Not only does this start a qualm about what we enjoy if we like his poetry, it also draws attention to the fact that the 'poetic' features of his work challenging to translators are embroiled with the least admirable aspects of his cultural example. It should remind us too that the

[60] Paterson, *Orpheus*, p. 76.
[61] William Shakespeare, *The Complete Sonnets and Poems*, ed. Colin Burrow (Oxford: Oxford University Press, 2002), p. 669.
[62] Hamburger, *An Unofficial Rilke*, p. 17.

'figurative' and 'tropical' features of poems are not free-floating values. It doesn't increase the 'poetry' in a work to play up that aspect at the expense of 'meaningful propositions'. The value of a poem resides, inseparably from its meaning-music, in what it can be understood to say.

As a result of an unusual childhood including a dramatic departure from Austria for the United States in 1938, fascinatingly described in her memoir *The Vienna Paradox*,[63] Perloff is bilingual in German and English, well placed to experience the drawbacks of Rilke in the one, or, as she also shows, Lowell in the other. Yet equally she doesn't have to depend on a German Lowell or an English Rilke. What Frost and Perloff appear to defend when they emphasize the untranslatable nature of the 'poetry' is the access granted to mother tongue speakers. Even if they don't actively promulgate it, poet and critic consort with linguistic manifest destinies, 'The Gift Outright', as it were.[64] Granted, there's nothing to touch an original, though this can't exclude exceptional cases where a translation proves a finer poem. Nor does it follow that native speakers are bound to fathom literary texts in their language better than 'foreigners'. To appreciate a poem you have to apply yourself, and being a native speaker is no guarantee you'll do that well enough. Moreover, while some of us through the chances of birth or life have multilingualism thrust upon us, many don't; nor are any of us so linguistically capable as to circumvent entirely the Babel of global tongues. If world poetry is to be more than a closed book, in Frost's sense, there need to be translations, losses and all. Again we face the paradox: the untranslatable is not only in need of translation; it is translated.

Discussing the matter of work preservation in his *Languages of Art*, Nelson Goodman confronts a partially analogous problem that arises with the performance of scored music:

> Since complete compliance with the score is the only requirement for a genuine instance of a work, the most miserable performance without actual mistakes does count as such an instance, while the most brilliant performance with a single wrong note does not. Could we not bring our theoretical vocabulary into better agreement with common practice and common sense by allowing some limited degree of deviation in performances admitted as instances of a work?

Goodman answers his question in the negative because 'If we allow the least deviation, all assurance of work-preservation and score-preservation is lost; for by a series of one-note errors of omission, addition, and modification, we can go all the way from Beethoven's *Fifth Symphony* to *Three Blind Mice*.'[65] This funny example only underlines the gulf between theoretical

---

63 See Marjorie Perloff, *The Vienna Paradox: A Memoir* (New York: New Directions, 2004).

64 See Robert Frost, 'The Gift Outright', *Collected Poems, Prose, & Plays*, ed. Richard Poirier and Mark Richardson (New York: Library of America, 1995), p. 316.

65 Nelson Goodman, *Languages of Art: An Approach to a Theory of Symbols* (1976; 2nd edn., Indianapolis, IN, and Cambridge: Hackett, 1988), p. 186. For a recent

vocabulary and practice, for even a Portsmouth Sinfonia performance of the former work would not, I expect, be reduced to a rendition of the latter. Fortunately, translating means altering, and in translations exact preservation of the original work cannot be a criterion for success or failure. In an aphorism criticizing, Frost-fashion, 'nearly all translators of poetry' for failing 'to understand the poem's incarnation in its tongue is *all there is of it*, as a painting to its paint', Paterson adds 'They do no more than look at the *Mona Lisa*, then make a picture of a woman smiling.'[66] Original poems are not unique artworks like paintings. Thanks to the printing press, they exist in identical multiple copies. Still, they do have the individuality, though not the uniqueness, of an art object such as the *Mona Lisa* by Leonardo da Vinci (and neither, for that reason, do they have its incalculable rarity value). Translations are multiple approximations, like performances of Max Schelling's opera *Mona Lisa*, or renditions of 'Mona Lisa', the song best known in Nat King Cole's version. The eyes' movement from original poem to translation, in an *en face* edition, involves registering the difference between a work loosely analogous to a unique artwork like the *Mona Lisa* in the Louvre, and a token of a type artwork — like one derived from the score of Beethoven's Fifth, including all the different interpretations of it in performance. Though a translation doesn't change the original poem itself, and in one sense this is plainly the case, in another it is not quite accurate. What translations of a poem do is to take the original text as a type from which tokens in other languages can be derived. The unique artwork's becoming a blueprint or score is illustrated in those anthologies that present different translations of the same poem, rivals from the same or different periods.[67]

Gass touches a number of Goodman's bases when writing that some translators 'would rather be original than right; they insist on repainting the stolen horse; "it's my translation," they say as they sign it, as if their work were the work of art. How should we fare if printers did the same, putting out their own *Lost Paradise*, their personalized versions of *As You Prefer It*?'[68] We should fare as readers did when Tottel revised Wyatt's 'They fle from me that sometyme did me seke' before anthologizing it in his *Miscellany*. Yet, equally, one possible analogy for Goodman's 'the most miserable performance without actual mistakes', namely the prose paraphrases at the page foot in those Penguin editions of poetry in other

discussion of Goodman's famous passage and related issues, see Lydia Goehr, 'Three Blind Mice: Goodman, McLuhan, and Adorno on the Art of Music and Listening in the Age of Global Transmission', *New German Critique* 104, vol. 35 no. 2 (Summer 2008).

[66] Don Paterson, *The Book of Shadows* (London: Picador, 2004), p. 45.

[67] See, for example, Charles Tomlinson (ed.), *The Oxford Book of Verse in English Translation* (Oxford: Oxford University Press, 1980); Adrian Poole and Jeremy Maule (ed.), *The Oxford Book of Classical Verse in Translation* (Oxford: Oxford University Press, 1995); and the Penguin Poets in Translation series.

[68] Gass, *Reading Rilke*, p. 69.

languages, turn out not to be, again strictly speaking, performances of the work at all — which may be why they have been so helpfully inspiring for poets attempting versions. The gulf between the poem and the prose has begged for reparative revision.

Translations, like performances of scores, are always interpretive variations; none of them can be perfect matches. The relative preservation of the work in performance is achieved by skills that respond imaginatively and creatively to the promptings of the score, or the original. Just as we can enjoy variant performances of a much loved work, perhaps one whose score we can sightread, so too different translations can be appreciated for their variant solutions to the same challenges. Translations are not exactly competing to match their originals, because that's impossible; they are creating variants from it that may or may not please with their fidelity, subtlety of interpretation, and imaginativeness in rendering tricky passages. A poetry translation might aspire to be a convincing transcription for another instrument, an analogy Paterson uses when describing his versions of Machado as 'something like piano transcriptions of guitar music'.[69] If a poetic translation's equivalent to a performance of the Fifth Symphony sounds like 'Three Blind Mice', that's an implicit judgment on the playing (not the score). The 'poetry', or the 'poetic', is translatable when the word 'translation' is back from its holidays and properly understood as interpretive performance on another instrument. The original cannot, by definition, be reproduced in the second language; but it can be variously approached, and its loss can be complexly, and both more and less faithfully, compensated for. Like Gass's objection to translators who would 'rather be original than right', with the proviso that 'right' means 'as accurate as practically possible', my objection to Lowell's *Imitations* amounts to a revulsion at his translations not being sufficiently imitative of their originals.

For long stretches *Reading Rilke: Reflections on the Problems of Translation* is not about the problems of translation, but, rather, the problems of reading Rilke. Gass's book contains many highly wrought and well-meaning passages of what the Wittgenstein of the *Tractatus* might have included under the rubric of his final sentence 'Wovon man nicht sprechen kann, darüber muss man schweigen'. Those things about which we either cannot do other than be silent, or must strive not to enter with our meaningless talk, include all ethics and aesthetics.[70] Gass writes:

> Beauty, in Angels and elsewhere, is the revelation of a wholly inhuman perfection, for art, as Rilke wrote, goes against the grain of nature and transcends man. Just as, in Plato, any apprehension of the Forms is achieved through a deadly separation of the rational soul from the influence of the body, so in these *Elegies* a glimpse of such purity is possible only by means of a vertiginous breach in the self as might be

[69] Don Paterson, *The Eye: A Version of Machado* (London: Faber & Faber, 1999), p. 58.
[70] Wittgenstein, *Tractatus*, 6.421, pp. 182–83.

made by a mighty quake of earth — one which can close as abruptly as it opened.[71]

This is not the only available description of the beautiful, and Stendhal's describing it as 'une promesse de bonheur'[72] at least allows that people can display in life what art might aspire to evoke. Still, if beauty in art is 'the revelation of a wholly inhuman perfection' we need hardly be surprised that it proves untranslatable. As Gass describes poets at work, to be visited with this vision of beauty and perfection, they would have to suffer the little death of inspiration. Yet if you need a definition of *Kitsch*, this flirtation with death as a source of absolute values, ones not so much discovered and tested in the vicissitudes of lived experience as fixedly authorized by some arbitrary higher power, this is a place to start. Robert Hass noted in his introduction to the Mitchell *Selected Poems of Rainer Maria Rilke* that this poet's theme is 'the abandonment of ordinary life for the sake of a spiritual quest',[73] and to this we might add Hamburger's point that for Rilke 'Music (rhythm) is the untrammelled superabundance of God, who has not exhausted himself in phenomena'.[74] Over and over, readers encounter Rilke's self-alienating tendency to attribute ordinary human capacities, in impossibly idealized form, to an evoked divinity of questionable provenance. It happens towards the end of 'Liebes-Lied', from early in the *Neue Gedichte*, where, having described the two lovers as '*one* voice' produced by bowing two strings, the speaker asks 'Auf welches Instrument sind wir gespannt? / Und welcher Geiger hat uns in der Hand?' The poet projects the two people's love as played not by themselves but by a mysterious spiritual fiddler. Rilke doesn't answer his questions about what instrument and what violinist; the poem expires in a sigh: 'O süßes Lied.'[75]

Gass writes that 'art ... goes against the grain of nature and transcends man', inserting the words 'as Rilke wrote' to step away from affirming the absolute he seems to stand by, while, in effect, articulating just such a would-be truth. He asserts as a current verity what may rather be a bundle of cruelly unhelpful contradictions and conundrums. He had earlier written that with 'a romantic naiveté for which we may feel some nostalgia ... Rilke struggled his entire life to be a poet' and as 'A high priest of the poet's art, he takes the European lyric to new levels of achievement — forming with Valéry and Yeats perhaps, a true triune god — and creates the texts of a worthy religion at last, one which we may wholeheartedly admire, in part because we are not required to believe in it or pay it tithes.'[76] Sentimentality

---

[71] Gass, *Reading Rilke*, p. 68.
[72] Cited in a criticism of Kantian disinterestedness by Friedrich Nietzsche, *On the Genealogy of Morals*, trans. Douglas Smith (Oxford: Oxford University Press, 1996), p. 83.
[73] Robert Hass, Introduction, *The Selected Poetry of Rainer Maria Rilke*, trans. Mitchell, p. xviii.
[74] Hamburger, *An Unofficial Rilke*, p. 12.
[75] Rilke, *Die Gedichte*, p. 428.
[76] Gass, *Reading Rilke*, pp. 68, 23, and 33.

is playing at having an emotion without being willing to pay for it; but Gass in effect believes and pays, writing in his preface that the poet's 'work has taught me what real art ought to be; how it can matter to a life through its lifetime; how commitment can course like blood through the body of your words until the writing stirs, rises, opens its eyes'.[77] I would like to conclude by sketching a different sense of how the art of poetry, and poetry in translation, can 'matter to a life through its lifetime'.

IV

In *After Babel*, George Steiner argues that European literature changed at about the time of the Franco-Prussian War in 1870: 'When literature seeks to break its public linguistic mould and become idiolect, when it seeks untranslatability, we have entered a new world of feeling.'[78] While Steiner has noticed something significant, is it possible to say that there is ever a 'public linguistic mould'? I wouldn't want to venture the opinion that Shakespeare's blank verse in the late romances or Milton's 'Babylonish dialect' in *Paradise Lost* were no more nor less than that. Nor would I feel confident in suggesting that Coleridge's poetry was written in one, or Keats's. Translators from any period must be attending to the authorial ideolect of their originals. Nevertheless, perhaps poets during the last thirty years of the nineteenth century were more unusually attuned to the unique music of their individual styles. If so, the Symbolists and the Aesthetic Movement mark the apotheosis of the 'poetry is untranslatable' argument. Mallarmé, notwithstanding, made a study of the English language, and aesthetes such as Rossetti were pioneering translators from the Italian, inspiring modernists to initiate a literary internationalism founded upon the art of translation as they variously understood it.

Two of Gass's holy trinity had already belatedly advised us to look to life for inspiration. 'We must try to live!' Paul Valéry urges in the final verse of *Le cemetière marin*, an exclamation that springs from the sound of the preceding phase, 'The wind lifts!': 'Le vent se lève! ... Il faut tenter de vivre!'[79] Rilke on his deathbed was, Gass tells us, translating Valéry's poem. W. B. Yeats's 'The Circus Animals' Desertion' concludes: 'I must lie down where all the ladders start, / In the foul rag-and-bone shop of the heart.'[80] These writers are tiptoeing away from the consequences of what Wallace Stevens, himself announcing a nineteenth-century theme as if it were a new discovery, wrote in his *Adagia*: 'After one has abandoned a belief in god,

---

[77] Ibid. pp. xv–xvi.

[78] George Steiner, *After Babel: Aspects of Language and Translation* (Oxford: Oxford University Press, 1975), p. 183.

[79] Paul Valéry, 'Le cemetière marin', *Oeuvres*, vol. 1, ed. Jean Hytier (Paris: Gallimard, 1957), p. 151.

[80] W. B. Yeats, 'The Circus Animals' Desertion', *The Collected Poems*, 2nd edn., ed. Richard J. Finneran (Basingstoke: Macmillan, 1991), p. 348.

poetry is that essence which takes its place as life's redemption.'[81] Those who are religious believers do not need poetry as a substitute religion; and those who feel they must, or would prefer, to live without such beliefs, don't need one either. Art isn't even an alternative to religion; it is more like, as Richard Wollheim asserted in *Art and Its Objects*, borrowing his term from the later Wittgenstein, 'a form of life'.[82] Discussing aesthetics with his Cambridge students in the 1930s, the Austrian philosopher discouraged attempts to find an essential definition for the 'beautiful', preferring to ask how the word is used, what role 'beauty' and the 'beautiful' play in life — definitions that will vary and alter between cultures, large and local, as well as through time. So you can know it by looking at and reflecting upon specific cases in embedded experience.[83]

Gass is clear-eyed about how Rilke's life does not offer us any Jamesian self- or other-sacrificing Lesson of the Master. He announces this theme in the first half of the sentence from his preface cited above: 'The poet himself is as close to me as any human being has ever been; not because he has allowed himself — now a shade — at last to be loved; and not because I have been able to obey the stern command from his archaic torso of Apollo to change my life, nor because his person was always so admirable it had to be imitated'.[84] Yet you can only be close to a 'poet himself' if he allows you to be so in his life. After reading Gass's biographical sketches, I would suggest that Rilke's life is a how-not-to-do-it for poets who aspire to be reasonably decent wives, husbands, parents, relatives, colleagues and friends. Gass knows in detail how Rilke had commitment issues with regard to everything except his art: his life's central crisis occurred when he feared it had abandoned *him*.[85]

In a passage of imaginative identification with his subject's emotional complexities, Gass offers a gloss on a familiar phrase in German:

> *Ich liebe dich.* No sentence pronounced by a judge could be more threatening. It means that you are about to receive a gift you may not want. It means that someone is making it very easy for you to injure them — if they are not making it inevitable — and in that way controlling your behaviour.[86]

The words don't mean what Gass says they do: people can mean that by using them in that way, or to that end. There's no reason why this famous phrase cannot be simultaneously murmured after reciprocally satisfying

81 Wallace Stevens, 'Adagia', *Collected Poetry and Prose*, ed. Frank Kermode and Joan Richardson (New York: Library of America, 1997), p. 901.
82 Richard Wollheim, *Art and Its Objects* (2nd edn., Cambridge: Cambridge University Press, 1980), pp. 104 ff.
83 Ludwig Wittgenstein, *Lectures and Conversations on Aesthetics, Psychology and Religious Belief*, ed. Cyril Barrett (Oxford, Blackwell, 1966), pp. 1-3.
84 Gass, *Reading Rilke*, p. xv.
85 See also Donald Prater, *A Ringing Glass: The Life of Rainer Maria Rilke* (Oxford: Oxford University Press, 1986), pp. 70 ff.
86 Gass, *Reading Rilke*, p. 23.

lovemaking. In his 'Paris Diary' (1930), Benjamin reports Adrienne Monnier's saying 'very beautifully of him' that Rilke 'seems to have given everyone who knew him the feeling that he was profoundly involved in everything they did'.[87] It must have been an effect of his social style, not an index of his involvements. The poet's attempt at parenthood and domesticity quickly collapsed, as Gass notes: 'We need not describe the layer of boring chores, the clutter of mismated china, sticky pots, and soiled silver, annoying habits and nervous tics, which will cloud the rich cloth when reality arrives'.[88] The detail of the china catches Clara and Rainer's ill-paired state, while Gass offers this vignette as one *Dinggedichte* that his poet could not write.

Rilke's prolonged crisis was to be of significance for the art of poetry. His sense, as he asserts at the close of the 'Archäischer Torso Apollos', that 'Du mußt dein Leben ändern' [You must change your life], his alter-ego's 'learning to see' in *The Notebooks of Malte Laurids Brigge*, his attempts to move beyond the work of seeing to that of the heart in 'Wendung' [Turning-point], whether he succeeded or failed, produced staying examples and enduring influences. Still, the great improvement in concreteness and occasioned utterance that occurred in his poetry at the time of the widely influential *Neue Gedichte* shouldn't encourage us to exaggerate their 'thing-ness'. His legacy has been the *Dinggedichte*; but those famous works ('Der Panther', 'Römische Fontäne', 'Orpheus. Eurydike. Hermes', 'Buddha in Glorie'), they're *Kunstgedichte*. Their objects, as in 'Der Tod des Dichters', are frequently art objects, a Rodin sculpture in that instance. Rilke finds occasions in things because confronted, startled, and trapped by them; as in 'Der Panther', material objects and others form bars to his cage, and the world beyond this symbol for the poet's self is first nullified, then annihilated by his look. Even his most world-embracing works sublime things with the poetic techniques of his subjectivity; and in this they contribute to an aesthetic spiritualizing, one which simultaneously makes a fetish of the artwork's unique and 'untranslatable' perfection. Do we really feel nostalgia now for this?

An indicator for such processes taking place in those crisis-ridden years was the assertion that artworks have, or had, because now they were losing it thanks to mechanical reproduction, an 'aura' — a term Benjamin drew from the poet Stefan George and his circle. Yet engravings and etchings had been mechanically reproduced for centuries before the arrival of industrialized mass production, as had literary texts after the introduction of the printing press. Whatever clings, or clung, to works of art cannot be lost by translation either, manifestly a non-mechanical and inexact mode for reproducing a work in another medium. Might that 'aura' not be a word for the value we attribute to artworks as they help us imaginatively live our lives? While those who can read and appreciate an original may collaborate

---

[87] Adrienne Monnier, in Walter Benjamin, 'Paris Diary', *Selected Writings*, vol. 2 part 1, p. 347.
[88] Gass, *Reading Rilke*, p. 22.

with the text to produce such an aura of value (and will likely feel its loss in encountering a translation of the same work), those who cannot access the source poem may find such specific value in a translation.

Gass alludes to 'O sage, Dichter, was du tust?' when suggesting that 'on the page, in a poem, the contradictions which were his chief affliction could be reconciled.'[89] Clive Wilmer's version *'after Rilke'*, from *Of Earthly Paradise* (1992), is also skillfully half-rhymed:

> Say, poet, what it is you do. — *I praise.*
> How can you look into the monster's gaze
> And accept what has death in it? — *I praise.*
> But, poet, the anonymous and those
> With no name, how do you call on them? — *I praise.*
> What right have you though, in each changed disguise,
> In each new mask, to trust your truth? — *I praise.*
> Both calm and violent things know you for theirs,
> Both star and storm: how so? *Because I praise.*[90]

In 'The Translator's Apology' Wilmer alludes to Ernest Dowson's 'I have been faithful to thee, Cynara! in my fashion',[91] typecasting the translator as a lovelorn decadent poet ('I have been faithful to the text, after my own fashion'). This translating poet's pursuit of 'some other dusky beauty' is then said temporarily to mislead him from 'Truth', or 'that perfect form' to which he would attempt to stay 'in perfect constancy',[92] reenacting thus the terms of Rilke's own *fin-de-siècle* yearnings for and fallings from ideal realms of gods and angels. But there is, I'm afraid, no *perfect* constancy in life. It's because translation, of poetry or anything else for that matter, can never generate exact reproductions that it requires exacting art and is such an art; it's because it cannot be exact that, like the playing of scored music, the variable fidelity of a performance may be evaluated, and so valued. Wilmer's version, to pause on it a moment, appears to be moving finely until that 'know you for theirs'. *The Penguin Book of German Verse* (1957) by Leonard Forster, a likely source for Wilmer's wording, has 'And how is it that both calm and violent things, like star and storm, know you for their own?'[93] Gass's more direct, paraphrasing version has 'And that the calm as well as the crazed / know you like star and storm?'[94] Wilmer's slightly odd wording, close to the original's sense, loses touch with usage momentarily; still, hanging on, I get to 'how so?' and am once again felicitously in the land of the living. Such translations occasion understanding and gratitude.

[89] Gass, *Reading Rilke*, p. 170.
[90] Clive Wilmer, *Of Earthly Paradise* (Manchester: Carcanet Press, 1992), p. 77.
[91] Ernest Dowson, 'Non Sum Qualis Eram Bonae Sub Regno Cynarae', *The Poems*, ed. Mark Longaker (Philadelphia: University of Pennsylvania Press, 1963), p. 58.
[92] Clive Wilmer, 'The Translator's Apology', *Agenda* vol. 42 no. 2 (Autumn 2006), p. 141.
[93] Leonard Forster (ed. and trans.), *The Penguin Book of German Verse* (Harmondsworth: Penguin Books, 1957), p. 399.
[94] Gass, *Reading Rilke*, p. 171.

But is Rilke's 'O sage, Dichter, was du tust?' the kind of poem Helen Vendler in *The Art of Shakespeare's Sonnets* says cannot exist, a dialogic lyric? There are two contrasting reasons why it just might not be: because the poet, though not exactly 'represented as alone with his thoughts' as Vendler describes all lyrics,[95] did write both sides to shape his complex statement; and because the responding phrases, which Wilmer prints in italics above, can't help sounding (and may in the original have been meant to sound) not so much Gass's 'contradictions ... reconciled'[96] as someone reiterating his point in the face of the other's implications. It's certainly possible to feel that 'Ich rühme' is a confidently evasive response to an interviewer's questioning. Confronted with the thoroughly implied grim vicissitudes of life, to praise appears a grandly accepting affirmation, but it is a choice among other possibilities for what poets can, and this poet did, do — evoke, satirize, comfort, or lament; and it is an unresponsively slogan-like one, a way, curiously enough, of refusing life by converting it into another distant god. Hamburger has suggested that his 'becoming a little human' would have required Rilke's 'ceasing to write'.[97] He couldn't or didn't want to do it; but his example has encouraged many who came after him to try and integrate the practice of these arts with the living of an ordinarily responsible life. Good poems and translations can help us to work at this not least because, as Goethe put it in his 'Dreistigkeit' from the *West-östlicher Divan,* before he sings and before he stops — 'Eh er singt und eh er aufhört, / Muß der Dichter leben' — the poet has to live.[98]

---

[95] Helen Vendler, *The Art of Shakespeare's Sonnets* (Cambridge, MA: Harvard University Press, 1997), p. 19.

[96] Gass, *Reading Rilke,* p. 170.

[97] Hamburger, *An Unofficial Rilke,* p. 16.

[98] Johann Wolfgang von Goethe, 'Dreistigkeit', *West-östlicher Divan,* ed. Hans Albert Maier, Text (Tübingen: Max Niemeyer, 1965), p. 25.

CHAPTER 4

The Art of the Impossible

I

In Mary Elizabeth Braddon's *Aurora Floyd*, the eponymous heroine's cousin Lucy feels for Talbot, the man she loves, intuiting from his behaviour that Aurora has rejected his marriage proposal. Yet her feelings are themselves misunderstood, for Talbot 'could read pity in that tender look, but possessed no lexicon by which he could translate its deeper meaning.'[1] Earlier the same man is described as falling in love with Aurora before he realizes it: 'Lucy knew, in short, that which as yet Talbot did not know himself: she knew that he was fast falling over head and ears in love with her cousin'.[2] Some of us, according to the novelist, are better translators of others' emotions; some of us, she assumes, aren't good at translating our own. 'Love / translates / as love', Matthew Mead writes in 'Translator to Translated', his poem address to Johannes Brobowski.[3] But consider uses of the word 'love' in relation to different people. If I say 'I love you' and then again 'I love you', but on each occasion the 'you' is another person who relates to me differently, wouldn't the differences concealed by the same second-person pronoun 'you' inflect the emotions represented by the same verb 'love'? Altering the object of such verbs can dramatically change their implications ('I love ice cream' or 'I love my country', for example). They might inflect the subject pronoun 'I': the feelings we call love can have the power to sustain or attack the cohesiveness of our identities. Changing the person you love is not separable from wishing to change the person you are. In such situations, I might have to give myself a good talking to, so as to reach an understanding of my own emotions; might, as it were, have to

---

[1] Mary Elizabeth Braddon, *Aurora Floyd*, ed. P. D. Edwards (Oxford: Oxford University Press, 1996), p. 70.

[2] Ibid. p. 55.

[3] Matthew Mead, *The Autumn-Born in Autumn: Selected Poems* (London: Anvil Press, 2008), p. 36.

translate myself twice into English (with the risks of schoolboy howlers — rendering 'infatuation' as 'love'). Without such attempted translations, how am I to understand what's been happening in my own sentimental education?

Introducing *The Craft of Translation*, its co-editors write that 'Human emotions hardly change from one culture to another; what changes is the way one perceives these emotions and how one places them within the natural environment of a country.'[4] Many believe this and hope it's true, but Georg Christoph Lichtenberg, reflecting perhaps on *Schadenfreude*, noted that 'on many occasions on which an Englishman has not even thought of laughing, a German does not laugh because he knows it is unseemly.'[5] While the editors of *The Craft of Translation* and the author of *Aurora Floyd* underline how all-embracing is the subject announced by the second part of my main title '& Translation', Lichtenberg's remark subtly distinguishes between the impulse to laugh or its absence, the conscious awareness of that impulse, and the social training which excludes it from a potential occasion of amusement. So does the fact that English borrows a German word to express the idea of laughing at another's misfortune support the idea that this emotion, if an emotion, is shared between these two natural environments — or that it isn't?

Some translators, intent on promoting the importance of their work, have spoken up for the translatability of poetry in a manner that echoes this universality of human emotion belief. J. B. Trend writes of versions from the Spanish poet Juan Ramón Jiménez:

> It is not true that 'poems that are written in one language can only be enjoyed by a particular race or nationality'. Such poems are not poems in any true sense; for the genuine quality of poetry does not depend on the language in which it is written ... Poetry does not really depend on the colour or vowel harmony or beauty of the original verbal sounds, but on the colour of the poetic emotions; and in most modern poetry the nuance of the poetic emotions is more important than the nuance of the words.[6]

What's unlikely about this idea is that it acknowledges Kraus's or Frost's aphorism in the quotation it opposes, but thinks to get round it by assuming that the poetic emotions are not in the words of the original. Yet if they are not to be found there, where else can they be but in some similarly universal breast? Trend posits an intangible entity (poetic emotions) beyond the words and then allows that intangibility to be translatable. I'm not sure

---

[4] John Biguenet and Rainer Schulte (ed.), *The Craft of Translation* (Chicago: University of Chicago Press, 1989), p. xiv.
[5] Cited in J. P. Stern, *Lichtenberg: A Doctrine of Scattered Occasions Reconstructed from His Aphorisms and Reflections* (London: Thames and Hudson, 1963), p. 35.
[6] Juan Ramón Jiménez and Antonio Machado, *Selected Poems*, trans. J. B. Trend and J. L. Gili, and Charles Tomlinson and Henry Gifford (Harmondworth: Penguin Books, 1974), p. 15.

why it would need translating, though, if it were more important than the 'verbal sounds'; but then equally I'm not sure how it could be accessible without them — which brings me back to the Frost remark and a poem's sentence sounds.

I begin by briefly exploring a doubt and some of the issues that the editors of *The Craft of Translation* may be papering over, so as to identify further the relations of difference and similarity that their comment usefully raises for the art of translating poetry. They are surely right to imply that for translation to be attempted there must be some assumption of commensurate forms underlying the evident presence of striking differences, differences that tend to be more immediately evident than do the similarities in poetry from other cultures. Put briefly, what they call 'human emotions' and Trend calls 'poetic emotions' might be better understood as human purposes, for since human emotions are expressed in natural languages and culturally specific behaviour, it is a form of at best hopeful humanism or at worst colonizing ethnocentrism to assume that, behind all these differences of behaviour and expression, we all feel the same emotions. Where's the evidence? As with 'poetic emotion' it's presumably in the different expressions. By contrast, the evidence for identifiable human purposes (species survival, group cohesion preservation, the maintenance of historical memory and the projection of futurity, personal well-being, and many others) can be read off the specific life forms of a culture, then compared and contrasted with those of another.

W. H. Auden would probably have assumed that if I first fall in love with a French speaker and then with an English one, the feelings, expressed or otherwise, would not be quite the same, for he wrote in a piece on Paul Valéry that *'amour* and *love* are not synonymous'.[7] This may be not only because I would find myself in situations where the repertoires of behaviour, the possibilities for expressions of feeling, and the received definitions of emotions would be different, but also because body sensations and mental states don't occur with names attached to them: rather, we attach feeling and emotion vocabulary to them by an improvisatory activity that could also be called 'translation', and which will inevitably vary from one culture to another in relation to the linguistic and other means available. The contemporary Mexican poet Jennifer Clement's 'Making Love in Spanish' reports that in 'English / the objects in the room have no sex / and I only hear our voices', but 'in Spanish'

> the chairs — those little girls — chatter,
> and our shoes
> want to step, with adoration, on the body
> of light, lamplight,
> that falls across the floor.[8]

---

[7] W. H. Auden, 'Un Homme d'Esprit', *Forewords and Afterwords* selected by Edward Mendelson (London: Faber & Faber, 1973), p. 359.

[8] Jennifer Clement, *New and Selected Poems* (Exeter: Shearsman Books, 2008), p. 18.

Clement's lines might equally be contrasted too with the Cuban Rafael Alcides's poem in Spanish about a zeugmatic making love and spaghetti, one in which the earlier date of the poem's composition, the gender of its poet, and the different Spanish-speaking country in which it is set, all make the non-synonymous senses of the same words in contrastive usage contexts evident enough.[9] The situational coordinates in particular uses of Pablo Neruda's 'amor', Shakespeare's 'love', Goethe's 'Liebe', Paul Verlaine's 'amour', and Gaspara Stampa's 'amore' cannot be reduced the one to the other in the interests of a universal human emotion — because of the conditions in which these concepts arose and in which they were and, evolving, continue to be acted out and upon by historically specific persons. Though they can be listed as dictionary equivalents, they cannot be taken as synonymously defining the same emotion under different conditions, for the very reason that Donald Davidson offers for skepticism about assuming that the translation of a truth will automatically produce a truth, namely, that translations relate languages, while truth relates language to world. It could equally be argued that 'love' and its other language relatives do not even name identifiable emotions, but point to culturally diverse complexes of expectation and love-behaviour.

The editors of *The Craft of Translation* cite Hans-Georg Gadamer: 'Reading is already translation, and translation is translation for the second time ... The process of translating comprises in its essence the whole secret of human understanding of the world and of social communication.' They then conclude that Gadamer 'confirms one of the basic assumptions of translations studies, that all acts of communication are acts of translation.'[10] If this grandly announces the centrality of the subject area in which I have been trespassing, it simultaneously invites the thought that complete communication never happens. Such a totality might only be imagined as taking place between the angels in Heaven. Matthew Arnold, in 'On Translating Homer', asserted the need for transparency: the 'union of the translator with his original, which alone can produce a good translation' that 'takes place when the mist which stands between them — the mist of alien modes of thinking, speaking, and feeling on the translator's part ... disappears.'[11] Yet there are reasons for being grateful that we, and our texts,

[9] See Rafael Alcides, 'Aquellos espaguetis', *Agradecido como un perro* (Havana: Editorial Letras Cubanas, 1983), p. 119.

[10] Biguenet and Schulte (ed.), *The Craft of Translation*, citing without reference Hans-Georg Gadamer, 'To What Extent Does Language Prescribe Thinking?' p. ix. For a slightly different translation of the passages in context, see Hans-Georg Gadamer, *Truth and Method* trans. Garrett Braden and John Cumming (London: Sheed and Ward, 1975), p. 497. See, for example, Fritz Senn, *Joyce's Dislocations: Essays on Reading as Translation* ed. John Paul Riquelme (Baltimore and London: Johns Hopkins University Press, 1984).

[11] Matthew Arnold, 'On Translating Homer', *The Complete Prose Works of Matthew Arnold* vol. 1, On the Classical Tradition, ed. R. H. Super (Ann Arbor: University of Michigan Press, 1960), p. 103. For a discussion of Arnold's debate with John Henry Newman on translation, see Simon Dentith *Epic and Empire in Nineteenth-Century*

display at least semi-opacity, and that understandings are necessarily partial. One of these reasons is to be found in the identification of culturally collaborative and conflicted autonomy and negotiation in the spaces between us required for the interpretation of all language use. The constrained conditions in which we must live and work, with reference not only to poetry and translation, are more useful than if we happened to have access to an idealized transparency that would also render us even more vulnerable to the worst imaginable manipulation by demagogues.

Contrasting writing and painting, William Hazlitt said that 'One is never tired of painting, because you have to set down not what you knew already, but what you have just discovered. In the former case, you translate feelings into words; in the latter, names into things.'[12] Hazlitt alights on the word 'translate' to suggest the process of reproducing something that you already know, those feelings, in the medium of words. This is a summation of the assumptions that I'm not convinced by. Feelings, like texts for translation, are not something we know and then simply reproduce. Rather, what we feel is the difficult source text for a rendering that we make with the aim of better understanding the original, and of creating a version for our inner life that convinces us and, if we express it, convinces others with whom we live and work. Again, understanding translation in this sense, we notice how central to human life the activity of translating is, and how much even so important a matter as self-understanding can depend upon the degree of subtlety with which we can render our feelings and sensations into an articulated form that may be appreciated and interpreted by others.

Sensations are private, we say, in the sense that strictly speaking no one else can feel my love or my pain. Human nervous systems cannot be linked up like computer systems. But what if I say: 'Feel this, isn't it finely woven?' We both feel the same fabric. We don't have the literally same sensation, can never know for a fact that the two 'feels' were exactly the same; but we can agree that there have been experiences of the same textured object, and about which we can come to conclusions, such as whether we would like it for our living room curtains. Although our nervous systems are not and cannot be the same, when rendered as forms of speech and behaviour, the feelings have been made communicable and can't be called private. Translating a poem from one linguistic and cultural situation into another can be understood in such a light. We have to go ahead as if 'love' and 'amour' were appropriately similar, because, beyond sitting tight in pristine isolation, we have no alternative; and we have to translate as much of the context as we can so that the 'love' in the poem has a flavour of 'amour'

Britain (Cambridge: Cambridge University Press, 2006), pp. 50-58. See also my 'Envy, Gratitude, and Translation', *In the Circumstances: About Poetry and Poets* (Oxford: Oxford University Press, 1992), pp. 171-72.

[12] William Hazlitt, 'On the Pleasure of Painting', *Table Talk* (1824), *The Complete Works of William Hazlitt*, 21 vols,. ed. P. P. Howe (London and Toronto: J. M. Dent, 1930), viii, p. 7.

about it. This is less difficult than might be thought, because honestly made and presented translations render the historical and cultural situations in which the linguistic usage is taking place, and they expect to be read as other-language accounts of an elsewhere. Reading them requires an exercise of imaginative projection into the conditions of this other country.

Yet what provides the confidence or reassurance in going through this process, the confidence that the translation and the original are, effectively, talking about the same textured object? What prevents workers in this field from succumbing to what might be called translational despair? Most translators will have had such feelings, and *The Art of the Impossible* is meant to include within its range of senses implications about the ever-present possibility of exhausted and exasperated collapse. The suggestion that I'm going to follow is that translational confidence can be sustained because human situations are analogous, or can, at a minimum, be understood analogically, and because languages display family resemblances, so they appear, at least up to a point, to be talking to each other. No one is likely to underestimate the limits of extension in extended families. Whereas translations of passages between Romance languages can sometimes appear little more than transliterations (though we learn to beware of *faux amis*), translating from synthetic languages not in the Indo-European group can mean in effect writing a stylistically attentive paraphrase. However, analogously understood human situations and the family resemblances of languages are both at least to some extent possible because 'translation' also means human migration and linguistic evolution, with the subsequent sense that different forms of life are historically embedded contiguously in the etymologies of our words. Being themselves the complex products of innumerable translations, natural languages embody the possibility of translation within their networks of meaning and implication, and while this makes translation between members of the Indo-European group less taxing than translating from, for instance, Japanese, nevertheless, that language too has absorbed one of its writing systems from China, and is speckled with European loan-words, some of them dating back to the seventeenth century. Translation is approximation, and the evolution of human societies embodies ways of approach across vast distances to within minute degrees of proximity.

II

Poetry is then said to be untranslatable, or, more practically, poems are untranslatable, or, more subtly, in a poetic text *the poetry* is untranslatable, because it is the synthesized meeting point of at least five different aspects of uniqueness: (1) the entire structural, sonic, and semantic complex which is the language, or languages, in which the poem is written; (2) the particular historical state of that complex at the time the work was written; (3) the individual poet's deployed version of that language, his or her idiolect; (4)

the poetic voice, or style, of the poet (at that point in her or his creative life); and (5) the particular deployment of that idiom in this individual poem. Moreover, from Donald Davidson's philosophy, and especially his essay 'A Nice Derangement of Epitaphs',[13] I take the suggestion that the most restrictive cases listed above are defining for the more general ones. À propos of René Char, Maurice Blanchot has similarly remarked that since the poet is created by the poems he has written, 'ce qui est general depend de ce qui est unique.'[14] The life of language in use is demonstrated by our ability to understand, intuitively and in passing, the most unusual and even incorrect usages. As far as interpretation and translation are concerned the seeming exceptions don't prove the rule, they demonstrate the need for a more complex and subtle picture, one not presupposing a general set of rules that overrides apparent eccentricities. A tradition of usage may support this too. We say 'translated from *the* Italian, *the* Japanese, *the* Catalan' using a definite article, when 'translated from Italian' might seem more natural. This may be a short form for 'translated from the Italian of Dante Alighieri', a phrase in which the article can't be dropped because the language has been made definite by its attribution to a writer. Translators don't translate from the language as such, but from the unique idiolects in individual performances of their authors.

Unique individual usage (whether in daily conversation or the most elaborated of literary texts) sets the standard for how and what verbal communication requires. Literary or poetic language is not parasitic upon what is called ordinary speech: it's a test case for what is happening when any communication is issued and understanding achieved. Davidson illustrates this by drawing attention to our ability to catch the significance of malapropisms even though we may have never heard such nonce phrases, and may never hear them again. The same is true for words invented within a family circle, ones like 'quoof' in Paul Muldoon's poem of that name ('our family word / for the hot water bottle'), or 'umbling' in Gareth Reeves's 'Mimsy':

> Umbling was shifting something heavy
> little by little. Furniture is umbled.
> When we moved house there was much
> umbling and grumbling.[15]

These lines instance what Davidson calls a 'passing theory', an improvised contextual understanding, for a word that you will probably only ever encounter in Reeves's poem, and which, unless taken up and used in your own improvisatory linguistic circles, you will have no other use for than

---

[13] See the discussion of Humpty Dumpty's 'There's glory for you' in Donald Davidson, 'A Nice Derangement of Epitaphs', *Truth, Language, and History* (Oxford: Oxford University Press, 2005), pp. 97-98.

[14] Maurice Blanchot, 'René Char', *La part du feu* (Paris: Gallimard, 1949), p. 108.

[15] Gareth Reeves, *Listening In* (Manchester: Carcanet Press, 1993), p. 7. For 'Quoof', see Paul Muldoon, *Quoof* (London: Faber & Faber, 1983), p. 17.

in the understanding of that poem. A translator of 'Mimsy' would have to work back from the translation of 'grumbling' and hope for a similarly sounding nonce word that could conceivably be used for the pushing around of objects. You couldn't translate this literally if you tried, but you might be able to approximate it. In Italian, for example, an equivalent of 'to grumble' is 'brontolare', so 'umbling' could perhaps be 'ontolando' – and therein might reside one aspect to the art of the impossible, the happy point here being that, since 'umbling' doesn't have a dictionary existence, the translator has the pleasant task of inventing an equally plausible but similarly not-existent equivalent. *Finnegans Wake* has been translated into many of the world's languages, including Japanese. Once again, if poetry is what gets lost in translation and yet such translating of poetry continues apace notwithstanding Frost's (for him) convenient truth, then our theory and our practice are not conceptually integrated, are not properly understood in their co-existence. The case I attempt to develop here is not the one illustrated in chapter 2 (that poetry is what is lost in translation), or that explored in chapter 3 (that poetry can be translated, when we understand the word 'translate' aright), but the complex of these two, namely, that the strict impossibility of translating poetry is at the same time the condition making poetry need to be translated and what makes its translation an activity that can practically be done, and be practically done, and done practically.

As we saw in the last chapter, with the assertion that poetry, or poems, or the 'poetry' is untranslatable goes the supporting assertion, or, more usually, assumption, that other things are translatable. Recognizing the inaccuracy of this formulation (I have been arguing) is one way in which the apparent paradox can be dissolved. After all, if we look back at the five reasons for poetry's being untranslatable given above, it can be seen that they could be applied to the conditions not only of any piece of writing, but of any piece of language use. So we each use one, or sometimes more than one, unique native language when we speak; we use it at a specific moment in the history of its usage; we are each unique persons with individual versions of that language at that historical moment; we each have our specific eccentricities of usage, speech rhythm, syntax, and so on; and, finally, each of our utterances, however casual or banal, is a unique bit of play in what Wittgenstein called a language game. My first counter-assertion to those who insist that poetry is untranslatable is to accept their argument, but then ask them to note that the consequences of believing this to be true are that, when it comes to language use, we are all, in our different ways and to different degrees, poets.

The elaboration of poetry's not being translatable depends, as we have seen, upon various more or less sophisticated versions of the denotation and connotation distinction: the idea that there are the things that the words mean, and there are the metaphors, similes, idioms, the imagery and other more intangible implications which the words and usage also carry with them. The same words being used in or out of poems present the same translational difficulties, though not the same amount of time to solve them, whether you are acting as an interpreter at an official tea party or rendering a passage of poetic dialogue from, for instance, a verse play which includes a scene set at an official tea party. That the interpreter at the tea party will get over the momentary social difficulty of getting the sugar to the visiting dignitary only goes to suggest that when we say that prose or conversation is 'translatable', we are using the word in a slightly different sense — using it to mean that agreeably functioning equivalents can be found. Might there not equally be agreeably functioning equivalents when translating a poem?

Bernard Williams once commented on the possibility of drawing conclusions about Greek culture and ethics through a reading of the Homeric poems:

> We can, to a considerable degree of agreement, translate the poems into English. The firm conviction that we can do this is supported by the historical traditions that link us to the ancient world, by the fact that informed readers today are not arriving at these texts by historical parachute, but have learned ancient Greek from someone who learned ancient Greek from someone who ... This does not, of course, guarantee 'correctness', or remove huge interpretative and historical problems, but it does provide the absolutely essential foundation of conducting the operations of ideal anthropology on those works at a level at which they can produce results and make some sense. A jokey classical scholar of my acquaintance, in parody of the methods of deconstruction, cheerily suggested that the word 'album' in a poem by Horace might be taken to mean a book in which you stick photographs; it is quite instructive to consider how many reasons, of how many kinds, there are why this is not a good idea.[16]

A classical scholar did fail to appreciate Ezra Pound's anachronistic reference to a 'frigidaire patent' in his *Homage to Sextus Propertius*, though, supposing it a mistranslation; and the afterlife of that interdisciplinary quarrel still lingers in the literature.[17] Yet if we were not making the sorts of judgments that exclude the photo album from Horace, we would not be able to appreciate the tacit satirical role of Pound's historically 'inappropriate' choices for his homage to this poet of the Roman Empire.[18] Perhaps you had never encountered the expression 'ideal anthropology' before reading the passage above: the way that you went about assuming, with a fair likelihood of near accuracy, what Williams means by it, would serve to illustrate Davidson's observations on our invention of 'passing theories' so

[16] Bernard Williams, 'Understanding Homer: Literature, History and Ideal Anthropology', *The Sense of the Past: Essays in the History of Philosophy*, ed. Myles Burneat (Princeton and Oxford: Princeton University Press, 2006), p. 64.

[17] Ezra Pound, *Collected Shorter Poems* (London: Faber & Faber, 1968), p. 209.

[18] See A. David Moody, *Ezra Pound: Poet. A Portrait of the Man and his Work*, vol. 1: *The Young Genius 1885-1920* (Oxford: Oxford University Press, 2007), pp. 352-54.

as to understand idiolect, malapropism, nonce words, inventive usage, and other such linguistic phenomena.

Williams comes to the defence of poetry from other cultures and other periods as being translatable after alluding to the theory and thought experiment called 'radical translation' in twentieth-century philosophy of language. This idea of W. O. Quine's involves imagining the efforts of field researchers placed among a newly discovered tribe in which there is no knowledge whatsoever of the language or cultural conventions of these anthropologically pristine people.[19] On what basis do these researchers come to understand what their new acquaintances are saying (or, for that matter, vice versa) and how is it done? The conclusion is that there can be no secure grounds for guaranteeing correspondences between sounds and objects in a notionally shared visual field, or of guaranteeing consistency of reference between occasions when the sounds are made. Williams's argument about the Homeric poems depends upon our noting that 'the entire schematic situation of "radical translation" that has so interested philosophers, is itself in almost all cases a drastic exaggeration'.[20] His point is that in cases which are not a philosopher's thought experiment there will be innumerable relations of knowledge and tradition between historically, culturally, or geographically distant peoples and their texts to allow for the sorts of agreement that will likely exclude the photo album from the translation of Horace. Nevertheless, in a footnote, Williams also acknowledges the point of the schematic situation: 'The purely philosophical concentration on radical translation ... is a device for isolating what is taken for granted in interpreting anyone.'[21]

III

These reflections on the strictly untranslatable in every language use have been adapted from my own multicultural domestic experience, lately supported by Quine's theories of 'radical translation' and the 'inscrutability of reference', and its developments in Davidson's 'radical interpretation' and his 'principle of charity' for isolating what is required when anyone understands another speaker, the charity principle being a set of operative assumptions that this speaker is more or less rational, identifying an interlocutor, attempting to issue words for a purpose, and many more besides. 'I advocate', Davidson writes, 'the adoption of the principle of charity on an across-the-board basis', believing that the presence of this human practice means that 'the degree of indeterminacy will, I think, be less than Quine contemplates.'[22] Where

[19] See W. V. Quine, *Word and Object* (Cambridge, MA: MIT Press, 1960), chapter 2.
[20] Williams, 'Understanding Homer', p. 61.
[21] Ibid. p. 61n.
[22] Donald Davidson, 'Belief and the Basis of Meaning', *Inquiries into Truth and Interpretation* (1984), 2nd edn. (Oxford: Oxford University Press, 2001), p. 153.

Quine sought to identify an absolute zero for reference and communication, Davidson was exercised to explain why in practice we don't live there.

These philosophical arguments about translation and interpretation have been contested in the literature. Hans-Johann Glock, for instance, has attempted to show Quine was wrong to believe that 'radical translation begins at home' (that all verbal communication, even that between native speakers, requires a homophonic translation), or that Davidson's charity principle in interpreting others' utterances is not enough.[23] In short, he argues, 'translations must be done by people who already understand the language of the text to be translated'.[24] Yet this is not, in theory or practice, necessarily the case, and for a reason that Glock gives elsewhere when he notes that 'approaching a foreign text or culture, we must keep in mind the possibility that we might have something to learn'.[25] One of the things we may have to learn is the language, as Elizabeth Bishop, an unexpectedly long-term resident in Brazil, knew when setting out to translate *The Diary of 'Helena Morley'* (1957): 'I started it just to teach myself Portuguese, and then I decided it really might be quite successful in translation'.[26]

A defender of Quine's separates his theory from non-objectivity in the translation of poetry:

> Another common misunderstanding is that Quine is overdrama-tizing the familiar point that translation requires the exercise of judgment because there will always be a range of alternative yet inequivalent versions in one language of sentences from a language with different concepts and syntax. It would be silly to expect that a poem, for example, must have a uniquely correct translation. Now Quine's thesis does not depend on subtle nuances, so we can forget the special case of poetry.[27]

I take it that the reference to 'subtle nuances' here makes the point that there is nothing root and branch about asserting that such intangibles in a poem cannot be exactly conveyed in another language, with the background implication yet again that more straightforwardly functional usages can be exactly reproduced. Yet doubting this latter assumption has importance for the so-called 'special case' of poetry and its translation. In this book I am not going to forget the case of poetry, and am not going to be thinking of it as special either. If Quine's thesis has explanatory power, then it will have

---

23 See chapter 6, 'Radical Translation and Radical Interpretation', section 4: 'Charity Is Not Enough', Hans-Johann Glock, *Quine and Davidson on Language, Thought and Reality* (Cambridge: Cambridge University Press, 2003), pp. 194–99.

24 Hans-Johann Glock, *Quine and Davidson on Language, Thought and Reality* (Cambridge: Cambridge University Press, 2003), p. 204.

25 Ibid. p. 198.

26 Elizabeth Bishop and Robert Lowell, *Words in the Air: The Complete Correspondence*, ed. Thomas Travisano and Saskia Hamilton (New York: Farrar, Straus and Giroux, 2008), p. 154.

27 Robert Kirk, 'Indeterminacy of Translation' *The Cambridge Companion to Quine*, ed. Roger F. Gibson Jr. (Cambridge: Cambridge University Press, 2004), p. 152.

implications for the practice of translation, and for the translation of poetry too. What's more, the philosopher who notes that it would be 'silly to expect that a poem ... must have a uniquely correct translation' has already relieved himself of the inconvenient possibility that no piece of language use could have 'a uniquely correct translation', while, at the same time, revealing himself free from the mistaken assumption that there can be literal translations of poems that by definition are superior in accuracy to renderings which attempt, for instance, to imitate the formal structuring of the poem. Trying not to be silly in this way, and taking note of what Williams wrote about translating the Homeric poems, I would instead suggest the possibility that there can be a great range of more or less accurate translations. The exercises conducted by Gass in his book on translating Rilke where he compares and contrasts attempts at famous lines and verses do not, I suggest, so much reveal that none of them translates the German original, as that, with a remarkable overlap in vocabulary and implication, most of them do.

Quine's theory can, as noted above, be applied to the translations taking place between native speakers of the same language. Davidson's development of the thesis accepts that different linguistic formulations can express what are effectively the same beliefs and states of mind: 'Indeterminacy occurs whenever a vocabulary is rich enough to describe a phenomenon in more than one way.'[28] There are innumerable possible variant ways of rendering any line from another language into English. All translation requires choices to be made, and the translation of metrical rhyming poetry multiplies the number of issues involved in any decision to translate one way rather than another. If replicating translation is strictly impossible, reasonably approximate translation is taking place all the time. It is an essential requirement for any social exchange, and not only with someone who doesn't speak your native language. What we produce will not be exact back-translational replications, but interpretive approximations that suit individual cases and can be agreed through the acceptance of conventions and practices. Being a native speaker means having a vast set of abilities for performing these approximations, and a high confidence (but no absolute guarantee) of success. Davidson's ideas underline that all acts of understanding are interpretations, and that any communicative understanding can only be achieved when we charitably interpret. If we don't do that, then things can always go wrong, or be made to go wrong — as in the cases of misfits created by the willful construal of an unintended sense. 'Can you close the window?' I ask my dad. 'Yes, I can,' he replies, 'but I'm not going to.'

In 'The Social Aspect of Language', Davidson defends himself against the charge by Michael Dummett that 'whenever we understand a speaker we translate his words into our own', and he goes on: 'Translation is no part of the transaction between speaker and hearer that I call interpretation. Where

---

[28] Donald Davidson, 'Reply to Rorty', in Lewis Edwin Hahn (ed.), *The Philosophy of Donald Davidson* (Chicago and La Salle, IL: Open Court, 1999), p. 596.

translation of a sort may be involved is in the description the philosopher gives in his language of what the hearer makes of the speaker's utterances.'[29] Yet that Dummett may have mistaken him suggests the closeness of the words — as in the fact that an 'interpreter' is a person who does 'simultaneous translations' of what the dignitaries are saying to each other. Gadamer had assumed that interpretations of others' words are also understandable as translations, and Davidson does echo this idea in an essay on Gadamer and Plato when he inconsistently writes: 'Understanding, to my mind, is always a matter not only of interpretation but of translation, since we can never assume we mean the same thing by our words'.[30] What's more, there are cases in which to understand means to be able to do it yourself, and that means possessing the knowledge in terms you can yourself generate. So some philosophers of language support the belief that all acts of human communication involve the receiver interpreting the speaker's words, and that such interpretations are then reinforced and absorbed into the flow, or else referred back for clarification. This is a process that we can observe in our daily lives any time we find ourselves involved in new situations conversing with people we don't know well. More unusual situations, such as talking with non-native speakers, or living in a country where the native language is not your own, will render evident the activity of communicating as a series of approximate translations generated by interpretive activities. This is an experience that may occur when you are in a country where you stand out as not native, and are thus not expected to speak the language: occasions will arise when you are not understood at first even when you produce reasonably accurate, contextually appropriate versions of the language they speak. Not being heard with the necessary charity in place, you are not expected to be understood, and so, self-fulfillingly, you are not.

Poetry being lost in translation is, then, one case of all language use — where we are each involved daily in translational losses and gains. This is not to misunderstand Quine by reducing his theory to poetry's translational impossibility, but is an attempt to incorporate the case of poetry into the philosopher's version of meaning. The impossibility strictly to translate any utterance is the ground upon which its interpretation and recasting in the translated terms of the listener is necessary, and will be attempted. It's the strict impossibility of exactly reproducing pieces of language use as understandings that creates the space for interpretation and requires the alternative formulation, often a highly implicit or all but synonymous one. Irritated by readers who want to know what they meant by a certain phrase, poets have been known simply to repeat it (T. S. Eliot is said to have done this with 'Lady, three white leopards sat under a juniper tree').[31] Though such

---

[29] Donald Davidson, 'The Social Aspect of Language', *Truth, Language, and History* (Oxford: Oxford University Press, 2005), p. 112.

[30] Davidson, 'Gadamer and Plato's *Philebus*', *Truth, Language, and History*, p. 275.

[31] T. S. Eliot, 'Ash Wednesday', *Collected Poems 1909-1962* (London: Faber & Faber, 1963), p. 97.

behaviour effectively rebuffs the questioner and asks for attention to be paid to the experience of the words, it equally illustrates in the questioner's frustration that the same words repeated are not an interpretation. Just so, the exact reproduction of a line of poetry from another language would not be its translation. Equally, if you ask someone to show that they have understood something you have said, they won't necessarily demonstrate it by simply parroting your words back to you. You want to hear it in their words, and that requires that the understanding is a different formulation. The apparent paradox that poetry is untranslatable and forever being translated turns out to be a logical consequence: it is only because poetry cannot be reproduced whole in another language that it can be translated, meaning that it can be interpreted and rendered, with whatever results, in another language. It is as if the impossibility of doing it were the very grounds for its practical necessity. And this is true not only of poetry, but of all written and spoken language use.

This definitive mismatch, or lack of solid basis for claiming that a translation is literal, word for word, or exact, is the condition that allows for value to appear in the acts of interpretation and approximation that are usually understood by the phrase 'making a translation'. The only thing that can be said in favour of the horrid old saw that 'translations are like women, the more beautiful the more unfaithful' is that it touches on the matter of fidelity. Approximation means to get close to something, and there can be innumerable degrees and kinds of nearer or further approxi- mation. In any translation, and certainly the translation of poetry, the degrees of closeness are likely to vary from phrase to phrase, and even from word to word. Fidelity is judged by taking a reading of how these inevitably varying degrees of proximity are managed overall. One assumption of the old saw is that translations can have values attributed to them according to their behaviour. If it were possible to be absolutely literally accurate, there would be no space or reason for ethical values to locate themselves in the calibrations of greater or lesser fidelity to their source text. Thus I might conclude for the moment that if its not being translatable is one of the status claims that poetry might have made for it, then not only does this quality occasion the necessity of its eventual translation, but it also marks out the space for the poetry that might be found *in* the translation.

IV

To understand a poem at all, let alone to make a translation of it, requires the activation of a collaborative openness that resembles Davidson's 'charity' principle. Such charity assumes that the poet is behaving rationally and intending to communicate usefully when, for instance, appearing to perpetrate an oddity, as Elizabeth Bishop does in 'One Art' when she writes 'The art of losing isn't hard to master', the line depending on the eccentric usage of the 'art of' formula, one not usually used with a non-intentional verb such as 'to lose'. This usage can then fall under the category of 'joking' — one that itself expects a quick-witted adjustment to the frames of reference or usage.[32] Davidson's argument that idiolect performance takes precedence over convention-governed knowledge of a language has a direct bearing on the translating of the unique idiolect performances that are modern and contemporary lyric poems. Just as nothing (except everything you happen to know and your native wit) prepares you for the 'Jaberwocky' or *Finnegans Wake*, so, equally, nothing prepares you for any unusual line of poetry, such as Bishop's 'The art of losing isn't hard to master' — and, indeed, I have listened to a scholar translating this for his convenience into 'the art of coping with loss isn't hard to master', a version which, while relieving the line of its joking eccentricity of usage, delivers it into the realm (in my experience, at any rate) of the untrue. We need what Davidson calls a 'passing theory' to understand Bishop's use of non-intentional verbs in an intentional context, and the conscious formulation of such a theory would amount to a reading of the poem. Equally, if I were translating it into Italian, 'knowing English' would be necessary but not sufficient for getting the line. I would have to interpret its gesture, for, as Bishop is pretending to persuade herself, 'L'arte di perdere non è difficile da padroneggiare'.

Veronica Forrest-Thomson's interest in Wittgenstein, whose language philosophy prefigured a number of Davidson's most striking ideas and discriminations, can be found both in her poetry and her critical prose writings. She draws upon his work in the opening pages of *Poetic Artifice: A Theory of Twentieth-Century Poetry* and throughout the collection of poems pointedly entitled *Language Games*. Here is the second half of 'Phrase Book', a frighteningly witty poem partly prompted perhaps by Wittgenstein's remark about what happens to language when it *'goes on holiday'* — to Greece, for instance:

> World is a monstrous excrescence;
> his is following me everywhere, one
> Nescafé and twenty Athenes, everything
> green; I am not responsible for it.
> I don't want to speak to you.
> Leave me alone. I shall stay here.
> I refuse a green extension. Beware.
> I have paid you. I have paid you
> enough, sea, sun, and octopodi.
> It is raining cats and allomorphs.
>
> 'Where' is the British Embassy.[33]

The 'octopodi' are octopuses, and 'allomorphs' are morphemes that vary in sound but not in meaning (such as the past-tense 'ed' ending in 'fished'

32 Elizabeth Bishop, *Poems, Prose, Letters*, ed. Robert Giroux and Lloyd Schwarz (New York: Library of America, 2008), pp. 166–67.
33 Veronica Forrest-Thomson, *Selected Poems*, ed. Anthony Barnett (London: Invisible Books, 1999), p. 51.

and 'hunted'). 'Phrase Book' addresses the difficulties you can get into when in a linguistic space that is not your own, in this case Greek. Its title refers to the kinds of books you can buy in an airport when you set off, which contain phrases to be used in everyday situations, such as buying a coffee or a packet of cigarettes — though not usually including phrases to be used to stop the local boys from harassing you on the beach. Forrest-Thomson's poem knows that 'philosophical problems arise when language *goes on holiday*'[34] — but not only philosophical ones, or that 'the limits of the language (*the* language which I understand) mean the limits of *my* world'[35] — but that this wouldn't prevent me finding myself pestered in or, as Forrest-Thomson puts it, again alluding to the solipsistic realism of Wittgenstein's early philosophy, by someone else's 'world'.

William Empson's 'Aubade' is set in Japan when an exogamous couple, the speaker English and the woman Japanese, are awoken at dawn by an earthquake. Aside from the many other things that the poem does (evoking, for instance, Laurence Sterne's erotic use of the word 'translation' in *A Sentimental Journey*),[36] in the following lines it provides a compacted miniature of how people communicate by triangulating, in Davidson's sense,[37] situational facts and responses to them. Empson's poem plays upon the misinterpretations that will likely arise, implying compacted evidence for why they can be understood to be misinterpretations:

> It seemed quite safe till she got up and dressed.
> The guarded tourist makes the guide the test.
> Then I said The Garden? Laughing she said No.
> Taxi for her and for me healthy rest.
> It seemed the best thing to be up and go.
>
> The language problem but you have to try.
> Some solid ground for lying could she show?
> The heart of standing is we cannot fly.[38]

Let me try and translate these lines. 'It seemed quite safe till she got up and dressed': he thinks that she's rising and dressing because the earthquake is going to get more dangerous; but she's doing it because she does not wish to be found out (thanks to the earthquake) in her affair with the visiting lecturer. 'The guarded tourist makes the guide the test': he gets up too, and

[34] Ludwig Wittgenstein, *Philosophical Investigations*, 3rd edn., trans. G. E. M. Anscombe (Oxford: Blackwell, 2001), I, 38, p. 16e.

[35] Ludwig Wittgenstein, *Tractatus Logico-Philosophicus* (1922), trans. C. K. Ogden (London: Routledge, 1995), 5.62, p. 151.

[36] See Laurence Sterne, 'The Translation', *A Sentimental Journey*, ed. Graham Petrie (Harmondsworth: Penguin Books, 1967), pp. 78–80. These applications of the word are in my 'Unfaithful Translations', *Selected Poems 1976-2001* (Manchester: Carcanet, 2003), p. 57.

[37] See Davidson, 'The Third Man', *Truth, Language and History*, pp. 160–61.

[38] William Empson, *The Complete Poems*, ed. John Haffenden (Harmondsworth: Allen Lane, 2000), p. 69.

begins to dress, asking her if they should take shelter not in the house that might collapse but 'The Garden?' Her laughter and her 'No' make it clear to him that he has misunderstood the situation (as the old Tokyo saying goes: 'If you know you're in an earthquake, it's not dangerous'). 'Taxi for her and for me healthy rest': she is going to leave him in a hurry, but he can go back to bed. 'It seemed the best thing to be up and go': he had thought that the safest thing to do in an earthquake was to get up and out of the house, but he was wrong; for her, caught by this event in a compromising situation, it was definitely the best thing to leave immediately and return to where she should have been as fast as possible. 'The language problem but you have to try': communicating with people from other cultures is difficult, even if you are apparently speaking the same language, because for one of them it's a native language and for the other it's acquired by study and against the grain of embedded ways of thinking; nevertheless, by whatever means are available, and by triangulating the results with your own interpretations and the material situation, you can come to practical decisions, reassurances, and agreements. 'Some solid ground for lying could she show?' The question asks if she can show him a place where he can be physically safe if he goes back to bed, while also asking if she has got a good excuse for why she was not where she should have been when the earthquake struck. 'The heart of standing is you cannot fly' invites readers to consider that if discretion is the better part of valour, then the wise will only make a stand when they cannot escape. So she leaves, and he remains. Later in the poem these movements will be tacitly reversed: they separate more permanently when she stays in Japan and he leaves the country.[39] It should be clear from the above that while these lines can be translated into paraphrase exposition, they would be extremely difficult to approximate with an equivalent concision in a language that, for one instance, did not have the classic English love poetry pun on 'lie'.

Forrest-Thomson, both in her poetry and her criticism, was a follower of Empson, and wrote of his 'Manchouli', another poem located in Asia: 'Having thus established a continuity between the words of the poem and the world outside, Empson is in a position from which to proceed to modify, subtly to undermine, this mode of reading and the assumptions on which it relies.'[40] Her title 'Phrase Book' and the poem's conceit of citing, or appearing to cite, set sentences for tourists, along with its speaker's having recourse to a British Embassy when in trouble, locate her work with such triangulations of self, situation, and other, attempting however imperfectly to establish a shared space of communication: to fend off the local boys. It too is fraught with the need to fly for protection, when, in this case, threatened by the

[39] For an account of Empson's poem and its Japanese location, see my *Twentieth Century Poetry: Selves and Situations* (Oxford: Oxford University Press, 2005), pp. 11–18.
[40] Veronica Forrest-Thomson, *Poetic Artifice: A Theory of Twentieth-Century Poetry* (Manchester: Manchester University Press, 1978), pp. 53–57.

locals, into the arms of her country's representatives abroad. However, the sentences in a phrase book are not 'meant' (as are the sentences in a conversation or, for that matter, the dialogue in a novel). They are dummy sentences that you can 'mean' if the occasion arises and you have time to get the book out and mouth them. They do evoke forms of life because they are functionally occasion-specific. Forrest-Thomson uses the dummy sentence effect (language on holiday) to produce a dislocation in the subject that 'means' these sentences not naturally generated by a speaker in a situation. Language has gone *on holiday* in at least three different ways: the philosophical, the poetic-lyrical, and the subjective-experiential — linking it with the cultural-political via the first two senses. Yet, even when on holiday in an implication probably not intended by Wittgenstein, the senses of multiple viewpoint and interpretation in both Empson's and Forrest-Thomson's poems imply the existence of shared space, mutually identifiable objects, sexual desires between different language speakers, so as to disturb complacent assumptions about these things. They imply the existence of a shared world so that the troubling differences of meaning and understanding can be brought to light. Just as the establishment of shared reference points is essential to any communication, so too is it essential to translation.

Consider, for example, César Vallejo's famous sonnet 'Piedra negra sobre una piedra blanca' with its proper names, its deictic words, its definite and indefinite articles:

> Me moriré en París con aguacero,
> un día del cual tengo ya el recuerdo.
> Me moriré en París — y no me corro —
> talvez un jueves, como es hoy, de otoño.
>
> Jueves será, porque hoy, jueves, que proso
> estos versos, los húmeros me he puesto
> a la mala y, jamás como hoy, me he vuelto,
> con todo mi camino, a verme solo.
>
> César Vallejo ha muerto, le pegaban
> todos sin que él les haga nada;
> le daban duro con un palo y duro
>
> también con una soga; son testigos
> los días jueves y los huesos húmeros,
> la soledad, la lluvia, los caminos ...[41]

Comparing a few of the many attempts on this poem that are readily available naturally reveals both some variations and some consistencies

[41] César Vallejo, *'Spain, Take This Chalice from Me' and Other Poems*, trans. Margaret Sayers Peden, ed. Ilan Stavans (Harmondsworth: Penguin Books, 2008), p. 168. The poem is discussed in detail by Eugenio Florit and provided with a guide translation in Stanley Burnshaw (ed.), *The Poem Itself* (1960) (Fayetteville: University of Arkansas Press, 1995), pp. 224-25.

in the translations of the nouns, verbs, adjectives and adverbs. The last word of line 1, 'aguacero', I have found rendered in the following ways: 'a rainy day', 'hard dirty rain', 'a day the rain's been coming down hard', 'a showery day', and 'pouring rain'. The unusual verb phrase 'proso / estos versos' over the ends of lines 5 and 6 is given as 'setting down / these lines', 'I prose these lines', 'I make / and remake this poem', 'I write these lines', and 'I am / prosing these lines'. The anatomical term 'los húmeros', which appears in line 6 and differently in line 13, is translated the first time as 'my shoulder', 'my humeri', 'the very bones / in my forearms', 'my arm-bones', and once more 'my humeri'. The evocatively simple final line appears as 'the solitude, and the rain, and the roads', 'the loneliness, the rain, the roads', 'by loneliness, by heavy rain, by the aforementioned roads', 'and the rain, the loneliness, the roads', and 'the loneliness, the rain, the roads'.[42]

Nevertheless, everyone gets the place Vallejo will die as 'Paris', as he was to some two years after the presumed date of this sonnet's composition. Everyone has it taking place on a 'Thursday' in 'autumn' when there is some sort of 'rain' falling. Everyone has 'today' when he is composing 'these' lines or verses, or 'this' poem — that's to say, the one you are reading, or, more strictly, imagining yourself as reading while you read one or another translation. In the case of the bones in the forearm, the translators tend to shift the determiner so as to render the conventional definite article of a Latinate language with the conventional possessive pronoun of English, as in 'my' humeri. Similarly, in the final line, everyone except Paul Muldoon in his personalized variation uses three definite articles for 'the' solitude or loneliness, and 'the' rain, and 'the' roads. Muldoon, though, underlines one of the poem's ways for establishing a shared set of reference points when he adds an adjective, with a definite article too: 'the aforementioned roads'. Vallejo establishes his space shared with the reader not only by deploying proper nouns like 'Paris', deictic determiners like '*estos* versos', or definite articles like '*la* soledad' or '*los* caminos', but also by repeating terms so as, in effect, to confirm the relevant presence of the same objects by verbally pointing again. So the theme 'Me moriré en Paris' is repeated in lines 1 and 3; 'jueves', the day of the week, appears three times in lines 4 and 5; and the 'aguacero' of the first line, and the 'camino' of line 8 on which he sees himself 'solo', all return in 'la soledad, la lluvia, los caminos ...'. That the proper nouns, deictic words, and definite articles establish the hauntingly sharable performance of 'Piedra negra sobre una piedra blanca' is underlined

[42] The translations are by, in order, Robert Bly and John Knoepfle in *Twenty Poems of César Vallejo*, trans. John Knoepfle, James Wright, and Robert Bly (Madison, MN: Sixties Press, 1962), p. 59; Clayton Eshleman in César Vallejo, *Poemas Humanos / Human Poems* (London: Jonathan Cape, 1969), p. 117; Paul Muldoon, 'César Vallejo: *Testimony*', *The Annals of Chile* (London: Faber & Faber, 1994), p. 32; Valentino Gianuzzi and Michael Smith in César Vallejo, *Complete Later Poems 1923-1938* (Exeter: Shearsman Books, 2005), p. 105; and Margaret Sayers Peden in César Vallejo, *'Spain, Take This Chalice from Me' and Other Poems*, ed. Ilan Stavans (Harmondsworth: Penguin Books, 2008), p. 169.

by Donald Justice's 'Variations on a Text by Vallejo' where, more radically personalizing, he replaces 'Paris' with 'Miami', 'Thursday' with 'Sunday', and 'César Vallejo' with his own name here in this last verse:

> Donald Justice is dead. One Sunday the sun came out,
> It shone on the bay, it shone on the white buildings,
> The cars moved down the streets slowly as always, so many,
> Some with their headlights on in spite of the sun,
> And after a while the diggers with their shovels
> Walked back to the graveside through the sunlight,
> And one of them put his blade into the earth
> To lift a few clods of dirt, the black marl of Miami,
> And scattered the dirt, and spat,
> Turning away abruptly, out of respect.[43]

If you imagine translating these lines into Spanish, you might find it difficult to convey the apt echo of T. S. Eliot's 'I had not thought death had undone so many'[44] from *The Waste Land* at the end of Justice's third line, and you might have problems rendering all the nouns into a suitably rhythmic shape, but I suspect that you would not be especially troubled by 'Donald Justice', 'Sunday', 'Miami', and all of the definite articles that the poet uses to share his imagined death-day scenery with you.

V

By way of concluding, then, let me point to a defence for my use of the word *'Art'* in the subtitle, *The Art of the Impossible*, when it might be asserted that translation is not an art, but, as in the name of the volume of essays whose introduction I cited earlier, a craft.[45] An influential distinction between these two words was formulated by Collingwood, who wrote that what distinguishes a craft from an art is that the latter is the expression of an idea or conception, achieved in a medium of art, but not as a matching of a preconceived end with a means understood to be appropriate before the work has begun:

> In describing the power by which an artist constructs patterns in words or notes or brush-marks by the name of technique, therefore, this theory is misdescribing it by assimilating it to the skill by which a craftsman constructs appropriate means to a preconceived end. The patterns are no doubt real; the power by which the artist constructs them is no doubt a thing worthy of our attention; but we are only frustrating our study of it in advance if we approach it in the

---

[43] Donald Justice, *Collected Poems* (New York: Alfred A. Knopf, 2004), pp. 158–59.
[44] T. S. Eliot, *Collected Poems 1909-1962* (London: Faber & Faber, 1963), p. 65.
[45] See Donald Frame, 'Pleasures and Problems of Translation' in John Biguenet and Rainer Schulte (ed.), *The Craft of Translation* (Chicago: University of Chicago Press, 1989), pp. 71-74.

determination to treat it as if it were the conscious working-out of means to the achievement of a conscious purpose, or in other words technique.[46]

Though Vittorio Sereni wrote that a 'translation is born, in contact with the foreign text, with the power, the irresistibility of the original inspiration',[47] Gilberto Lonardi has suggested of Sereni's exemplary efforts that 'the exercise of translating, often admirable in its turn, will also perhaps be a way of lightening and getting round, more or less provisionally, the stress itself of poetic "responsibility"'.[48] Translating a poem, and certainly completing a translation of a poem, requires an interpretive conception, an interpretation of an experience, that of reading the poem, which, while not necessarily fully formed before the activity is begun, nevertheless has to be present as a motivating force — an urge to translate, which, as Sereni notes, can be as insistently nagging as that which prompts the writing of a poem. As various poet-translators' oeuvres illustrate, this motivating force is not distinct from the complexities of life, of reading, and other prior experiences that would be driving them forward in their own work. While a craft aspect of translating may be more enabling in being to the fore when translating, helping to ease in a poet such as Sereni a burdensome sense of duty towards poetry through his own efforts, and, as I explore in chapter 6, prompting a facilitating return to his own work, the impetus to translate and the forming conception of the work being translated need not be different in kind from the impetus and dawning realization that goes to making a work of your own. It is on the basis of such a belief that I recognize Collingwood's distinction and deploy it to support the assertion that translating poetry *is* an art — one unlike politics in the familiar saying, but as international politics (dependent on translators and interpreters) might more aim to be, it has to be an *'Art of the Impossible'*.

Don Paterson has another aphorism in which he imagines anachronistically acquainting 'Borges with the internet' or 'da Vinci with digital imaging', then adds 'though such things might have dismantled them as artists, as realizations of their necessary *impossibles*.'[49] One such impossible is the complex of cultural and linguistic differences that shapes the conditions in which the translator's art must reside. Within this necessary and therefore enabling impossibility all sorts of things can be done. Let me, then, conclude this chapter with some attempts at Stéphane Mallarmé's 'Brise marine':

---

[46] See R. G. Collingwood, *The Principles of Art* (Oxford: Oxford University Press, 1938), pp. 28-29.

[47] Vittorio Sereni, 'Premessa', *Il musicante di Saint-Merry* (1981), 2nd edn., introduction by P. V. Mendaldo (Turin: Einaudi, 2001), p. xxxii.

[48] Gilberto Lonardi, 'Introduzione', Vittorio Sereni, *Il grande amico: Poesie 1935-1981* (Milano: Rizzoli, 1990), p. 8.

[49] Don Paterson, *The Book of Shadows* (London: Picador, 2004), p. 173.

La chair est triste, hélas! et j'ai lu tous les livres.
Fuir! là-bas fuir! Je sens que des oiseaux sont ivres
D'être parmi l'écume inconnue et les cieux!
Rien, ni les vieux jardins reflétés par les yeux
Ne retiendra ce cœur qui dans la mer se trempe
Ô nuits! ni la clarté déserte de ma lampe
Sur le vide papier que la blancheur défend,
Et ni la jeune femme allaitant son enfant.
Je partirai! Steamer balançant ta mâture,
Lève l'ancre pour une exotique nature!

Un Ennui, désolé par les cruels espoirs,
Croit encore à l'adieu suprême des mouchoirs!
Et, peut-être, les mâts, invitant les orages
Sont-ils de ceux qu'un vent penche sur les naufrages
Perdus, sans mâts, sans mâts, ni fertiles ilots ...
Mais, ô mon cœur, entends le chant des matelots![50]

This much-translated poem has usually been presented in English under the title 'Sea Breeze':

The flesh is sad — and I've read every book.
O to escape — to get away! Birds look
as though they're drunk for unknown spray and skies.
No ancient gardens mirrored in the eyes,
nothing can hold this heart steeped in the sea —
nor my lamp's desolate luminosity
nor the blank paper guarded by its white
nor the young wife feeding her child, O night!
Away! You steamer with your swaying helm,
raise anchor for some more exotic realm!
Ennui, crushed down by cruel hopes, still relies
on handkerchiefs' definitive goodbyes!
Is this the kind of squall-inviting mast
that storm-winds buckle above shipwrecks cast
away — no mast, no islets flourishing? ...
Still, my soul, listen to the sailors' sing![51]

This translation by E. H. and A. M. Blackmore is published on a right-hand page facing its original, conveniently allowing readers with some French better to enjoy Mallarmé's poem, and to note any of the many ways in which the translation diverges from it. The immediate sense this version gives is of a coherent rendering with a firm rhythm and clearly sounding rhymes. It appears to come off well. Comparison of the Blackmores' version with a guide translation in a monograph on the poet illustrates how far

[50] Stéphane Mallarmé, *Oeuvres complètes*, ed. Henri Mondor and G. Jean-Aubry (Paris: Gallimard, 1945), p. 38.
[51] Stéphane Mallarmé, *Collected Poems and Other Verse*, trans. E. H. and A. M. Blackmore, introduced by Elizabeth McCombie (Oxford: Oxford University Press, 2006), p. 25.

they have gone in the effort to render poetry as poetry. Here is a supposedly 'literal', a non-rhyming rendition of Mallarmé's opening lines:

> The flesh is sorrowful, alas! And I've read all the books.
> Flee! Flee over there! I sense that the birds are intoxicated
> With being between the unknown foam and the skies![52]

Not only does 'sorrowful' mangle rhythm, it looks to be avoiding 'sad'. That the poet wants to 'Flee over there' sounds implausibly 'literal' because failing to get near an equivalent idiom in English. There's even a question of sense to address, for this version renders 'ivre / D'être' as 'intoxicated / With being' where the Blackmores have the apparently closer 'to be'. Are the birds drunk because they appear to have had too much of the drink, or do they appear dizzy with the desire for it? Since the poet's looking at them is emphasized in the original, the latter seems a more likely interpretation, because it echoes his equivocal desire to be off, while the envy of the birds underlined in the guide translation is implicit in the comparison.

The good translator of poetry understands not only the meaning of the words, but also the interaction between the words and their structuring. This understanding on the part of the translator, this respectful act of reading poetry, has to be conveyed in the translation too. Here the comparison with performing a piece of music is instructive: you don't simply have to get the notes right, you also have to integrate them into a rhythmic and expressive structure, one which in its emphases will inevitably be an act of interpretation. Broadly speaking, the better this can be done, the better the translation. Translators are in a different position to musicians and conductors, though: it isn't possible to play the poem's notes exactly because only some of the words have close equivalents, and if this fact is added to the differences of grammatical structuring between languages it can be seen that the rhythmic and expressive relationships of the parts can only approximate that produced by the original composer. Translations so often come to grief in Lowell's sense of the phrase because they can neither play the notes accurately nor effectively transpose into the new language their dynamic interaction. Affecting every line of the Blackmores' version is the decision to render alexandrine couplets as pentameters. Their version has a firmness approximating to the original, though not the same firmness, for they are required to condense Mallarmé's sense into a line that is two syllables shorter. This contributes to the more neatly versified feeling in the rendering. However, shortening the lines brings their paired rhymes into closer proximity. English heroic couplets are forever at risk of declining into glib epigram, and the Blackmores' version is faintly tarred with that historical brush. The iambic beat of the English also inevitably contrasts with the more fluid syllabics of the French, in which an alternating stress is far less marked.

---

[52] Rosemary Lloyd, *Mallarmé*, p. 70.

Closer comparison of their version with the original starts to reveal divergences of sense that have been accepted to facilitate the rhymes, producing what Nabokov would call a paraphrasing translation. This begins with the seemingly minor matter of turning Mallarmé's 'tous les livres' [all the books] into the singular 'every book', so as to rhyme perfectly with 'Birds look'. More dramatically, they introduce the words 'swaying helm' of the steamer (it would probably have been a 'turning wheel'), so as to relieve themselves of the 'mâture' and 'nature' rhyme in French by inventively recasting the latter as 'realm'. A similar invention renders 'fertile îlots' as 'islets flourishing', nicely preparing for the closing rhyme on 'sing' — which itself mildly paraphrases the 'songs of the sailors'. Looking at the last line, again, I wonder why they decided on 'Still, my soul' to render 'Mais, ô mon cœur'? The question is underlined by their translation of the next poem in their collection, 'Soupir', which begins 'Mon âme' and is translated by them as 'My soul'. As ever with pre-twentieth-century poetry there is the problem of what to do with exclamations. The Blackmores, reducing alexandrines to pentameters, opt for the editorial approach. So 'hélas!' disappears from the opening line. But why did Mallarmé include it? The opening of their translation is one of its weaker moments, because it seems oddly factual or informative: the flesh is sad, and he has read every book. The original is an expression of mood, or state of mind — an affect that the exclamation helps to locate, as does the more dismissively exaggerating 'all the books'. He hasn't; it just feels like that when he is in such a depressed, shiftless, or frustrated state.

Translations *are* likely to be slightly disappointing in this way — as Frost said they ought to be. They have turned an impossible and unreal aspiration into the textual proof of what was then practicable for them, and from that contrast an irritant desire is born — inviting us to approach the original and perhaps to try again. Here is 'Sea Breeze', Richard Wilbur's translation of 'Brise marine', which was 'written for the centenary of Stéphane Mallarmé', though not (let me underline) in response to the version above:

> The flesh grows weary. And books, I've read them all.
> Off, then, to where I glimpse through spray and squall
> Strange birds delighting in their unknown skies!
> No antique gardens mirrored in my eyes
> Can stay my sea-changed spirit, nor the light
> Of my abstracted lamp which shines (O Night!)
> On the guardian whiteness of the empty sheet,
> Nor the young wife who gives the babe her teat.
> Come, ship, whose masts now gently rock and sway,
> Raise anchor for a stranger world! Away!
>
> How strange that Boredom, all its hopes run dry,
> Still dreams of handkerchiefs that wave goodbye!
> Those gale-inviting masts might creak and bend
> In seas where many a craft has met its end,

> Dismasted, lost, with no green island near it ...
> But hear the sailors singing, O my spirit![53]

Wilbur's handling of his couplets, their end-stops and enjambments, is more rhythmically attuned than the Blackmores, but he too renders alexandrines as pentameters, making his rhymes click, and the sense units sound faintly pat, thus setting up the problem focused around his final rhyme, again avoiding the word 'heart' — which places a different part of Mallarmé's sentence in the concluding position. This again touches upon a crucial issue in how poems work: it's not only achieved through what they contain, but also through the ordering by means of which the significance elements are delivered.

Faintly disappointed once again, especially in the final couplet and rhyme, I might try myself, with implicit apologies, and gratitude for all the words borrowed or re-echoed, because, as we have seen, compared translations often share a remarkable amount of vocabulary, and so here is a translation called, for the sake of variety and distinctness, 'Marine Breeze':

> My flesh is sad, alas! and I've read all the books.
> Escape! fly away! I sense how each bird looks
> Enraptured to be among unknown foam and skies!
> Nothing, not the old gardens mirrored in my eyes
> Will hold this heart that is soaked in the sea,
> O nights, nor the lamp's deserted clarity
> Upon the blank paper defended by its white,
> Nor the young wife breastfeeding her little mite.
> I'll leave! Steamer swaying your mast-work, your
> Anchor, haul it up for a more exotic nature!
>
> An Ennui, made wretched by cruel hopes, still tries
> To believe in handkerchiefs' ultimate goodbyes!
> And, maybe, the masts, those calls to be storm-tossed,
> Are such as a wind bends on the wrecks lost
> Without masts, without masts, nor fertile islands ...
> But, heart, o my heart, how the sailors' song resounds!

The paraphrasing rhyme of 'islands' and 'resounds', with its contrastive stresses, may not be to everyone's taste. The apostrophes may be thought inappropriately archaizing. The opportunely rhyming 'little mite' might be thought unsuitably colloquial, or the repetition of 'heart' over-pitched. Yet it's in the nature of art objects to be evaluated (you can't have value-free art). The difference between poems and translations is that post facto *mot juste* claims have even less evidence to attach to: translations perpetually invite the thought that they can be phrased differently — and because they are performances, tokens of types, they appear more evidently approximate.

[53] Stéphane Mallarmé (trans. Richard Wilbur), 'Sea Breeze', *Mallarmé in the Twentieth Century*, ed. Robert Greer Cohn and Gerald Gilespie (Madison and Teaneck, NJ: Fairleigh Dickinson University Press, 1998), p.7. I have corrected line 9 to read 'How strange' rather than the apparent misprint 'Now strange'.

None of this am I urging as a counsel of despair, but to look again and try once more. Originals don't need reproducing; but retranslating is natural to *The Art of the Impossible*.[54]

What these various versions of Mallarmé's poem draw attention to is the high level of agreement about how the poem may be rendered in English, the range of words that might be called upon to convey its sequence of events, helped by the cross-channel poetic exchanges (emblematically represented in his French by the word 'steamer'), that links Mallarmé with the developments of poetry in English during the last century. Though none of the above versions are exactly the same, at certain points they use the same words, or near synonyms, and their similarities are striking. They can also be compared and contrasted, with admiration, perhaps, for how their writers have finessed the most difficult moments in the original, or with that disappointment to which Frost refers, and which may well prompt us to look at and work on its original — whether as readers or translating writers. The poem cannot, then, be exactly translated into English. Frost is right: there is no substitute for the original. Yet multiple translations of famous poems exist, transformations of a unique original into a range of contiguous interpretive performances, some of them distinctly good in their own right, and in any exploration of poetry and translation this fact must also be acknowledged as a part of the cultural landscape. Thus, what I have been arguing for, to this point, is the existence of a level playing field in which neither linguistic skills nor the arts of poetic composition can be used to relieve the translation from the bright illumination of both those evaluative desk lamps. The grounds for what can be achieved in the art of the impossible are the same as the grounds for saying that it can't be done.

I have thus been trying to identify a qualitative distinction between seeing two objects, the poem and its translation, as either the same or different, and seeing the two objects as relevantly similar in their evident differences. The translation of poetry is said to be impossible because poem and translation are thought about in the first way as either the same (impossible), or different (and therefore no translation), while if they are thought about in the second way the impossibility is retained in the evident differences and this forms, simultaneously, the grounds for translation to have taken place, and to be identified, in the relevant similarities. (What counts as relevant will depend on cases and will continue to arise in debates about the qualities a particular translation displays or fails to display.) The first way of thinking makes it impossible for communication to happen between people or cultures that decide they are unique and hold nothing

---

[54] For other versions of 'Brise marine', see *Mallarmé: The Poems*, trans. Keith Bosley (Harmondsworth: Penguin Books, 1977), p. 91, and Stéphane Mallarmé, *Collected Poems*, trans. Henry Weinfield (Berkeley and Los Angeles: University of California Press, 1995), p. 22; and for prose guide translations, see *Mallarmé*, trans. Anthony Hartley (Harmondsworth: Penguin Books, 1965), p. 29, and *French Poetry 1820-1950*, trans. William Rees (Harmondsworth: Penguin Book, 1990), pp. 195-96.

in common with others. The latter makes this impossibility the grounds for shared understandings that do not require either to believe there is anything strictly the same about them. Nor do their understandings of each other, agreed to be relevantly similar, require either of the two to impose their understanding on the other, while neither can suppose that their understandings escape wholly from the shaping terms of their own cultural situations. Thinking in this way recognizes that cultural formation is porous, never complete, and always open to revision. Not only does translation, seen in these lights, contribute to the shaping of intercultural understandings agreed to be relevantly similar, it instances any and all occasions of communication in which none of the parties is obliged to submit to assumptions, from any quarter, of either sameness or difference. Another way to put this would be to say that translation, interpretation, communication, and understanding are extendedly metaphorical. I now turn to exploring some of the larger implications in such a view of *Poetry & Translation*.

CHAPTER 5

Nostalgia for World Culture

I

Remembering the murderous nineteen-thirties, Nadezhda Mandelstam reports her husband's answer to a question about Acmeism, the poetic alliance he had belonged to in his youth, a group that included Anna Akhmatova and her husband Nicolay Gumilyov:

> To the question: 'What is Acmeism?' M. once replied: 'Nostalgia for world culture.' This was in the thirties, either in the Press House in Leningrad or at the lecture he gave to the Voronezh branch of the Union of Writers — on the same occasion when he also declared that he would disown neither the living nor the dead. Shortly after this he wrote: 'And bright nostalgia does not let me leave the still young Voronezh hills for those of all mankind so bright in Italy.'[1]

As his wife's collocated quotations imply, the terms for Osip Mandelstam's nostalgia were his inability to travel. The chapter in which this is reported is entitled 'Italy', and she notes that he had been there briefly in his youth but had almost forgotten it by the time he made these remarks. Mandelstam's response to the poetry of Dante and Ariosto is a part of his St Petersburg ambience: a Russia opened up to the world. The word 'nostalgia', a 'disease of the soul' (as a Soviet party member defined the word for me in 1980), implies a desired homecoming to world culture on the part of the poet whose exile in Stalin's Soviet Union was both real and soon-to-be fatal. If Mandelstam's present reputation could constitute such a homecoming, then it is thanks to admirers of his poetry, such as Paul Celan,[2] who have felt they were able to translate or collaborate on translations of it with contemporary poets — for Mandelstam is another twentieth-century author whose work

---

[1] Nadezhda Mandelstam, *Hope Against Hope: A Memoir*, trans. Max Hayward (London: Collins Harvill, 1989), pp. 246-47.
[2] For Celan as a translator of Mandelstam, see John Felstiner, *Paul Celan: Poet, Survivor, Jew* (New Haven and London: Yale University Press, 1995), pp. 128-36.

has conveyed his long-range heart largely in translation, as poems such as Seamus Heaney's 'Exposure' make amply clear.[3]

Over a century before Mandelstam expressed his 'Nostalgia for world culture', in 1827 Goethe had written in the journal he edited, *Über Kunst und Altertum*, that he foresaw the appearance of a *'Weltliteratur'*, a world literature. Though he did not invent the compound noun (Wieland had used it more than fourteen years earlier, and he was not the first), nevertheless it was Goethe who is most widely associated with the term, not least because of the international reach his own writing had — its weaving together, for instance, of distance, exile, and longing in one of his best-known poems, composed 'in 1782 or, more probably, 1783, in his last truly lyrical outburst for several years to come':[4]

> Kennst du das Land, wo die Zitronen blühn,
> Im dunkeln Laub die Gold-Orangen glühn,
> Ein sanfter Wind vom blauen Himmel weht,
> Die Myrte still und hoch der Lorbeer steht,
> Kennst du es wohl?
> > Dahin! Dahin
> Möcht ich mit dir, o mein Geliebter, ziehn.[5]

Samuel Taylor Coleridge attempted a translation of the poem in about 1828. He completed a draft of the first two stanzas from Goethe's three-verse poem, with its refrain that varies on each appearance:

> Know'st thou the Land where the pale Citrons blow,
> And Golden Fruits thro' dark-green foliage glow?
> O soft the breeze that breathes from that blue Sky!
> Still stand the Myrtles and the Laurels high.
> Know'st thou it well? O thither, Friend!
> Thither with thee, Beloved! would I wend.
>
> Know'st thou the house? On Columns rests its Height:
> Shines the Saloon: the chambers glisten bright:
> And Marble Figures stand and look at *me* —
> Ah thou poor Child! what have they done to thee!
> Know'st thou it well? O thither, Friend!
> Thither with thee, Protector! would I wend.
>
> Know'st though the road? — &c —[6]

---

[3] Seamus Heaney, *North* (London: Faber & Faber, 1975), pp. 72-73. For 'long-range heart': see Peter Riley, 'Osip Mandelshtam's "Poetry about the Unknown Soldier": A Version Made in Memory of John Riley', *For John Riley*, ed. Tim Longville (Leeds and Wirksworth: Grosseteste, 1979), p. 27.

[4] Nicolas Boyle, *Goethe: The Poet and the Age*, vol. 1: *The Poetry of Desire* (Oxford: Oxford University Press, 1991), p. 355.

[5] [Johann Wolfgang von] Goethe, *Selected Verse*, ed. and trans. David Luke (Harmondsworth: Penguin Books, 1964), p. 85.

[6] Samuel Taylor Coleridge, *Poetical Works I: Poems (Reading Text)*, part 2, ed. J. C. C. Mays (Princeton, NJ: Princeton University Press, 2001), p. 1018.

Perhaps that '— &c —' indicates Coleridge's loss of patience with the struggle to find equivalents for stanzas that by the third are evidently variations on a theme, a characteristic of the work which has helped to make it a favourite with composers from Franz Schubert to Hugo Wolf. The poem appears at the head of the first chapter in book 3 of *Wilhelm Meisters Lehrejahre* (1795-96), where Mignon sings it twice to the eponymous hero. As the narrative makes clear, though we have just read it in German, the poem is to be imagined as heard by Wilhelm in Mignon's 'Italian original' that 'is not communicated to us'.[7] Though Goethe appears to have written 'Kennst du das Land?' as an original poem in his own language, possibly inspired by his desire to visit Italy (fulfilled some four years after the poem's composition), it is offered as a translation from elsewhere. It thus exemplifies a subgenre of original works presented as if translated, of which Elizabeth Barrett Browning's *Sonnets from the Portuguese*, her love poems addressed to Robert Browning, are perhaps the most famous example in English poetry. Goethe's novel includes reflections on Wilhelm's problems encountered when rendering Mignon's song into German, given here in Thomas Carlyle's 1824 translation:

> The music and general expression of it pleased our friend extremely, though he could not understand all the words. He made her once more repeat the stanzas, and explain them; he wrote them down, and translated them into his native language. But the originality of its turn he could imitate only from afar; its childlike innocence of expression vanished from it in the process of reducing its broken phraseology into uniformity, and combining its disjointed parts.

Goethe economically conveys the familiar experience of feeling both the need and the restricted possibility of rearticulating in a different syntax the expressive parts of a poem when they have been disassembled in the transfer to another linguistic medium. The difficulties of translation can thus be evocatively expressive of both distance and responsibility. The passage concludes by underlining the place for which the gypsy Mignon (whose displacement is emphasized by her poor spoken German) famously longs in 'Kennst du das Land?' — the same country that was to prompt Mandelstam's nostalgia for world culture:

> On finishing her song for the second time, she stood silent for a moment, looking keenly at Wilhelm, and asked him, '*Know'st* thou the land?' 'It must mean Italy,' said Wilhelm: 'where didst thou get the little song?' 'Italy!' said Mignon with an earnest air: 'if thou go to Italy, take me along with thee; for I am cold here.'[8]

If the early sources of *Weltliteratur* in Goethe's work can be linked with his yearning to cross the Alps, it grew with the international reach of his ambitions for poetry in German, his Roman elegies, Venetian epigrams,

[7] Nicolas Boyle, *Goethe: The Poet and the Age*, vol. 1, p. 365.
[8] [Johann] Wolfgang von Goethe, *Wilhelm Meister*, trans. Thomas Carlyle (1824), 2 vols. (London: J. M. Dent, 1912), i, pp. 125-2

and, most sustained, his *West-östlicher Divan* (1814–1827), a collection of verse with a commentary written under the influence of Persian poetry. This theme in his oeuvre has been interpreted as a political project as well as a cultural one, a project in which translation and inter-cultural understanding might contribute to World Peace.[9] The difficulty of the idea for Goethe lay in the need to keep it clear of a narrow political co-option that would identify it with global imperialism. An opposite danger, of its appropriation by aestheticism, can be heard in Théophile Gautier's use of the *West-östlicher Divan* as a model for an art-for-art's-sake detachment. In his sonnet 'Préface' to *Emaux et camées* (1852), he recalls that 'Pendant les guerres de l'empire, / Goethe, au bruit du canon brutal, / Fit *le Divan occidental*, / Fraîche oasis où l'art respire' [During the wars of the empire, / Goethe, at the sound of brutal canon, / Made *the West-Eastern Divan*, / Fresh oasis where art breathes]; while, at the start of his sestet, the poet compares himself to 'Goethe sur son divan /A Weimar'.[10]

The word 'divan' is itself an instance of the processes by which the resources of a natural language are evolved and enriched by translational borrowings from uses in other cultures, a process dependent on travel and trade. How else could the word in English for a piece of living room furniture be used with that compounded adjective as the title for a collection of poems in German? How could the word be cognate with the French 'douane' and the Italian 'dogana', meaning 'customs' — places where you pay taxes to cross borders? Its movement across language barriers from Persian had evidently involved taxing the word's meanings in unexpected ways. The *OED*'s answer is that the two seemingly unrelated senses developed around bureaucratic situations in which there were both bundles of papers (by extension, collections of poems) and pieces of lounging furniture upon which to deal with such documents. Edwin Morgan was playing on at least two of its meanings (as was Gautier), and suggesting their common source, when he composed an extended love poem in the 1970s wittily entitled 'The New Divan'.[11]

If the danger of partisan political appropriation in the idea of a world literature was to be manifested in the history of the following century, and emblematically in the rhetoric and policy of the Third Reich (or, for that matter, of an Empire upon which the sun would never set), it had already been foreshadowed in the contradictory history and fate of Napoleonic Europe. Such circumstances would also urge poets such as Gautier to take culturally critical refuge in the garret of a disengaged aestheticism. Yet if the various forms of imperialism that flourished for longer or shorter

[9] David Barry, 'Faustian Pursuits: The Political-Cultural Dimension of Goethe's Weltliteratur and the Tragedy of Translation', *German Quarterly* vol. 74 no. 2 (Spring, 2001), pp. 164–85.

[10] Théophile Gautier, *Émaux et camées*, ed. Claudine Gothor-Mersch (Paris: Gallimard, 1981), p. 25.

[11] Edwin Morgan, *The New Divan* (Manchester: Carcanet Press, 1977), pp. 7–56.

periods in the nineteenth and twentieth centuries have underlined the dangers of such an idea as subservient to political imperatives, they simultaneously emphasized the continuing relevance and urgency of Goethe's original vision — one in which, as the cognate senses of the word suggest, to understand the poetry and art of another culture is to contribute to a cultural understanding that may foster the acknowledgement and appreciation of irreducible differences, and, by acknowledging such differences, contribute to a spirit of cooperation in international affairs. It might be added that no matter what the difficulties facing such a vision are, and the history of the last two centuries can furnish innumerable examples, its desire to have 'to understand' inflect 'to be understanding of' hasn't yet been bettered. In an era of precarious and equivocal globalism its potentials, for better or worse, are likely to be ever more needed and tested.

To preserve its integrity as a positive value the idea of world literature has both to assume and cultivate a world of differences, and, to that end, to resist the unreflective imposition of exclusive norms. The impossibility of translation, understood as the divergences of cultural and linguistic conditions across which any translation is attempted, collaborates with the idea of world culture, or *Weltliteratur*, in being the term by which the differences strictly inexpressible in other words are both acknowledged and made approximately available for understanding. To those who reply that if it is approximate it cannot be understanding, I would recall for them that understanding is itself necessarily approximate because it means others' ability to demonstrate the internalizing of knowledge or capacity in their own self-generated terms and actions. If it is an understanding it must be an approximation. Translation makes a world culture thinkable, but the impossibility of translation, as defined here, makes it 'nostalgia' for what must be a never complete return home. The art of the impossible is one crucial way in which we continue to hope and strive for an idea, one necessary for the overcoming of ignorant nationalistic and, by extension, imperialistic assertions, while its strict impossibility prevents a succumbing to the presumption of capture implied by transparency assumptions of translation as replicating transfer or complete delivery of literal meaning.

A crucial condition for Mandelstam's nostalgia and Goethe's political-cultural project is the existence of one world in which this culture could occur. Though the 'nostalgia', the longing for a world of differences, dialogically communicating and at peace, is expressed by the strict impossibility of translation, yet still this sense of longing also requires the idea that we do live in one world, one composed of innumerable differences. The existence of such a world is, though, a contested idea — as we shall see. Equally, those who feel Mandelstam's nostalgia, a nostalgia for Goethe's idea which had been formulated in response to a resurgent nationalism in the wake of Napoleon's defeat, and one that has equally to be contrasted with illusions of world political or military domination (as Mandelstam's living in Stalin's Soviet Union underlines), they need a trans-cultural communication focused around the theme of poetry, and poetry in translation, precisely because of

Frost's preemptive aphorism, and its emphasis on a national culture: 'We must remember', he wrote in 1957 to the poets of Korea, 'that one may be national without being poetical, but one can't be poetical without being national.'[12] Yet among the incidental pleasures of speaking English now is the fact that there is no nation state named England for which it is the official language. There is a small country; but that is a different matter.

In a review of Daniel Weissbort's selection from Ted Hughes's translations, Martin Dodsworth rejects Hughes's theory of translation with its assertions of both literalness and a trans-cultural universalism: 'But word-for-word literalness is an impossibility,' he writes, 'because there is no exact calibration between languages' — turning then to truths mythically embodied in the Tower of Babel story:

> If Hughes was able to overlook them it was because he tended to look through words to a 'universal' grammar of myth underlying poetry. Among his many, often helpful appendices, Weissbort gives us Hughes's programme note for the Poetry International '67, in which he writes of poetry as 'a Universal language of understanding, coherent behind the many languages in which we can all hope to meet'. The invented language of *Orghast*, of which Weissbort gives us a morsel (though it is hardly translation) plainly relates to this idea of the 'Universal' language. Hughes described it as 'stripping off the intrusive, formal, merely communicative or intercommunicative element of language — that intellectual and loaded side of language'.[13]

Hughes's version of world culture sidestepped the linguistic specificity that stands in its way, promoting the poetic to that part of the mind or self or world in which we are all a single organic humanity behind the supposedly superimposed levels of linguistically and socially divided societies. Given the fear that nostalgia for world culture or *Weltliteratur* may be annexed by imperialistic homogeneity, or dominance by a single set of ideas, Hughes's universalism appears to imply as much and adds an irrationalism for good measure. Such mythical universalism with its indifference to specificities of language and culture, its practical unrealism, invites the dismissive ripostes of a Larkin ('*Foreign* poetry? No!'), occasioning reversions to national isolationism. Like the invented languages of Esperanto or Volapuk, Hughesian internationalism slides away on the traction-free slope of no actual speech communities, seemingly uninterested in grounding comparisons and contrasts between language uses and cultural conditions. His noble hope for 'global unity' to be achieved by finding 'in poetry a

---

12 Robert Frost, 'Message to the Poets of Korea' (1957), *The Collected Prose of Robert Frost*, ed. Mark Richardson (Cambridge, MA: Harvard University Press, 2008), p. 182.

13 Martin Dodsworth, 'The God of Details', *Agenda* vol. 43 no. 1 (Autumn 2007), p. 27. See Ted Hughes, 'Poetry International '67: Programme Note', *Selected Translations*, ed. Daniel Weissbort (London: Faber & Faber, 2006), pp. 199–200.

single common language of fellow feeling ... of shared essential humanity' longs for a state of affairs in which there would be no need for translation because differences would be done away with in what he elsewhere calls '*agape* as a world republic'.[14] In the absence of any such transcendental spirit glue, translators of poetry attempt to show and invite understanding of culturally different speech forms.

A contrasting way to resist cultural homogenizing and preserve the valued possibility of distinctly different outlooks is by multiplying worlds, taking the word 'world' to mean an extreme equivalent of a *Weltanschauung*, or worldview. Yet this preserves what are taken to be incommensurable worldviews at the cost of assuming that these 'worlds' cannot, or can barely and imperfectly, communicate with one other. Donald Davidson argues that to say someone is living in 'another world' would be to say that the translation of terms between that conceptual scheme and our own cannot be done.[15] My skepticism about whether we may be sure that others' words, whether in the same or other languages, can express the same feelings or emotions was a way of clarifying what interpretation and translation must mean, not, as I hope the subsequent discussion suggested, a way of reducing to nothing the possibilities for mutual understanding. Quite the contrary: if we do not presume to be reproducing another's words exactly in a translation or interpretation, then we have a rich vocabulary of means at our disposal for conveying a sense of them. The 'many worlds' account of consciousness offers little grounds for how cultural negotiations, even of unopposed parties, would take place. In this chapter I describe drawbacks in opting for a multiple worlds philosophy and the difficulties it presents for understanding the non-paradoxical interdependence of translation's strict impossibility and its ubiquitous practice.

Among the most symbolically present of figures at the first Poetry Internationals of the 1960s was Allen Ginsberg. In a recent literary critical essay he is treated as an emblematic instance of how we cannot be living in a single world — by means of comments on a remark he made when visiting Liverpool in 1965. So writing at about the time that the city, whose university press publish this book, was European Capital of Culture, I take the opportunity to address issues involved in Mandelstam's nostalgia for world culture by looking at Liverpool as a city in the world. If there is to be a world culture or *Weltliteratur*, there has to be a single world in which this literature and culture could be recognized to be evolving, one in which the kinds of local triangulation we saw in the previous chapter can contribute to understandings of the situations in which texts are located

---

[14] Hughes, 'Poetry International '67: Programme Note', headnote to 'Orghast', and 'Modern Poetry in Translation (1982): Introduction', *Selected Translations*, pp. 200, 70, 202.
[15] See Donald Davidson, 'On the Very Idea of a Conceptual Scheme', *Inquiries into Truth and Interpretation* (1984), 2nd edn. (Oxford: Oxford University Press, 2001), pp. 183-98.

and to which they, complexly and from oblique angles, relate. I explore the conflict between these views of the 'one world or many' debate, and argue that the singularity of this world is not compromised by variety and incommensurability in it. Rather, the presence of such features is among the characteristics that make it one world.

Do the problems of translating poetry support the idea that there are many worlds, or that there is one world of many differences? Imagine the situation in which you are that Italian writer having a problem with rendering a particular phrase from a villanelle in English. Being a translator who has a wide knowledge of poetry in your own and other languages will give you some advantages in understanding the original over even a native speaker who 'doesn't like poetry', doesn't happen to be so inward with this form of life. I take it in writing like this that even when there are striking differences between the poetry in your tradition and that in the tradition from which you are translating, and when there are striking differences between the oeuvre of the poet you are translating and other contemporaneous work produced in the same culture (e.g. Emily Dickinson's poetry, or William Blake's), nevertheless, in order to understand it, and translate it, you will still have to appreciate those differences within a set of background similarities — ones that allow you to identify the text you are translating as a poem at all, ones that make intelligible written linguistic performances of the poem category, ones that assume human intentions and purposes as these can be embodied in poems, and many others. Imagine, once more, that you are translating 'The art of losing isn't hard to master', and, not quite catching the point of the line in the entire assemblage of Bishop's 'One Art', you translate the phrase as an equivalent of 'The art of coping with loss isn't difficult to master'. Translation is interpretation, but to translate Bishop's line, in its context of inter-cultural and intercontinental losses, would naturalize what she is saying to the point of expressing an untruth, and, by taking the comic paradox out of the line, weaken the deft balance acted out in the entire poem:

> Then practice losing farther, losing faster:
> places, and names, and where it was you meant
> to travel. None of these will bring disaster.
>
> I lost my mother's watch. And look! My last, or
> next-to-last, of three loved houses went.
> The art of losing isn't hard to master.
>
> I lost two cities, lovely ones. And, vaster,
> some realms I owned, two rivers, a continent.
> I miss them, but it wasn't a disaster.[16]

The joke is continued here in that it's difficult to see how you can 'practice' a non-intentional action. The word 'farther' here is probably an

---

[16] Elizabeth Bishop, *Poems, Prose, Letters*, ed. Robert Giroux and Lloyd Schwarz (New York: Library of America, 2008), pp. 166–67.

untranslatable auditory pun, for an earlier draft has 'further'.[17] The poem's implicit geography takes in Nova Scotia and Massachusetts (sites of her childhood's death of father and mother's mental illness), Rio de Janeiro and Ouro Preto, the Amazon and the São Francisco (her Brazilian years with their complex love-life); and the planned travels include a visit to Europe that never happened.[18] These geographical locations, their loss, and the memory of their loss, all require the existence of a single physical and human world in which the journeys could or could not be made, the places visited and inhabited or not, both for there to be something to remember and for those memories to be painful. Equally, the art of the impossible as it fits into a nostalgia for world culture requires the effortful preservation of the irreducible difference in a poetic gesture such as Bishop's, the act of using a non-intentional verb in a way that implies the achievement of intentional control, while understanding it within a frame of similarities: strategies for managing life's damages, such as pretending to having more control over situations than you actually have as a way of getting through them. What's more, in translating this line you would have to produce something in the second language that, while it conveys the sense of the line, and retains the significantly odd grammar, also expresses its oddness in a line that has the casually natural flavour of something anyone might happen to say. The line's relation to English embodies just such interplay of natural similarity and idiolect difference.

II

Life is full of shocks, such as those registered via loss in Bishop's 'One Art', or Empson's 'Aubade' and Forrest-Thomson's 'Phrase Book' or, for that matter, Jo Shapcott's Gulf War poem of the same name.[19] As these poems differently illustrate, such shocks can more frighteningly occur when out of familiar language areas. Nearer to home, there's an unusual and repeatedly disturbing shock described by Muriel Spark in *The Prime of Miss Jean Brodie*:

> And many times throughout her life Sandy knew with a shock, when speaking to people whose childhood had been in Edinburgh, that there were other people's Edinburghs quite different from hers, and with which she held only the names of districts and streets and monuments in common.[20]

---

[17] See 'Drafts of "One Art"', Elizabeth Bishop, *Edgar Allan Poe & the Juke-Box: Uncollected Poems, Drafts, and Fragments*, ed. Alice Quinn (New York: Farrar, Straus and Giroux, 2006), p. 223 ff. The handwritten change of 'further' to 'farther' occurs on draft 13.

[18] See my 'Elizabeth Bishop's Art', *Twentieth Century Poetry: Selves and Situations* (Oxford: Oxford University Press, 2005), pp. 106–10.

[19] See Jo Shapcott, *Phrase Book* (Oxford: Oxford University Press, 1992), pp. 26–27.

[20] Muriel Spark, *The Prime of Miss Jean Brodie* (Harmondsworth: Penguin Books, 1965), p. 33.

'Sandy Stranger' is this character's name, though by the time she has these many shocks Miss Jean Brodie's star pupil has been translated into the cloistered Sister Helena of the Transfiguration; and Sandy is also the unexpectedly famous author of an 'odd psychological treatise on the nature of moral perception called *The Transfiguration of the Commonplace*',[21] a title taken in acknowledged theft by the philosopher Arthur C. Danto for a real book on the aesthetics of readymade, or readymade-like, art. Still, in Spark's novel Stranger is the name, and stranger — I imagine we're to think — the nature. To know that there are 'other people's Edinburghs' with 'a shock' at all is odd, in that it hardly seems a surprise that people have different experiences of places; while its coming as a shock suggests Sandy had believed, and kept falling back into the belief, that experience of place is unitary. Not only is it strange she knows this with a shock, but stranger that she is thus shocked 'many times throughout her life'.

Spark expresses this sudden awareness of difference to present Sandy's experience as unusual by contrasting it with a less strange way of talking. She is 'speaking to people whose childhood had been in Edinburgh', which sounds unexceptional enough; but this use of the place name in the singular then sets up the oddity of 'other people's Edinburghs', a plural form my spell-checker underlines in red. Her phrase 'quite different' equivocates plausibly between 'fairly different' and 'totally different', a range occasioning the explanatory qualification that what she and the other people shared was 'only the names of districts and streets and monuments'. Spark is establishing Sandy's experience as both perfectly possible, something anyone might feel, and distinctly unusual, allowing a reader to slide without a thought of disbelief from the obvious to the weird. If we take it that Sandy's Edinburgh is more or less completely different from other people's and that it really is *only* the names that she held in common with them, then she's living close to solipsism and madness, while if she merely notices that our experiences vary then she is being reminded of something most of us know — so her strangeness resides in this being a discovery for her. Readers are also invited to enjoy the frisson of wondering if madness lies in the way of what we more or less take for granted.

'Similarly, there were other people's nineteen-thirties,' Sandy reflects, as if to remind us of the cruel fates of Osip Mandelstam and millions of others. She is introducing a report on one of her visitors, whose childhood had taken place in Edinburgh:

> Sandy, who was now some years Sister Helena of the Transfiguration, clutched the bars of the grille as was her way, and peered at him through her little faint eyes and asked him to describe his schooldays and his school, and the Edinburgh he had known. And it turned out, once more, that his was a different Edinburgh from Sandy's.[22]

---

[21] Ibid. p. 35.
[22] Ibid. p. 34.

Cities like Edinburgh are large places with various districts of different characters, ones often separated not only by physical distances, but also by cultural, class, and gender ones too. The man she is talking to through the literal and symbolic 'bars of her grille' (as if she were also in a prison or cage like Rilke's panther) had been to a boys' school and was a boarder, whereas Sandy had been a day pupil at a school for girls. That would be enough in itself to give them different childhoods, but in ways that should shock nobody. We have different experiences of the world because we experience different parts of it, whether because you grew up in the other hemisphere, or in the next street. These sorts of differences can be of great interest to people comparing and contrasting their lives in a town or the past; and in this sense 'the Edinburgh he had known' does not mean that he and Sandy grew up in different Edinburghs, but that they had understandably various experiences of the same city. This is certainly how Spark presents the man's idea of his childhood:

> 'But Edinburgh,' said the man, 'was a beautiful city, more beautiful then than it is now. Of course, the slums have been cleared. The Old Town was always my favourite. We used to love to explore the Grassmarket and so on. Architecturally speaking, there is no finer sight in Europe.'

The place name is firmly in the singular, a capital city with a history of change, and of aesthetic evaluation, the former being something that the man takes for granted as a prerequisite for the latter. Needless to say, there might be citizens from elsewhere of a similarly *campanilista* mentality who would find their own city one which offers 'no finer sight in Europe.' Again, this should not surprise, opinions and tastes differing widely, and frequently accounted for by such indications as where people grew up, or what kind of education they received. Yet the way Spark expresses such differences when referring them to the mind of her central character once again pushes the account of it a little beyond the style of ordinary varieties of experience: 'And it turned out, once more, that his was a different Edinburgh from Sandy's.'

Here the imputation and implication of subjectivity is more extreme, echoing back to 'there were other people's Edinburghs quite different from hers, and with which she held only the names of districts and streets and monuments in common.' If you were walking along the Royal Mile with Sandy Stranger, although you would both pass place names like the 'Heart of Midlothian' or 'John Knox House', you and Sandy would have distinctly different experiences and, on that account, could be said to be inhabiting, as you walked towards your Edinburghs' Castles, two 'quite different' places which happen to share the name 'Edinburgh'. There are strands of philosophical thought and reflection that appear to support such a version of isolated and incommensurate experience — exemplified, for instance, by William Blake's aphorism from *The Marriage of Heaven and Hell* that 'A fool sees not the same tree that a wise man sees', or Ludwig Wittgenstein's remark in his *Tractatus* that 'Die Welt des Glücklichen ist eine andere als die des Unglücklichen' [the world of the happy person is an other than that of the unhappy].[23]

Blake's sentence seems to say that there are two trees and the two men see different ones, but if so, it would not serve as a statement differentiating the two men; that is, we understand it to mean that they both look at the same tree, but one of them sees it with the eyes of a wise man and the other sees it with the eyes of a fool. If the tree were not the same one, the contrast would not work, because each of them would be seeing the tree in his own way and to the best of his ability. Their experiences of trees would, in this sense, be incomparably the same. Wittgenstein's remark about the world of the happy and the unhappy man has similar features, and for it to be a contrast between the men, they have to inhabit the same world under different aspects. Otherwise they would be each as happy or as unhappy as they happen to be according to their own lights and in 'the world of' each person. The contrast of 'happy' and 'unhappy' could not take place if they were each living in worlds of their own. Wouldn't Blake's wise man, being wise, be able to see, or at least imagine, the tree of the foolish man? If Wittgenstein's happy man were also sensitive, might he not be able to imagine the world of the unhappy one? I wouldn't myself think much of his happy world if it didn't include a sense of what the unhappy man's world is – and vice versa. How would he distinguish his happiness from self-delusion? We might also note that, strictly speaking, the two men looking at the tree in Blake's aphorism will not have exactly the same experiences of the tree, especially if they are looking at it simultaneously, because they cannot occupy the same physical space as they look.

Some philosophers have been pushed to think and formulate distinct sets of objects to avoid the problem that Sandy Stranger's Edinburgh would have to be a materially different object for her to refer to 'my Edinburgh'.[24] In 'I love Edinburgh' and 'Take the train from King's Cross if you want to visit Edinburgh', the second is supposed to refer to the material object in space, while the former is said to refer to an intensional object, the object of an idea or opinion or point of view. What relationship, if any, does there have to be between material objects and intensional objects for the latter to have sense? What does it mean to be able to write not merely 'an idea or opinion or point of view', but 'an idea or opinion or point of view *of or about something*'? Further, since most people not professional philosophers, or their fellow travellers, remain blissfully unaware that intensional objects exist at all, in so far as they can be said to, how do ordinary language

---

[23] William Blake, 'Proverbs of Hell', *The Marriage of Heaven and Hell*, ed. Geoffrey Keynes (Oxford: Oxford University Press, 1975), p. xviii. Wittgenstein, *Tractatus*, pp. 184–85.

[24] For an account of 'abstract objects', see W. V. Quine, 'Things and Their Place in Theories', *Theories and Things* (Cambridge, MA: Harvard University Press, 1981), pp. 1–23.

users manage to get through life without thinking that there are as many Edinburghs, Liverpools, Londons, and everything else under the sun, as there are people to experience them?

III

That brief passage in *The Prime of Miss Jean Brodie* appears strikingly to contradict the assumption that there is only one world — and that all of us who happen to be alive now are living in it. If there is no such single world, then there can be no *Weltliteratur* or world culture, and nostalgia for it will be no more than empty hankering. Spark's passage acknowledges, by expressing the recognition as a continuing shock, the possibility of other worlds, better worlds, or similar conceptual entities that can be called 'worlds' in English. Eric Griffiths has staged a subtle apologia for Sister Helena's way of talking.[25] The poet and critic John Ash was once mildly criticized by me for formulating praise of Roy Fisher (used on a number of his jacket blurbs) in the following terms: 'In a better world he would be as widely known and highly praised as Seamus Heaney and Ted Hughes'.[26] Not only did I not know of any 'better world' of literary reputations, but also the notion of 'a better world' seemed, haplessly perhaps, a means for pushing such a world off even as it was invoked. Griffiths, contesting the idea that there is a single world, or that to appeal to the existence of such a world is to deny the possibility of various conceptual entities conventionally called 'worlds' (e.g. the literary world), notes of the criticism levelled at Ash that 'there are no "*wholly* imaginary, alternative places" (my emphasis)', and adds that 'what Ash or anyone desires under the description "a better world" is never *sheer* figment.'[27] Yet we may distinguish between the imaginative content of Ash's sentence, his desire that Fisher be better known, which need not be a figment, and his 'better world' formula (or, equally, his polemical contrast of Fisher's with others' reputations) which remains a figment, and must do for the bite of the polemic against the then current state of affairs to function. Ash used the 'better world' formula, after all, to mean that Fisher should by rights be as famous as the other two in *this* world. My argument was with the formula, not the wish. Taking issue with Griffiths in support of Goethe's idea and Mandelstam's nostalgia, I have three questions: (1) Does the linguistic fact that the word 'world' can have multiple references, can be used in the plural, and can be used metaphorically or in science fiction have a bearing upon the issue of whether there is or is not epistemologically

[25] Eric Griffiths, 'Blanks, misgivings, fallings from us', *The Salt Companion to Peter Robinson*, ed. Adam Piette and Katy Price (Cambridge and Perth: Salt Publications, 2007), pp. 55-83.

[26] Peter Robinson, Introduction, *The Thing about Roy Fisher: Critical Studies*, ed. John Kerrigan and Peter Robinson (Liverpool: Liverpool University Press, 2000), p. 1.

[27] Griffiths, 'Blanks', p. 57.

and ontologically one world in which we live? (2) Can people be sensibly, though usually pejoratively, said to live in worlds of their own without there being one world to which the differences can be referenced? (3) Does the world with its names of districts and streets and monuments in Edinburgh, for instance, because it is independent of us therefore display no consciousness or viewpoint?

At one point in his essay Griffiths asserts of my recourse to John Searle for support that 'even so accomplished a philosophical argument as Searle's can't withstand and dismiss centuries of usage' and he lists twelve distinguishable meanings for the word 'world'.[28] But the *OED* does not include notes on whether the referents of its words exist, or whether conceptualizations containing them are true. It differentiates meanings on the basis of recorded usage. The *OED* defines the word 'love', but says nothing about whether when I say 'I love you' my 'love' actually exists, or, if it exists, that it is a 'true love' or if, sadly, it is the selfish performance attributed to the phrase 'Ich liebe dich' by William Gass. The word 'soul' has meanings given in the *OED*, but the dictionary doesn't note whether it is true that human beings have souls given to them by God. The word 'alchemy' is accurately defined by the *OED* but that does not make it any more likely that we can create gold out of base metals. That English grammar allows us to use the word 'world' in the plural, or with an indefinite article, or as a possessed object, has no bearing on the truth or not of our living in a single world or in innumerable worlds. A language is the mutual creation of all the people who speak, have spoken, and indeed will speak it. Over many centuries, they have wanted and needed words and phrases that will allow them to say what has come to be thought error, falsehood, self-delusion, and utter rubbish — and their achievements in this enterprise are also gratefully enshrined in the *OED*. There are bound to be occasions when, as a native speaker, I too will exclaim that 'So-and-so is living in a world of his own'. Yet as Davidson has remarked: 'what is the common reference point, or system of coordinates, to which each scheme is relative? Without a good answer to this question, the claim that each of us in some sense inhabits his own world loses its intelligibility'.[29] One of his explicators has noted that he 'thus takes the supposition that there are "different worlds" for different cultures, or that there is "incommensurability" between one literary tradition and another, to be either literal nonsense or a hyperbolic way of saying that people and traditions can be very different.'[30] The use of the word 'world' in the plural does not give the game away, as it were, and show that, however much I might want (supported by John Searle) to deny it, there really are many 'worlds' because we imply there are by that usage.

[28] Ibid. p. 58.
[29] Donald Davidson, 'The Myth of the Subjective', *Subjective, Intersubjective, Objective* (Oxford: Oxford University Press, 2001), p. 39.
[30] Samuel C. Wheeler III, 'Language and Literature', *Donald Davidson*, ed. Kirk Ludwig (Cambridge: Cambridge University Press, 2003), p. 188.

Rather, the usage depends upon a background assumption that however many metaphorical or extended-usage 'worlds' there may be, the related meanings of these 'worlds' depend upon the assumption of a singular world, in relation to which such extended senses can be referenced or applied: 'Since there is at most one world', Davidson notes, 'these pluralities are metaphorical or merely imagined.'[31] I don't like 'merely' here, but let's forgive the argumentative flourish.

Discussing Wordsworth's 'The Sailor's Mother', Griffiths shows himself able to slide across these two dependent ways of thinking, namely, an intelligible description which idiomatically attributes life in a 'world of his or her own' to someone — and yet one which relies, for the contrast implied, on the background assumption of there being the one world in which both persons live. After quoting 'She answered soon as she the question heard, / "A simple burden, Sir, a little Singing-bird"', Griffiths suggests that 'Hers is a voice which admonishes Wordsworth from another world', not only the world of her distinctive human experiences as figured by her 'burden', but also, he notes, by 'yet a third world of vocalization, the wordless chirping of the "Singing-bird".'[32] However, a couple of pages later he notes that 'Wordsworth's interview with the sailor's mother comes to us (as it came to him) down a crackly line, through much interference from the divergent routes the two of them have taken through the world, from their pasts which coincide only now in these fumbled utterances, and from the individual Background skills each has picked up on his or her way.' However different the 'worlds' from which Wordsworth's, the mother's, and the bird's vocalization have come, suddenly they are coinciding on their paths through what Griffiths refers to here as 'the world'. 'Instead of living in different worlds', as Davidson notes of scientists who are working within different conceptual schemes, they may 'be only words apart.'[33] Once again, 'only' may be misjudged.

Wordsworth's poem does not imagine the encountering figures and the bird as inhabiting different worlds. To conceive of the encounter and exchange in this way is to disable the cultural work, a form of translation, which it attempts. In the earliest draft of the poem the sailor's mother tells the poem's speaker about the pedestrian journey that she has been taking: twice across the Pennines from the northwest coast to the northeast: she lives in Mary-port and has travelled as far as Hull, and most of the way back, for she has reached the road between Grasmere and Ambleside. She also tells him that her son was 'cast away' (a phrase recalling Cowper's poem 'The Castaway', but also implying that he has been discarded, thrown away) in Denmark — and it has been argued elsewhere that there is here an allusion to the Battle of Copenhagen, won by the signal-ignoring Nelson some eleven months before Wordsworth's poem

---

[31] Davidson, 'On the Very Idea of a Conceptual Scheme', p. 187.
[32] Griffiths, 'Blanks', p. 67.
[33] Davidson, 'On the Very Idea of a Conceptual Scheme', p. 189.

was drafted.[34] 'The Sailor's Mother' dramatizes the speaker's complex of success and failure in his attempt to translate her into terms that he understands. In the first stanza she is an impressive figure (with 'a Roman Matron's gait' — Roman mothers being famous for their stoicism in sacrificing their sons for the empire). Yet she 'begg'd an alms, like one of low estate',[35] and asserting that despite this fact 'nor did my pride abate', he asks her what she is carrying hidden under her cloak — some ad hoc means testing on his part.

The sailor's mother is then represented as immediately understanding her interlocutor's implication without any such 'crackly line' as Griffiths anachronistically imagines: 'She answer'd soon as she the question heard'. Prompted to account for the swollen shape under her cloak, she then tells him about the caged bird she is carrying home, a memento of her dead son borne in the place of her womb. The art of the poem is to imitate the woman's reply (to translate her into rhyming stanzas), reinforcing the speaker's original assumption about her dignity and stoicism, but expressing it not in his abstracting and analogy-forming mode, but in a translation-like approximation of her own directly apologetic words. The sense of difference between them, of their not belonging to the same socio-linguistic groups, is made manifest — and was a cause of some critical conflict between Coleridge and its poet that emerged in the *Biographia Literaria*. But if the speaker and the sailor's mother, and indeed her son's bird, do not belong to the same world, then the poem's troubling differences need not register. The poem's place names could be treated in Sister Helena's way (different Mary-ports, Hulls, and Denmarks), but by naming these geographical spots — and Wordsworth composed poems on the naming of places — the speaker assumes, and reasonably, that her listener will know how far she has walked.

There is one further point of contention which emerges when Griffiths, finding support in Searle, goes on to tell us what 'the world' should be understood to mean. He cites the American philosopher: 'In short, it is only from a point of view that we represent reality, but ontologically objective reality does not have a point of view.' To which Griffiths wittily adds: '"Ontologically objective reality" comes out sounding remarkably clueless, for everyone has a "point of view" these days', and he clarifies matters when explaining that what he means by a 'world' is the equivalent of a 'point of view' from which each of us may represent reality, and so 'Ontologically objective reality does not have such a world, because it *is* the world.'[36] However, that formula suggests some strain, for, shorn of the

---

[34] See my 'Reparation and "The Sailor's Mother"', *In the Circumstances: About Poems and Poets* (Oxford: Oxford University Press, 1992), pp. 9–22.

[35] William Wordsworth, *Poems, in Two Volumes, and Other Poems, 1800–1807*, ed. Jared Curtis (Ithaca, NY: Cornell University Press, 1983), pp. 77–79. I cite the earliest text.

[36] Griffiths, 'Blanks', p. 79.

explanation that a 'world' may be understood as a 'point of view', the phrase 'reality does not have ... a world' sounds (as it is probably meant to for *reductio* purposes) bizarre. At which point, perhaps, it might seem we could even agree to differ, might agree that words such as 'we all vocalize in our own "world" and there is also "the world" in which those worlds move around' is a near equivalent of my preferred 'there is the world in which we, with all our various outlooks, move around'.

It would thus appear we might agree that since no two people can stand in exactly the same spot at the same time, in order for us to meet, e.g., outside the Adelphi Hotel in Liverpool, we have to understand 'outside the Adelphi' as not *exactly* the same spot (otherwise, strictly speaking, we could never meet *there*). So it's not that this one world's non-existence is demonstrated by the fact that we all have a unique and different view. Rather, 'the world' exists independently of us not least because we each view it, however slightly, differently. You may have noticed that my concern about this matter of 'one world or many' is not merely a question of phraseology, but, rather, that those who prefer the 'many worlds' philosophies also tend to denigrate the 'one world' school of thought by denying the accessibility of that cherished object. Griffiths falls into this category, because while it seems he is willing to acknowledge the existence of that ontologically dumb reality, he maintains that there is a strict separation between 'the world' (which inaccessibly expresses nothing) and us birds, poets, translators, critics, readers, sailors' mothers, and such like, who do express things in our innumerable worlds. My understanding of these matters has been strengthened by reading Davidson's theory of 'triangulation' in the communication of responses to what occurs in the visual fields of two adjacent people. His observations not only allow access to the world, but also show how it is there because we can share talk about it, and we can share talk about it because it is there. If there is room for disagreement, then we must be living in no other world than this.

IV

'Literal meanings are not always unambiguous,' Griffiths helpfully reminds us, 'nor are words, even when used literally, ever self-interpreting.'[37] Let me further relate the existence of no other world than this to matters of translation, and the question, already aired, about what it could mean to say that a translation is literal. In an anthology of English renderings from Dante Alighieri, Griffiths and his co-editor Matthew Reynolds make use of the word when discussing relationships between their samples and the Italian original. Back in 1760, for example, William Huggins offered a version of the first twenty-one lines of Canto IX from Dante's *Purgatorio*, which he claimed was done 'As literally as possible'. The editors of *Dante*

[37] Ibid. p. 64.

in English comment on this fond hope: '*wild and thorny way* Huggins does translate quite literally but not "as literally as possible": the Italian has no 'way', wild or otherwise, but a 'harsh desert' because Dante knew that it was there the Israelites received the manna — see Exodus 16'.[38] So the editors take it that there can be literal translations of poetry as complex as Dante's. All translations are vulnerable to depredation from the fine changes that occur day by day in the spoken idioms of natural languages. Nevertheless, this does not mean that because languages have changed we are no longer living in the same world as Dante (we may be living in a different cultural, political, and historical era, also metaphorically called 'a world', but that's another matter, and is in any case fairly continuous with ours, as in the present existence of the language Dante helped to bring into being, the cities of Florence, Verona, and Ravenna where he lived, and the Catholic Church). One of the many reasons why it is possible figuratively to say that Dante is our contemporary will be because you can go and climb the stairs in Verona upon which he trod, you can read the poems by Arnaut Daniel that he read, just as you can walk round the arena that Goethe commented on in his *Italienische Reise*. That you can also visit the *stadio* where neither ever set foot does not mean that going to watch a football match in Verona involves entering another world.

These editors, Griffiths and Reynolds, are much exercised in their notes on the translations they select with occasions where the translator embroiders or elaborates on the original Italian. In doing so they often implicitly, sometimes explicitly, and understandably claim to know what the original means. To this end, they draw upon the kinds of continuities of cultural knowledge that allowed Bernard Williams's classicist friend to joke that the Latin for 'album' in a poem by Horace could be an object in which to preserve photographs. Take, for example, the following lines from *Inferno* 30 as rendered by James Montgomery in 1841:

'One's the false woman who accused young Joseph,
And t'other Sinon, the false Greek at Troy,
Who, in the excruciating pangs of putrid fever,
Send up such steam.'

The volume's two editors remark: 'Montgomery refines on Dante's "coarser vein"; the original means "their fever is so sharp they throw out a fug"'.[39] The phrase 'coarser vein' is pounced on from Montgomery's introductory words to his translation. What concerns me is the assumption that, by contrast with the anthologized version they are annotating, Dante's text 'means' the translation that the editors offer. Let's imagine for a moment that we don't know a word of Italian, that Dante's is a closed book to us. What would we think of their translation? The editors' offering has three

[38] Eric Griffiths and Matthew Reynolds (eds.), *Dante in English* (Harmondsworth: Penguin Books, 2005), p. 45.
[39] Ibid. p. 81.

119

uncertainties of touch. Do English speakers usually describe fevers as sharp? We understand what *they* mean or we can guess, but there may be colloquial strain between noun and adjective. More serious, the verb 'throw out' is inherently ambiguous between 'put forth' and 'discard', and we might ask if the original has such an ambiguity. The word 'fug' is highly usage-specific, perhaps of Northern dialectal origins, and might require some translating itself. You could think that Montgomery's is a better translation because it has some rhythm, some alliteration, and presents a vividly painful picture of that moment in the canto. It's presumably not like Dante because written in mid-Victorian English, and so we wouldn't expect it to be. But then neither is the offering by the editors for what 'the original means'. What Dante's lines may mean is an Italian-speaking reader's understanding of —

> ['] L'una è la falsa ch'accusò Giuseppo;
> l'altr'è il falso Sinòn Greco da Troia:
> per febbre aguta gittan tanto leppo'.[40]

If you interpret or translate it, then, as in Robin Kirkpatrick's 2006 version, it will be different: 'Joseph was falsely charged by that "she" there./ The other, just as false, is Sinon (Trojan-Greek!)./ Their biting fever brews that curdled reek.'[41] What Dante's lines are said by Griffiths and Reynolds to mean is an interpretation, a paraphrase in another language, selecting some aspects of the original for foregrounding in other words; that's to say, it's a competing translation. One thing, though, that I suggest the original does not 'mean' is an ambiguously formulated, un-rhythmical summary in English. If Natalino Sapegno's notes are to be trusted, 'fug' isn't even that close to 'leppo', for it is glossed as 'puzza di arso unto, come quando lo fuoco s'appiglia alla pentola o alla padella' [smell of oily burning, as when the fire gets hold of the pot or the pan].[42] *OED* gives 'fug' as a 'thick, close, stuffy atmosphere, esp. that of a room overcrowded and with little or no ventilation' whose earliest citation is 1888 (post-dating Montgomery's version by some decades), while 'leppo' appears in current dictionaries, citing the line from Dante, as 'vapore puzzolente' [stinking steam]. It is this adjective in its verb form that provides Ciaran Carson with a rhyme in his direct and ballad-like rendering of the lines:

> ['] This one's lies put Joseph in the clink;
> the other's Sinon, lying Trojan Greek;
> they burn with fever, which is why they stink.[43]

Yet (and this is the point to emphasize) to claim that a rendering of Dante's phrase is 'literal' you must assume your English refers to a space continuous

[40] Dante Alighieri, *Inferno* 30, ll. 97–99.
[41] Dante Alighieri, *The Divine Comedy I: Inferno*, trans. Robin Kirkpatrick (Harmondsworth: Penguin Books, 2006), p. 269.
[42] Dante Alighieri, *La divina commedia*, ed. Natalino Sapegno, vol. 1: *Inferno* (2nd edn., Florence: 'La Nuova Italia' Editrice, 1968), p. 337.
[43] Ciaran Carson, *The Inferno of Dante Alighieri* (New York: New York Review Books, 2002), p. 211.

with, coherently homologous with, that of Dante's Italian: you have to be both writing of the one world with its fires and smokes and pans and crowded rooms and stinks. Nor should this surprise in a volume that pays its anthologizing tribute to a key text, *La divina commedia*, in the tradition of a world religion that is called Catholic because it believes itself to be the true faith of all the populations of the world, and, as a consequence, continues to fund missions for the conversion of the heathen.

Quite apart from any failure of editorial tact or taste involved in nit-picking at the texts you have presented to readers, there lies the issue of what a 'literal' translation is, and what is implied when someone claims to say what the original poem 'means'. As Griffiths reminded us above, the literal meaning of a word is not as plain an entity as it may seem. 'For a *large* class of cases — though not for all — in which we employ the word "meaning" it can be defined thus: the meaning of a word is its use in a language', Wittgenstein remarked, with a qualification that is not always included in its aphoristic citations.[44] This being so, the meanings of words are often so highly inflected by the specific usage situations in which we find them that what counts as a literal meaning in one context won't be in another. Rather, the notion of 'literal' meaning is a convenient way of prioritizing senses, and while such prioritizing has its uses, we might note that poetry is one of the places where equivocation about priorities of sense also has its uses.

In another of their notes, the *Dante in English* editors comment on the line 'The murmuring rivulets down the verdant hills' as follows: '*murmuring* the standard-issue epithet has no equivalent in the original *verdant* Dante's hills are just plain green ("*verdi*")'.[45] Yet, for speakers of the language conversing in Italian, the word 'green' just doesn't come into it. Strictly speaking, 'verdi colli' [l. 64] are not 'green hills'; that they are closely approximate expressions for comparable experiences of geographically different topography with their own flora is closer to it. What's more, Montgomery is, to the best of his ability, attempting to produce lines that in mid-Victorian England would be appreciated as at least poetry-like. He puts in 'murmuring' because he's a post-Keatsian, perhaps, to fill out his pentameter; and he chooses to translate 'verdi' as 'verdant' because it approximates the sound of the original, perhaps, and because it gives him a trochaic structure that melds conventionally with the stressed monosyllable 'hills'. In this respect too, Dante's 'colli' are not 'just plain green', for Dante is adapting his phrase from the sonic structures of Italian to the particular sonic contours of his own hendecasyllabic lines. He has two disyllabic words with echoic endings. To render 'verdi colli' as 'green hills' (in a translation that aspires to the condition of being a poem) would require an approach to the patterning of English verse not apparently available to Montgomery. Though this may be

44 Ludwig Wittgenstein, *Philosophical Investigations*, trans. G. E. M. Anscombe (3rd edn., Oxford: Blackwell, 2001), I, 43, p. 18e.
45 Griffiths and Reynolds, *Dante in English*, p. 80.

their point, what the editors say is that he fails to match Dante's sense in the deployment of his two adjectives.

A further problem with the idea of the 'literal' translation is that those who refer to such versions tend to assume that what is literal will be accurate, something that by no means follows in the transfer from one language to another. To take one final example from the editors' picky persecution of Montgomery's efforts, where Dante has 'Ma s'io vedessi qui l'anima trista / di Guido' (ll. 76-77) and his translator has 'Yet could I spy the woeful ghost of Guido', the editors note: '*woeful ghost* the original means "sad soul"'.[46] Similar claims can be made for the usefulness of 'woeful' as were made above for 'verdant'. Two-syllable adjectives help anchor an iambic rhythm. That Montgomery's choice of noun is also objected to is probably more a theological issue. The editors don't appear to like the way that in the mid-Victorian version the figure in Hell is more like a mock-gothic ghost of Christmas past than a mediaeval Catholic soul in torment. Yet, once again, there are problems about what the original is said to mean. After all, 'sad' is a particularly lame and colloquially ambiguous adjective in English, and a 'sad' figure could be a mildly pathetic creature, not what Dante's lines suggest, while 'soul' in English may not necessarily or even readily conjure up a figure or presence in the way that 'ghost' will. It can be used in expressions like 'not a soul', meaning nobody, but only when the context implies the absence of actual bodies. Let's consider the theological issue. We're reading a translation of *Inferno* 30 written by that famous Italian Catholic poet, Dante Alighieri. In the first canticle of his poem, as people reading it in translation tend to know, he meets the dead in the various circles of Hell to which they have been consigned by him according to his interpretation of the mediaeval Catholic God that we mid-Victorian Anglicans (with our many differences) also worship. In Montgomery's translation, the 'ghost of Guido' must mean his post-mortem divinely judged state. For all practical purposes here, 'ghost' is a synonym for 'soul' and can be understood as such by anyone reading with a little faith, hope, and, above all, charity. If 'woeful ghost' is not a perfect rendering of the original phrase, then that's only because there are no perfect matches, and practically any phrase in a translation can be contested and retranslated. Montgomery's noun and epithet may not be what is called a 'literal translation' of the Dante, but let me suggest that in the context of his version his is a reasonably accurate one. As anthologies like *Dante in English* amply demonstrate, it's in the nature of translated poetry that there are legitimately various versions fruitfully co-existing over time.

Thus, to conclude, just as I cannot and would not want to deny that the word 'world' can be used figuratively or in the plural, so I would not suggest that people can't sensibly and intelligently use the word 'literal' for the translation of a word or a phrase or poem. Yet to use the word to privilege a particular word-choice does not magically access perfect replication of

---

[46] Ibid. p. 81.

sense between languages. What I would equally assert is that if you want to claim that you know what a literal meaning is, then you must assume such sufficient continuities between your linguistic competence and that of your original to presuppose the existence of a single world in which they can both function. However, it does not by any means follow that the possibility of multiple translations of the same line of poetry with various claims to fidelity and accuracy forces us to assume the existence of as many worlds as there are translators to make them, or, indeed, readers to interpret those translations. A literal translation that requires a single world in which its claim can have a space to make sense must equally take its place in that one world as a way among many of rendering the original. It cannot claim privilege as a loss-free match — not least in poetry, where such literal translations tend to have so little by way of auditory felicity.

V

Griffiths begins his essay in defence of 'worlds' by having a little fun at Ginsberg's expense. During the last week of May 1965, the Beat poet visited the place that in 2008 became European Capital of Culture, and reportedly said that Liverpool was 'at the present moment the centre of the consciousness of the human universe'. Born and brought up in the same city, Griffiths comments (wittily invoking the local newspaper called the *Liverpool Echo*):

> This is a sentiment to which not every bosom has returned a Liverpool echo. I was there at the time and found his view hard to share, especially when arguing with my mother. Frank Kermode, though thrilled to step off the Isle of Man Ferry at the Pier Head, failed to spot evidence of Liverpool's centrality: 'I have known the place myself without ever quite perceiving this'.[47]

The twelve-year-old Griffiths, arguing with his mum, is unlikely to have heard Ginsberg's remark at the time, since it was first made public in Edward Lucie-Smith's *The Liverpool Scene* (1967) — but it has since entered the mythology of the place.[48] By citing the remark not from Ginsberg but from Ron Ward in a 2003 issue of *Auto Model Review*, Griffiths tees up his point that 'Allen Ginsberg and Ron Ward appear to converge on Liverpool as the centre of consciousness but "Liverpool" to one means "the place where Dinky Toys began" and means something quite other to the other. They don't, as we say, "mean the same thing by 'Liverpool'"'.[49] I disagree.

[47] Griffiths, 'Blanks', p. 55.
[48] See Simon Warner, 'Raising the Consciousness? Revisiting Allen Ginsberg's Trip in 1965', *Centre of the Creative Universe: Liverpool and the Avant-garde*, ed. Christoph Grunenberg and Robert Knifton (Liverpool: Liverpool University Press, 2007), p. 96.
[49] Ibid. pp. 56–57.

Ginsberg appears to mean: *the city* where I have had such an exciting time I want to give it this bit of hip-jive praise; while Ward appears to mean: *the city* so described by Ginsberg where the great Dinky Toys also happen to have been made. Though the one may have cared for model cars as little or as much as the other does for Beat poetry, it is the same city to which they refer by using the word 'Liverpool'.

What's more, even if Ginsberg isn't familiar with the work of Ward, and so it can't be a part of his world because the poet died in April 1997, the same cannot be said for Ron, since he cites Allen. The city to which Ginsberg hyperbolically refers is the one to which Ward can allude in appropriating those words to praise model car manufacturing. Something similar might be said for Kermode, since he takes Ginsberg to be referring to 'the place' that 'I have known', even if in a way that the critic finds amusingly beyond his ken. Once again, if Ginsberg and Ward didn't mean the same thing by Liverpool (namely, that it is a city where things that they each value have happened) then there would be no point using the term. They could, for instance, have referred to a grid reference on the South Lancashire plain; but that would not have conveyed what both of them intended.[50] Ginsberg and Ward can imply different things by, of, or about 'Liverpool', just as football fans at Anfield can mean eleven men in red shirts by it, but only with reference to 'Liverpool' as the proper name of a seaport in the North West of England.

In the exhibition catalogue for *Centre of the Creative Universe: Liverpool and the Avant-garde*, Simon Warner has attempted, by contextuali-zation and with historical research, to show Ginsberg the Davidson-like charity of being assumed to have rationally intended something by his pronouncement. Warner canvasses a range of possibilities. Adrian Henri, the Liverpool poet and painter, was sensibly sure that he had the world fame of the Beatles in mind. Others note the importance to Ginsberg of the city's nightlife, its many opportunities to sample homegrown pop music in the company of lively and attractive young people — and ones, in particular, of the male sex. Ginsberg had been recently ejected from both Cuba and Prague for advocating gay liberation in the Communist bloc. It appears he found musically hip young Liverpudlians, 'children of Albion', who were thankfully not so culturally constrained. Griffiths denigrates Ginsberg's comment further by his suggestion that being at the centre of consciousness was a condition which came with the presence of Ginsberg in person. Yet the poet had enough sense of his relative significance to enjoy attaching himself to the Beatles' moment. This is underlined by his not going to Liverpool to perform in a large venue to a mass of fans. He gave a small reading in Wilson's bookshop in Hardman Street.[51]

---

[50] For translation entering into talk about the locations of cities, see Davidson, 'Indeterminism and Antirealism', *Subjective, Intersubjective, Objective*, pp. 78–79.

[51] See Warner, 'Raising the Consciousness? Revisiting Allen Ginsberg's Trip in 1965', p. 100.

My third question was: does the world with its shared names (the 'names of districts and streets and monuments in Edinburgh', or Liverpool for that matter) have no consciousness or viewpoint? There is no way to talk about this without manifesting one of my own. Yet my suggestion is this: if the ontologically objective world could not manifest purpose, have purpose meaningfully identified in it, and show cause and effect of its own, it could not be represented with and from our various points of view. Among the many reasons why 'ontologically objective reality' cannot be said to have no point of view is that any individual person who happens to be walking through districts, on streets, and past monuments (Ginsberg in Hardman Street as it might be) can also count as a part of such a reality distinct from your consciousness of it (whether you happened to be there to walk past him or not). Ontologically objective reality therefore also contains the entire human population of the world that in turn includes the points of view of all those millions of individuals, including Ginsberg's in May 1965. This doesn't yet assert that such a reality has its own unique point of view, but it does assert that ontologically objective reality manifests viewpoints and signs of viewpoints — as in traffic lights, No Parking lines, adverts, house numbers, street names, graffiti, and innumerable other objects. Griffiths might acknowledge this; but he would need to conjure 'a world of vocalization' for the Highway Code in order to explain the existence of a Give Way sign, and such a 'world' would not explain why anyone could feel compelled to stop for the traffic, or for the absence of traffic, as law-abiding drivers do. Searle's theory of institutional facts is one attempt to account for the shared meaning of such signs and tokens.

But perhaps 'ontologically objective reality' means everything except human beings and their consciousnesses and artifacts. Griffiths also assumes the 'world' of the bird's song in 'The Sailor's Mother'. He cites Mary Midgley to support him with her view that 'The world in which the kestrel moves, the world that it sees, is, and always will be, entirely beyond us. That there are such worlds all around us is an essential feature of our world.'[52] Perhaps I could suggest, though, that if in 'our world' we can know that the kestrel's world is entirely beyond us, then, it isn't so entirely beyond because we can both imagine what it might be like to be a kestrel, and know that we'll never know for sure. Because we can do that, we can also resist the temptation to possess the world with Midgley's pronoun 'our'. What imagining might involve is, after all, sharing with kestrels the need to eat, to defecate, to generate, to protect our young, to defend ourselves, and such like — while, in moving and seeing, the kestrel will be manifesting, as we are when doing such things, what Schopenhauer called the world's will. Similar assertions and imaginative actions can be engaged in for grass, trees, the sea, the elements, and so on. After all, we also share the world with Pantheists and Buddhists.

Thus, if for convenience we divide Liverpool into the natural and the

[52] Griffiths, 'Blanks', p. 61.

man-made, both of these spheres can be thought to have 'point of view' in that the natural manifests itself as forms of energy, growth, and decay, seeking to propagate and sustain itself, while the man-made shows point of view in its intentional design. The bombed-out St Luke's church on the corner of Berry Street and Leece Street in Liverpool, for instance, displays a number of points of view in this respect: the one shown in the architectural design by John Foster of the Anglican church, begun in 1811 and consecrated in 1831, its purpose in being built; a second, its present roofless shell, shows the point of view of the Luftwaffe, and behind them Hitler, who hit it with incendiary bombs on one night, 5 May 1941; and a third shows the point of view of the city in preserving the ruined church as both a memorial to what Liverpool had endured during the Blitz and a sign of its being undefeated.[53] A fourth point of view can be seen in the leaves, grass, and weeds around the church taking advantage of the park's preserved space to propagate and spread. Nor do we have to include my point of view to capture these four as 'my world'. My existence and its limited point of view (I was brought up in Anglican vicarages in a fairly leafy Liverpool not policed by the Gestapo) are more entailed by theirs than the other way round. Ontologically objective reality contains point of view because nature manifests the energies of growth, reproduction, and decay, while objects and environments created by human design manifest our varieties of outlook and viewpoint.

The bombed-out church in Liverpool gets us back to the nineteen-thirties and their consequences in the following decade. It also brings us back to Goethe, Mandelstam, and nostalgia for world culture. Extreme separations of consciousness — my world, your world — do (as Griffiths points out) have evident equivalents in fiercely contested differences of religious and political opinion and value, something painfully evident at most times, but unusually so for the citizens of Europe's cultured cities during the nineteen-thirties: '"Tell me, Sister Helena, what would you say was your greatest influence during the 'thirties? I mean, during your teens. Did you read Auden and Eliot?" "No," said Sandy.' Spark's 'and' in her 'Auden and Eliot' cunningly reconciles oeuvres and careers that in the 1930s were, politically, distinct. Reading Eliot's early poems might have helped Sandy be less shocked by the thought of other people's Edinburghs. The last of his 'Preludes' contrasts the 'conscience of a blackened street / Impatient to assume the world' and the 'worlds' that 'revolve like ancient women / Gathering fuel in vacant lots.'[54] Auden's 'Spain' (1937) included a possessive form of the word, 'Yesterday the bustling world of the navigators', while the last verse of his 'September 1, 1939' begins with 'Defenceless under the night / Our world in stupor lies', a verb in which two relevant senses are activated at Auden's line-ending:

---

[53] For the role of such objects in post-war states of affairs, see Elaine Scarry, *The Body in Pain: The Making and Unmaking of the World* (New York: Oxford University Press, 1985), p. 114.

[54] T. S. Eliot, *Collected Poems 1909–1962* (London: Faber & Faber, 1963), pp. 24 and 25.

'We boys were very keen on Auden and that group of course. We
wanted to go and fight in the Spanish Civil War. On the Republican
side, of course. Did you take sides in the Spanish Civil War at your
school?'

'Well, not exactly,' said Sandy. 'It was all different for us.'

'You weren't a Catholic then, of course?'

'No,' said Sandy.

But it appears Sister Helena is being a bit economical with the truth
when she says 'not exactly' — because, as we find out, it appears to be as a
consequence of someone going to fight in the Spanish Civil War and being
killed before she gets there that Sandy decides to act against the compulsive
interfering of her charismatic teacher in the young lives of those within the
Brodie set. Certainly Sandy suggests to the headmistress, Miss McKay, that
she try politics instead of sex as her reason for getting rid of Miss Brodie. We
are informed that 'Everyone, including Joyce Emily, was anti-Franco if they
were anything at all.' But then comes the further shock:

> One day it was realized that Joyce Emily had not been at school for
> some days, and soon someone else was occupying her desk. No one
> knew why she had left until, six weeks later, it was reported that she
> had run away to Spain and had been killed in an accident when the
> train she was travelling in had been attacked.[55]

If the train was attacked, of course, then her death was not an accident but
a further manifestation of 'point of view'. What persuaded Joyce Emily to
go to Spain, and on whose side, is explained later in a conversation between
Miss Jean Brodie after her prime, in enforced retirement, and Sandy, her
unknown betrayer, who may have even taken the veil in a closed order as
a form of self-punishment. Here she is listening to Miss Brodie before that
happens:

> '... sometimes I regretted urging young Joyce Emily to go to Spain to
> fight for Franco, she would have done admirably for him, a girl of
> instinct, a — '
> 'Did she go and fight for Franco?' said Sandy.
> 'That was the intention. I made her see sense. However, she didn't
> have the chance to fight at all, poor girl.'[56]

'I made her see sense': whether we imagine ourselves as living in one or
in many worlds may appear yet another barely comprehensible debate that
philosophers, and their students, engage in by way of education. Yet as the
imaginary example of Joyce Emily and the real one of Osip Mandelstam
imply, when it comes to the infliction of pain and the causing of death,
those who effect it and those who suffer are, entirely independently of
what they may or may not be thinking and believing, indissolubly linked
together in the world. Pain is caused and felt in the world, the world where

[55] Spark, *Brodie*, p. 118.
[56] Ibid. p. 124.

our actions have consequences. The acknowledgement of our inhabiting this one world is a prerequisite for moral and ethical life, and this includes those morals and ethics propagated (not always in the best, or even good, faith) by world religions.

At the end of the final stanza to 'Of the Last Verses in the Book', Edmund Waller writes of the dying: 'Leaving the old, both worlds at once they view, / That stand upon the threshold of the new',[57] while Patrick McGuinness wonders across an enjambment 'if the best of here translates / to there'.[58] Sister Helena, a Catholic convert like her author, would be expected to believe in such a better world beyond the no other world than this whose singularity I have been defending; and Griffiths, himself such a convert, would likely want to assert that this entity is not a *'sheer* figment'. Nor is it that the word 'world' can't be used for what is or isn't beyond the sky, as Waller elegantly shows in his poem. Naturally I hesitate to speculate on the possible contents of the fictional Sister Helena's non-existent 'odd moral treatise' with its suggestive title *The Transfiguration of the Commonplace*; but if it happened to argue that moral consciousness required the commonplace to be transfigured by faith or belief, then I would happily agree — if it were reciprocally understood that such transfigurations require the recognition and acceptance of the 'commonplace' as a space not only banally familiar but truly held 'in common' by us all. Without such, its transfiguration (or, I would add, its translation) can have no meaning; and the entry into the moral life implied by it can have no location in which to demonstrate, by means, and with results, that may be appreciated by others, the value of having such a moral sense or ethical life. Without such a common place, this one world I have been defending, there can be no recognized human rights, no international law, no war crimes tribunals with legitimacy beyond 'might is right'. Mandelstam's nostalgia for world culture is an aspiration for such a cherished place to be held in common by and for all.

[57] Edmund Waller, *The Poems*, 2 vols., ed. G. Thorn Drury (London: A. H. Bullen, 1901), ii, p. 144.
[58] Patrick McGuinness, 'The White Place', *The Canals of Mars* (Manchester: Carcanet Press, 2004), p. 12.

CHAPTER 6

Translating the 'Foreign'

I

'I wonder if you read much foreign poetry?' '*Foreign* poetry? No!'[1] Philip Larkin's reply to Ian Hamilton's question has not only been taken as expressing an attitude to reading poetry written in other languages, but as a riposte which (in just three words) catches Larkin's adopted posture of the little Englander. While it has not been difficult to show that his reply will mislead, if taken as conveying information about some of his reading experiences and their impact on his poetry, it has been less easy to relieve Larkin of the prejudicial in the formulation of that reply. The publication of his letters has even tended to reinforce the assumption that it is prejudicial in a way continuous with some of the poet's beliefs outside the area of poetry in other languages.[2] He is not, after all, merely saying that he doesn't read poetry that happens not to have been written originally in English, and nor is he saying that he doesn't read translations of such poetry because it can be (in Frost's sense) a disappointing experience. Rather, as suggested in the first chapter, he appears to be leaping on Hamilton's conventional use of the word 'foreign' to indicate 'not in English' and relishing the chance to say he doesn't read poetry written by poets who don't happen to be English-born.[3]

---

[1] Ian Hamilton, 'Four Conversations', *London Magazine* vol. 4 no. 8, November 1964, and collected in Philip Larkin, *Further Requirements: Interviews, Broadcasts, Statements and Books Reviews*, ed. Anthony Thwaite (London: Faber & Faber, 2001), p. 25.

[2] See, for example, the comment on Vikram Seth, *Selected Letters of Philip Larkin 1940-1985*, ed. Anthony Thwaite (London: Faber & Faber, 1992), p. 704.

[3] Larkin appears to have thought that 'the foreign' began not at the political borders of the United Kingdom, or at the geographical limits of the British Isles, but at historically fought-over edges of England. See 'The Importance of Elsewhere', *The Whitsun Weddings* (London: Faber & Faber, 1964), p. 34, which articulates a contrast with Northern Ireland, or his being photographed beside an 'England' boundary marker in *Larkin at Sixty* ed. Anthony Thwaite (London: Faber & Faber, 1982), facing p. 60.

The world has changed in various ways since 1964, at least to the point where the public relations department at Lufthansa could during the 1990s respond to an identified rise in nationalistic sentiment among their fellow countrymen by producing an advertising campaign in which, because of the airline's global reach, their crews were described as 'foreigners every day' — the visuals enforcing the idea that, despite other possible conclusions, this experience made them welcoming of everybody. If we are all foreigners every day (whether we happen to have experiences that bring it home to us or not) the term can no longer have discriminating force. Yet in a field where poets can both translate and be translated, this reversibly discriminatory concept of the 'foreign' is fairly regularly offered as a seemingly positive term in just such cultural exchanges.

David Constantine has, for example, written in his lecture 'Translation Is Good for You' of how 'for the nation, especially if that nation is English-speaking, the continual shock of the foreign is absolutely indispensable.'[4] It would not be difficult to rephrase this statement so the idea of a shocking difference were not founded on the simplified and simplifying contrast of the nation and the foreign, upon a politically defined version of the 'us' and 'them' discrimination. In the interests of a more accurate description of the people who live in a particular country that has its own national government, and of the vitality in the language or, usually now, array of languages that they speak, such a reformulation of benefits might help to understand the activity of translation, and the translation of poetry, within a multiculturally evolving and complex area of human interaction. One of the consequences of such a re-description would be that the contrasting term, the 'foreign', would also grow more differentiated and be seen to overlap with its supposed opposite in innumerable ways. Similarly, in such a situation of multiple dialogues between languages and cultures, the sense of 'shock' would be better understood as a vivifying of cultural activity through the stimulation of contrasting examples in which, as we saw with the case of a poet such as C. P. Cavafy (to whom I return here), both differences and similarities can be usefully registered. A further danger with a picture in which a nation is shocked by the foreign is that this nation will unite in the face of the other and drive it out, a national-defensive role the word 'foreign' has also been called upon to play.

Commenting on the formation of cultural identities in *The Scandals of Translation*, Lawrence Venuti describes a situation that deploys bare contrasts like Constantine's to stage its polemic:

> Translation wields enormous power in constructing representations of foreign cultures. The selection of foreign texts and the development of translation strategies can establish peculiarly domestic canons for foreign literatures, canons that conform to domestic aesthetic values and therefore reveal exclusions and admissions, centers and

---

[4] David Constantine, 'Translation Is Good for You', *A Living Language: Newcastle/Bloodaxe Poetry Lectures* (Tarset: Bloodaxe, 2004), p. 25.

peripheries that deviate from those current in the foreign language. Foreign literatures tend to be dehistoricized by the selection of texts for translation, removed from the foreign literary traditions where they draw their significance. And foreign texts are often rewritten to conform to styles and themes that *currently* prevail in domestic literatures, much to the disadvantage of more historicized translation discourses that recover styles and themes from earlier moments in domestic traditions.[5]

Venuti could, without difficulty, exemplify these various sins of omission and commission, not least by pointing readers to his translations of Antonia Pozzi's poems, where, in an *en face* edition, his approach 'affiliates her poetry with' the styles of H. D., Amy Lowell, Mina Loy, and Lorine Niedecker, and thus 'supplies what she lacked in Italian: a tradition of modernist women poets.'[6] To a large extent his polemic, one with which I sympathize, is not against translators, their familiarizing or foreignizing efforts, nor those who buy and read translations, but against the chronic complacency and lack of interest in cultural difference in dominant Anglophone cultures such as his own. What concerns me about the passage is its reiteration of the adjective 'foreign', a word which appears seven times in four sentences, the sequence 'foreign language. Foreign literatures ... foreign literary traditions ... And foreign texts' being a particularly relentless one-note samba. Such writing reinforces an oversimplified division between one culture and another that is contradicted by daily experience at the levels of individual encounter, borrowings of words, recognitions of divergent behaviour patterns, and market choices. More damaging to Venuti's and Constantine's polemics, such simplified contrasts between the 'domestic' and the 'foreign' reinforce the prejudicial opposition that they write to counteract. Such largely nuance-free divisions between peoples, ideas, and cultural objects tend to be the trade barriers that acts of translation attempt to resist, to overcome, or, as I hope, to complicate out of existence.

One key problem with 'the foreign' as a way of thinking about translation is that it sets the drama of difference (Venuti's subtitle is *Towards an Ethics of Difference*) on the contrasted stages of the original language culture and the translation language culture. This tends to occlude the conflicts that not only mark, but also define the original text's language in its relations with its culture, and, further, the multitude of similarities in difference between the original's culture and the translation's that make the art of translation possible at all. The former are conflicts that a good translation, exploring such similarities and differences, will be seeking to convey in rendering the original's particular idiolect. Venuti usefully notes that 'Foreign literatures tend to be dehistoricized by the selection of texts for translation, removed

---

[5] Lawrence Venuti, *The Scandals of Translation: Towards an Ethics of Difference* (London: Routledge, 1998), p. 67.

[6] Antonia Pozzi, *Breath: Poems and Letters*, ed. and trans. Lawrence Venuti (Middletown, CT: Wesleyan University Press, 2002), p. xxii.

from the foreign literary traditions where they draw their significance.' Yet the twice-used adjective 'foreign' lumps together all other literatures as the 'not ours' and equally dehistoricizes them by foregrounding their categorically alien condition. This reiteration conceals the conflict that not only marks but also defines the original's idiolect in its relations with its culture — conflict that, as I say, would at best be articulated in a translation. Such complexity tends especially, but by no means uniquely, to be embodied in poetry — because of its all but obligatory, and stylistically emphasized, 'slight angle to the universe', to recall Forster's phrase characterizing Cavafy and his work. If the translator cannot convey that 'angle' of relationship, then a crucial point of the original is lost, and those who like to read poetry, whether in original languages or translation, will likely be reading precisely to appreciate that 'angle'. To translate such a sense of difference within the cultural situation of the original is to perform an act of imagination not only in relation to the original, but also in relation to the cultural conditions of the translation language, for it is to imagine the 'receiver' culture as also fraught with its own conflicts in which and towards which poets' words can obliquely locate themselves. To imagine the translation of poetry in this light is to find the unfamiliar in the apparently 'domestic', and to recognize the similarities and influences from your own culture within the so-called 'foreign'. Among the reasons why I looked at translations of Cavafy in the opening chapter is that in his life and work he exemplified to an unusual degree complexities such as these that can be found in any valuable poet's oeuvre and its situations.

Can the activity of translation, and the ways it is understood, be detached from the prejudicial notion of the 'foreign'? Arguments have been made for the value of the translator's work as equivalent to a Russian Formalist 'making strange', namely 'making foreign', or, 'foreignization'. This is said to be a method for resisting 'domestication', 'naturalization', or 'annexation' by the target culture, and is an equivalent in translation studies to the vanguard stylist's resistance to 'recuperation'. Once again, the idea depends upon an inert and undifferentiated contrasting term to give it salience and privilege: the concept of 'foreignization' requires for its visibility the contrastive sense of writers and readers at home in, or native to, a language or culture. The archaic binary structure of foreigner, stranger, or alien confronting and activating those who are comfortably and, in Constantine's sense, complacently in the home place oversimplifies the understanding of translation and relations between languages and cultures. It also underestimates the likely readership for poetry in translation.

It is hardly unusual to find that poets such as Cavafy, Mandelstam, and Pessoa wrote out of conditions and manifested in their writings ways in which they were complexly not at home in their supposed native places and languages. Such poets have expressed a marginalized sexual life with an unusually shame-free frankness, or brought a necessary freedom of lyrical utterance into direct conflict with a totalitarian regime, or mitigated cultural isolation by invented an entire school of imaginary poets, and attempting to write literature in three languages. Yet, despite such exemplary cases, it appears as if translators and their theories are still and forever awaiting the arrival of Cavafy's barbarians, whose attention spans will have such a useful effect on the language of our politicians: '— And why don't our worthy orators, as always, come out / to deliver their speeches, to have their usual say?' A voice replies: 'Because the barbarians will arrive today; / and they get bored with eloquence and orations.' Cavafy's famous poem ends by inviting us to think about a life without the enemies that give us our contrastive identity: 'And now, what will become of us without barbarians? / Those people were some kind of solution.'[7] Equally, what would become of translation without foreigners and the foreign?

To identify a more illuminatingly various picture what's needed is to consider the distinct location that any significant poet's work occupies in its own culture. 'Non lo amo il mio tempo, non lo amo' [I don't like my times, I don't like them], Vittorio Sereni wrote in the early 1960s.[8] If poetry is understood, however indirectly or unpredictably, as an Arnoldian criticism of life, then the approach it asks readers to adopt will expect them to appreciate the angles that this work takes up towards its occasions. That the poetry to be translated is not simply at home in its own culture will not exclude it from appearing unusual when translated, but part of that strangeness will derive from its own specificity in the circumstances of its original writing and publication. To register such original and unique strangeness the translator from another culture will have to work through a familiarizing dialogue with the source texts and, when living, their author, to achieve an equivalent distinctness for the translation, a distinctness whose coordinates will be drawn more from tensions in relations between the original and its cultural situation than between those of the source and target linguistic cultures. Translating the original's 'slight angle to the universe' is an invitation to the target culture to understand the work of the original in its situation by means of analogically conflicted relations within the second language area. The original's complexes of similarity in difference are thus themselves placed in relation to sets of similarly different cultural relations.

In 'Translation Is Good for You', Constantine offers a portrait of the translator's relation to the original that is adapted from a Keatsian creative psychology as explored in the young poet's own letters: 'Using the terms I have borrowed and applied from Keats, we may say that Hölderlin allowed the identity of Pindar's Greek to press upon him almost to the point of his own annihilation; but came through the ordeal, into his own vernacular,

---

[7] C. P. Cavafy, *The Collected Poems*, trans. Evangelos Sachperoglou, Greek text ed. Anthony Hirst, introduction by Peter Mackridge (Oxford: Oxford University Press, 2007), p. 17.

[8] Vittorio Sereni, *Poesie*, ed. Dante Isella (Milan: Mondadori, 1995), p. 147, translated in *The Selected Poetry and Prose of Vittorio Sereni*, ed. and trans. Peter Robinson and Marcus Perryman (Chicago: University of Chicago Press, 2006), pp. 154-55.

by an equal act of self-assertion.'[9] The vocabulary of Constantine's metaphor derives from Hölderlin's own: 'Translation does our language good, like gymnastics', he wrote. 'It gets beautifully supple when forced to accommodate itself thus to foreign beauty and greatness and also often to foreign whims.' Hölderlin sounds a further warning note when adding that if language 'serves too long abroad there's a danger, I think, that it won't quite ever again do what we want it to do: be the free and pure and one and only appropriate expression of the spirit within.'[10] For Hölderlin, as Constantine also points out, the 'foreign' began at the borders of Swabia in a not yet united Germany. Given his years of mental instability and decay, this fear of self-annihilation or loss of a unique language that would answer to his spirit has a poignant ring. Keats's sense of self-transcendence when with a beautiful lady in a room of people was not so total as to prevent him from being highly conscious of what was happening — as his letter describing the experience makes plain: 'I am at such times too much occupied in admiring to be awkward or on a tremble. I forget myself entirely because I live in her.'[11] For Keats to assert as much requires him to have forgotten himself and to be aware of it: 'I am at such times'. Constantine's account of translating sounds too painfully like total warfare. The enemy language threatens to annihilate its 'target' culture, and then the receiver language, in danger of being overrun in the ordeal, having perhaps 'served too long abroad', as Hölderlin has it, valiantly reasserts itself.

Perhaps Constantine, if pressed, wouldn't recommend Hölderlin's translation method to ordinary mortals. But why does he imagine that such or similar struggles need to be undergone? He adds that 'for the nation, especially if that nation is English-speaking, the continual shock of the foreign is absolutely indispensable.'[12] I know we're talking about reading poetry, but, following out the analogy, this sounds bizarrely like the idea that a good war would cleanse the nation of its complacency. Once again, we can sense that, however well meaning the argument may be, it is conducted in terms that 'consort with the enemy'. Why does the 'nation' have to raise its ugly head at such a moment? Why do texts in other languages have to be called 'foreign' — and even by so fine a translator and co-editor of *Modern Poetry in Translation*? My preference would be for a sense of translation that emphasizes the degree of attention to similarity in difference, and vice versa, required to effect an understanding, for readers either without or who would appreciate help with the relevant language, of writing from another culture more or less related to their own. That might be helpful for them as people in the complexly conflicted states of their

[9] David Constantine, 'Translation Is Good for You', *A Living Language*, p. 20.

[10] Hölderlin to Neuffer, July 1794, cited in David Constantine, *Hölderlin* (Oxford: Oxford University Press, 1988), p. 53 and translated on pp. 340-41.

[11] To George and Georgina Keats, 14-31 October 1818, *The Letters of John Keats*, ed. Maurice Buxton Forman, 4th edn. (London: Oxford University Press, 1952), p. 232.

[12] David Constantine, 'Translation Is Good for You', *A Living Language*, p. 25.

daily lives. Artworks from other cultures can, after all, come to our aid in distress. The benefit of translation needn't only come from shock tactics. Nations, in my experience, are only too fatally able to look after themselves — not least by the annexation of a selection from the cultural products made within their own territorial limits for the purposes of self-flattering identity formation or its reinforcement.

Yet in some cases, a marginalized or colonized nation can have its claims to autonomy and its proper history reasserted by the equivocal means of translation. For Welsh, Scots, and Irish poets it's possible to have claims made for their separateness by its communication in English translation, or, equally, to refuse translation as an enactment of the same idea.[13] However politically complex these issues may be, it is nonetheless clear that within the United Kingdom when translating from one of its native languages into another, 'foreignness' is neither a necessary nor a sufficient condition for the classification of artworks with originals in another tongue. The same could be said for the translations of regional dialect poetry into Italian usually offered at the foot of the page in contemporary editions.[14] However strange, these are not what we loosely call 'foreign languages.' Something similar can be said of translations from an earlier state of the same language into a later one. Among both Dryden's and Wordsworth's translations are recastings of Chaucer — a form of translation that has returned to publishing fashion since Seamus Heaney's *Beowulf.*[15] What's more, in *Guesses at the Truth* (1827), Augustus Hare remarked that every age 'has a language of its own; and the difference in the words is often far greater than in the thoughts. The main employment of authors, in their collective capacity, is to translate the thoughts of other ages into the language of their own.'[16] Recalling Davidson's remarks about the importance of idiolect eccentricities in analyzing what is required for human language understanding, Hare's intuition may be applied to individual authors as well. They too have a language of their own (a signature style such as Dylan Thomas's), and, especially in the cases of

[13] See, for example, Nuala Ní Dhomhnaill, 'Mo Theaghlach', translated by Eiléan Ní Chuilleanáin as 'Household', *Pharaoh's Daughter* (Oldcastle, Co. Meath: Gallery Books, 1990), pp. 150-51.
[14] See, for example, Pier Paolo Pasolini, *La meglio gioventù*, ed. Antonia Arveda (Rome: Salerno Editrice, 1998).
[15] See John Dryden, 'The Wife of Bath Her Tale', *The Poems and Fables of John Dryden*, ed. James Kinsley (Oxford: Oxford University Press, 1970), pp. 778-92; and William Wordsworth, 'Selections from Chaucer: Modernised', *Poetical Works*, ed. Thomas Hutchinson, rev, ed. Ernest de Selincourt (Oxford: Oxford University Press, 1969), pp. 432-42. For more recent instances of translation from earlier states of the language, see Seamus Heaney, *Beowulf: A New Translation* (New York: Norton, 2000), Bernard O'Donoghue, *Sir Gawain and the Green Knight* (Harmondsworth: Penguin Books, 2006), and Simon Armitage, *Sir Gawain and the Green Knight* (London: Faber & Faber, 2007).
[16] Augustus Hare, *Guesses at the Truth* (1827), cited in John Gross (ed.), *The Oxford Book of Aphorisms* (Oxford: Oxford University Press, 1983), p. 282.

poetic oeuvres, the task of the translator is both to translate and, analogically, to preserve signs of that uniqueness. The significant contrast is not then merely between a familiar native language and a strange foreign original. The second language culture will only be importantly enriched if something of the contrast between the original's language culture and its unique contribution to that culture is communicated.

Constantine's writings about outsiders within cultures do suggest that he appreciates the importance of individual styles and unique situations in the translation of poetry, while his involvement in the poetry of Hölderlin, as both translator and commentator, is one of the places where he found an enormously significant fate to explore, a fate that would stand as exemplifying the uniqueness of significant writers' conflicted relations with their own cultures:

> Hölderlin formulated the obligation to engage with and assert oneself against the empirical world again and again in his letters from Frankfurt. He knew perfectly well that poetry and the spirit do not constitute a place apart into which it is permissible or even possible to flee; rather, they must fight for living space in the real world and there, at the very least, hold on; at the best they would advance somewhat, and by engaging critically and energetically with a hostile reality hope to affect it for the good.[17]

Once again, the critic's addiction to a figurative language derived from warfare is on display. Constantine cites the central character of Hölderlin's novel *Hyperion* complaining to the Germans that poets and artists, the good, must 'live in the world, as foreigners [or strangers] in their own houses', and he concludes his paragraph by noting that 'The lines of battle are pretty clearly drawn.'[18] This assumption of embattled exclusion reinforces the 'outsider' status at the very moment that it draws emotive sustenance from the excluded one. Outsiders provide insights only and precisely because we are not like them. Constantine, though, identifies with his subject: 'He pushes the mind to imagine a better state than benightedness, mercenary busyness, selfishness, and anxiety; and the verse itself then engenders the persuasion that these projections of betterment are indeed able to be pursued.'[19] Yet such engendering cannot strictly be provided if we do not also see how the outsiders are like us. Valuing the 'foreignness' of the texts from which he is translating, his commitment to the structurally excluded risks displaying a lack of conceptual flexibility to get beyond a world split, however well-meaning in its partitioning, between an 'us' and a 'them'. It's not that the so-called 'foreign' should be domesticated when brought over, but the complexities of its being a stranger at home, and, equally, a relative familiar abroad would mitigate the damagingly fixed definitional contrast.

[17] Constantine, *Hölderlin*, p. 59.
[18] Ibid.
[19] Ibid. p. 315.

'I haven't a thought in my head that could /sound like a line of Hölderlin',[20] John James writes in an elegy for Rolf Dieter Brinkmann, staging a moment of mental drama at what might be an emulative or even envious remoteness from the great German poet's inspiration. James's lines locate the poetic in a reversible distance that reaches back towards one version of German romanticism, and yet acknowledges itself forward from it. This makes us as properly strange to Hölderlin as he might seem to us. The Australian poet John Tranter sidesteps John James's problem in his poem 'After Hölderlin' from *Borrowed Voices*, with a subtitle directing readers to 'Da ich ein Knabe war', whose opening stanza in Constantine's translation reads:

> When I was a boy
>   A god often rescued me
>   From the shouts and the rods of men
>   And I played among trees and flowers
>   Secure in their kindness
>   And the breezes of heaven
>   Were playing there too.[21]

Tranter's borrowing translates the contrast between punishment and play by locating it at a different stage in life, on the other side of the world, and over a hundred and fifty years later:

> When I was a young man, a drink
> often rescued me from the factory floor
> or the office routine. I dreamed
> in the mottled shade in many a beer garden
> among a kindness of bees and breezes,
> my lunch hour lengthening.

In the next verse, he longs for 'a movie theatre's satisfying gloom / where a little moon followed the usherette / up and down the blue carpeted stairs.'[22] This detail seems sponsored by Hölderlin's third stanza in which he exclaims: 'und, wie Endymion, /War ich dein Liebling, /Heilige Luna!' ['and like Endymion / I was your darling, Holy Luna'].[23] Though these lines might be of the kind that, like John James, you couldn't find in your head, neither (for different reasons) could Hölderlin have found thoughts of Tranter's 'factory floor' or 'movie theatre's satisfying gloom' in his. Foreignness as a category in the discussion of translation gives precedence to the at-home-ness of the receiver language's culture even when it is supposing its contribution able to refresh that culture with the other litera-ture's 'unheimlich' linguistic difference. That giving of precedence delivers

---

[20] John James, 'Rough', *Collected Poems* (Great Wilbraham: Salt Publications, 2002), p. 114.
[21] Friedrich Hölderlin, *Selected Poems*, trans. David Constantine, 2nd expanded edn. (Newcastle upon Tyne: Bloodaxe Books, 1996), p. 13
[22] John Tranter, *Borrowed Voices* (Nottingham: Shoestring Press, 2002), p. 14.
[23] Friedrich Hölderlin, *Selected Poems and Fragments*, trans. Michael Hamburger, ed. Jeremy Adler (Harmondsworth: Penguin Books, 1998), pp. 28-29.

poetry back to the 'Geschrei und der Ruthe der Menschen' [the shouts and the rods of men]. Poetry's transformative capacities are being disabled by the very contrastive structure that serves to highlight them.

At the close of his lectures, Constantine aligns himself with poetry's being an Audenesque 'way of happening'[24] and asserts that 'We are, when we read poetry, during the reading of the poem and lingeringly for some while after, more wakeful, alert and various in our humanity than in our practical lives we are mostly allowed to be.'[25] Much as, in the encouragement of a shared humanity, I would collaborate with his hopes, and agreeing that we are often not allowed to exercise full humanity in the daily round, I fear that reading, and reading poetry in particular, has to have a more lasting and identity-shaping transformative influence on the mind, the body, and the nervous system. This is how Constantine describes the role of poetry and literature in Hölderlin's life: 'I am inclined to think it proves Hölderlin's seriousness and the wholeness of his vocation from the start that his models and favourite predecessors in literature touched so closely on his moral and sentimental life. It proves that his writing was never an activity apart.'[26] Taken in occasional doses from a store apart, poetry (and poetry in translation) would be a form of ethical or aesthetic caffeine — one which fades only too soon when we cross another conventional divide, and return to our practical lives. If Constantine's model in his lecture were the true one, under the benign influence of the translated poem we are reading the author's humanity is brought home to us even through the representation of her or his shocking foreignness; but once back in our practical lives we decline into our, however enforced, Podsnap-like conventionality in which foreignness is the mark of that part of humanity which, however implausibly, we don't share.

Constantine's final two sentences bring him back to what Ezra Pound's *Mauberley* called the 'relation / of the state to the individual'.[27] 'Any further stage,' he writes, 'any conversion of this alerted present state into action, into behaviour, is the responsibility of the citizen. And the poet, like the reader, is always a citizen.'[28] But poets, like the rest of us, are to imagine themselves as citizens of what? Now it seems ever more pressing that if we are to be 'wakeful, alert and various', whether as poets or readers, and necessarily as people, then we will have to become not merely citizens of some town or city in a unitary nation with its national language, but (to borrow a title of

[24] W. H. Auden, 'In Memory of W. B. Yeats', *The English Auden: Poems, Essays and Dramatic Writings 1927-1939*, ed. Edward Mendelson (London: Faber & Faber, 1977), p. 242, and see my *Poetry, Poets, Readers: Making Things Happen* (Oxford: Oxford University Press, 2002), pp. 29-58.

[25] Constantine, 'Poetry of the Present', *A Living Language*, p. 59.

[26] Constantine, *Hölderlin*, p. 11. For poetry changing permanently our relations to the world, see my *Poetry, Poets, Readers: Making Things Happen* (Oxford: Oxford University Press, 2002).

[27] Ezra Pound, 'Hugh Selwyn Mauberley', *Collected Shorter Poems* (London: Faber & Faber, 1968), p. 201.

[28] Constantine, 'Poetry of the Present', *A Living Language*, p. 59.

Oliver Goldsmith's) citizens of the world — a place in which, since we are all always foreigners to somebody somewhere, that word might helpfully drop from the equation.

II

To go beyond 'the foreign', then, I suggested we attempt to find out about the precise angles to the universe that are expressed in poems from other languages. In his note to the first edition of Vittorio Sereni's *Gli immediati dintorni*, Giacomo Debenedetti observed that 'the poetic translations included here, even in their fidelity and lyrical effectiveness, signify certain moments of Sereni's identified with other poets' moments'.[29] Debenedetti's word to describe Sereni's translating occasions is appropriate enough for his relations with Pound. Sereni renders his title 'Impressions of François-Marie Arouet (de Voltaire)' as 'Momenti di', while 'The Psychological Hour' becomes 'il momento psicologico'.[30] Sereni's translation of Pound's 'Villanelle: The Psychological Hour' can be shown to display both 'fidelity and lyrical effectiveness': it is faithful to its original and has an attuned rhythm and diction of its own. Yet, imbued with implications derived from its place in the poet's own work, its 'lyrical effectiveness' delicately manifests such 'momenti di Sereni' in analogically conflicted lexical choices and rhythmic patterns. 'Villanella: il momento psicologico' has a simultaneously double significance. In exploring the poet's motivations for translating, and considering why, in a letter of 8 January 1956 to Alessandro Parronchi, he expressed dissatisfaction with his work, writing that 'the greatest love I put into the *Villanelle*, perhaps the least successful', I show one conflicted angle to the universe that an original poem embodies and that its translation, released from reductively fixed contrasts, can attempt to convey as responsively as possible.[31]

This Italian version of Pound's poem, which doesn't appear in Sereni's selected translations, *Il musicante di Saint-Merry*, superimposes two phases of war-related cultural crisis for twentieth-century poetry in Europe. Pound's poem, written when the author was aged thirty, in the summer or early

[29] Giacomo Debenedetti, 'Nota alla prima edizione', in Vittorio Sereni, *Gli immediati dintorni, primi e secondi* (Milan: Il Saggiatore, 1983), p. xvii.

[30] This and subsequent citations of 'Villanella: il momento psicologico' are from Vittorio Sereni, *La tentazione della prosa*, ed. Giovanna Raboni (Milan: Mondadori, 1998), pp. 48–49. A manuscript and a typescript of the translation are preserved in the Archivio Vittorio Sereni at Luino. These versions are both entitled 'Villanella: l'ora psicologica'. I am grateful to Barbara Colli for supplying photocopies of these papers.

[31] *Un tacito mistero: Il carteggio Vittorio Sereni-Alessandro Parronchi (1941-1982)*, ed. Barbara Colli and Giovanna Raboni (Milan: Feltrinelli, 2004), pp. 278–79. At the foot of the typescript preserved in the Archivio Vittorio Sereni is an undated note in the handwriting of the poet's wife Maria Luisa Sereni: 'from Pound — translation believed "not to have matched best intentions" 1955'.

autumn of 1915, responds to effects on the London literary scene of the first year of the Great War.[32] It dramatizes a moment of generational change, and the fear in its speaker that his style has become suddenly dated. The title itself articulates the anxiety in the shift of mode on each side of the colon: from the 1890s 'Villanelle' to the early modernist 'Psychological Hour'. The villanelle is another poetic form that enters English poetry via translation, this time from French. The generic title names a poem in nineteen lines with two refrains alternating in set positions, such as Elizabeth Bishop's 'One Art'. The name 'villanelle' derives from the Italian word 'villanella' that Sereni uses for his translation, meaning a village dance and song. Pound's poem is not in the strict villanelle form, but probably alludes to the word's original sense in the second part when asking: 'You have danced so stiffly?' This speaker's fear of becoming passé is associated in his 'Villanelle' with implications for his place in relation to social class and cultural power. It contains allusions to 'The Papers' by Henry James, a story concerning a young journalist couple and an older playwright who would like to be promoted by them. James Joyce's *A Portrait of the Artist as a Young Man* provided the example of a 'period' poem, the 'Villanelle of the Temptress', attributed to Stephen Dedalus for purposes of ironic distancing. The phrase 'Between the night and morning?' in Pound's poem silently evokes the line above it in W. B. Yeats's 'The People': 'The reputation of his lifetime lost / Between the night and morning.'[33] Sereni's translation unfortunately fails to report Pound's interpolated question mark.

The glancing styles in Pound's poem, though, preserve an impersonality by which the speaker might be yet another of the poet's early 'personae'. The word 'psychological' can suggest both 'state of mind' in general as well as a 'condition of mental well being or ill health'. The term underwent a rapid evolution between the moment when Pound adopted it from James's tale of 1903 in a cant phrase, 'the psychological hour', meaning the moment when the iron is hot — and when a forty-two-year-old Sereni made his translation for the 1955 Schiewiller homage to Pound on his 70th birthday. By then psychoanalysis had become an established intellectual and professional field.[34] Differences between the original and the translation may come from the greater degree of psychological identification with the speaker's predicament in Sereni's version than is the case in the Pound poem. It is as if notwithstanding the poem's final line ('Dear Pound, I am

[32] See my 'Not a Villanelle: Ezra Pound's Psychological Hour', *Twentieth Century Poetry: Selves and Situations* (Oxford: Oxford University Press, 2005), pp. 22–38.
[33] This and other citations of 'Villanelle: The Psychological Hour' are from Ezra Pound, *Personae: The Shorter Poems*, rev. edn., ed. L. Baechler and A. Walton Litz (New York: New Directions, 1990), pp. 155–56. For the lines from Yeats's 'The People', *The Variorum Edition of the Poems of W. B. Yeats*, ed. P. Allt and R. K. Alspach (New York: Macmillan, 1971), p. 351.
[34] The term 'psychological warfare', for example, entered the English language in 1940. See John Ayto, *Twentieth Century Words* (Oxford: Oxford University Press, 1999), p. 298.

leaving England'), Sereni takes the psychological hour more inwardly and personally than did the poem's own author.[35]

Sereni's urge to translate was connected, from the first, with a sense of anxiety and the need to perform acts of expiation. In the 'Premessa' to *Il musicante di Saint-Merry* the poet states: 'I had never thought of translating others' texts until a fellow prisoner, who read English much better than I, but did not have any experience of verse, passed me his literal version from a poem by E. A. Poe asking me to make of it an Italian poem for his own uses, naturally keeping an eye on the English original'.[36] Citing from memory the first two lines to his lost translation of 'The Conquering Worm' — 'Ecco si spiega una notturna danza / in cuore ai solitari ultimi anni' ('Lo! 'tis a gala night / Within the lonesome latter years!'), Sereni says he remembers them 'also because those, and those only, seemed to me to accord with the particular situation and states of soul in which we found ourselves then'.[37] His comment appears to be strictly excluding the burden of the American poem, as it might be understood from an Italian POW point of view in the spring of 1945. This burden ('That the play is the tragedy, "Man," / And its hero the Conquering Worm') might conceivably have been why his fellow prisoner was interested in having an Italian version. Sereni, though, was not at all inclined to identify Poe's conquering worm with his captors, about whom he writes with both admiration and gratitude in 'La cattura' [The Capture] and 'L'anno '45' [The Year '45].[38] This does not seem to have prevented the gothic trappings of Poe's text, which the poet had kept under his eye, from finding echoes in Sereni's poems of imprisonment. Comparison of 'The Conquering Worm' with the twelve sections of 'Diario d'Algeria' reveals several parallels in references to theatrical performance, the music of angels, a circle fixed to a single spot, and a ghostly image that writhes as the light goes. Sereni's echoes of Poe might then be nuanced refusals of loaded analogies.[39]

---

[35] For Pound's psychological self-awareness, see my 'Ezra Pound: Translation and Betrayal', *In the Circumstances: About Poetry and Poets* (Oxford: Oxford University Press, 1992), pp. 195–97.

[36] Vittorio Sereni, 'Premessa', *Il musicante di Saint-Merry* (Turin: Einaudi, 1981), p. v. See my discussion of René Char's *Feuillets d'Hypnos* 138 in 'Envy, Gratitude, and Translation', *In the Circumstances*, pp. 149–52.

[37] For 'The Conquering Worm', see Edgar Allan Poe, *The Complete Poems*, ed. T. O. Mabbott (Urbana and Chicago: University of Illinois Press, 2000), pp. 325–26.

[38] For Sereni's positive views of his captors, see *La tentazione della prosa*, pp. 153–60 and 83–86.

[39] For 'in a theatre, to see / A play of hopes and fears': the 'bravissima compagnia filodrammatica del campo', see 'Algeria '44', *La tentazione della prosa*, p. 19; for 'A blood red thing that writhes from out / The scenic solitude': 'Si torce, fiamma a lungo sul finire / un incolore giorno'; for 'An angel throng' and 'The music of the spheres': 'non è musica d'angeli'; for 'a circle that ever returneth in / To the self-same spot': 'ma immoto è il perno'; for 'its Phantom chased for evermore, / By a crowd that seize it not': 'ma sepolcrale il canto d'una torma / tedesca', see Poe, *The Complete Poems*, pp. 325–26, and Vittorio Sereni, *Poesie*, ed. Dante Isella (Milan: Mondadori, 1995), pp. 75, 76, 78 and 79.

'Came the war and ruined everything', Sereni states in 'Cominciavi' [You Began] — just as it had for writers and artists such as Pound, but not only for them of course, in the century's second decade. Sereni was twenty-seven when war finally came to Italy in 1940, part of a new literary generation in Milan, on the point of publishing his first book of poems. In this brief prose piece from 1960 he recalls how Milan seemed to him two decades before: 'a city ready for a new thrust forward, a living refutation of laughable Imperial destinies, a definite premise, on the contrary, despite everything and despite its own mistakes, for a European reality'.[40] This may have been wishful thinking about a past that could not be different; but that, in any case, is one of Sereni's subjects: the unquenchable hankering for a life that was not able to come into existence. When he came to translate the 'Villanelle', Sereni had experienced a more devastating dispersal than Pound's in 1914, one that led to the further abnegation of possibility in his imprisonment in Algeria between 1943 and 1945 — though it should be recalled that in 1955 Pound was himself incarcerated, as he had been since 1945, in St Elizabeth's Hospital, Washington, DC.[41]

Sereni's 'Villanella' has what Debenedetti called 'fidelity'. It remains close to the dispositions of meaningful shape in Pound's poem, while maintaining its own 'lyrical effectiveness'. Here is one of the transitions in the original from refrain-like italicized lines in an archaic mode to a taste of early twentieth-century London life:

> *Beauty is so rare a thing.*
> *So few drink of my fountain.*
>
> So much barren regret,
> So many hours wasted!
> And now I watch, from the window,
> the rain, the wandering busses.

Sereni's version is faithfully close to the sense of the original, achieving fidelity through a close identification with, a near self-recognition in, the translated poet's original occasion:

> *Così rara cosa è la bellezza.*
> *Alla mia fonte così pochi bevono.*
>
> O vacuo rimpianto,
> O molte mie ore sciupate!
> E dalla finestra ora guardo
> la pioggia, gli autobus raminghi.

Nevertheless, immediately after the refrain, Pound's exclamation has become an invocation; and the 'hours wasted' are emphatically identified by Sereni as 'mie ore sciupate' — as *mine*. This calls to mind the many occasions where

40 Sereni, *La tentazione della prosa*, p. 59.
41 See Humphrey Carpenter, *A Serious Character: The Life of Ezra Pound* (London: Faber and Faber, 1988), pp. 819-20.

Sereni discusses his inability to write — 'Quel film di Billy Wilder' (1951) about *The Lost Weekend*, 'Silenzio creativo' (1962), and his self-portrait essay, 'Autoritratto' (1978), from *Gli immediati dintorni*, for instance.[42] It also recalls the frustrated interior atmosphere of 'Le cenere' [The Ash] from 1958 where the poet asks if he is awaiting 'un qualche vento / di novità a muovermi la penna / e m'apra a una speranza?' [some breath of fresh air / to lift then set my pen in motion / and open me up to a hope?] Most directly, it evokes the lament over lost youth in 'Mille Miglia' — a poem conceived in the year of the Pound translations for the Schiewiller homage, but only written in 1956.[43]

When Sereni reorganized the contents of his first book *Frontiera* (1941) for the 1966 Schiewiller edition, he moved 'Inverno' [Winter] from the start of the second section to the beginning of the entire book. He thus placed as his first work a poem that contains the two key words ('bellezza' and 'fonte') in the translated refrain to Pound's 'Villanelle': 'le fonti dietro te' [fountains behind you] and 'la svelata bellezza dell'inverno' [the beauty of winter unveiled].[44] The first section of the 'Villanelle' concludes with a sorry and self-pitying cadence: *'Beauty would drink of my mind./* Youth would awhile forget / my youth is gone from me.' Sereni rendered the lines: *'Al mio spirito berrebbe la bellezza./* Per poco la gioventù scorderebbe / andata è da me la mia gioventù.' Sereni chooses to translate 'mind' with 'spirito'. He might have written 'Alla mia mente berrebbe la bellezza'. Pound's first two lines each begins with an abstraction, which is given a personal turn in the third: 'Beauty', 'Youth', and 'my youth'. Sereni loses this pattern, but substitutes for it a parallelism at the end of his first and third lines; he manages this by the adoption of a literary word order, where in both cases the noun is withheld to become the terminal word of each sentence. The literariness of these choices aptly imitates that of Pound's lines: 'spirito' has more associations than 'mente', covering a range of implications from the religious 'anima' [soul] to 'arguzia' [acuteness] and 'umorismo' [humour]. It also has a pedigree in classic Italian poetry — as in the last line of Petrarch's *Canzoniere*: 'ch 'accolga 'l mïo spirto ultimo in pace' [that he gather my last breath in peace].[45] However, in making such choices as 'spirito' for 'mind' and the change of rhythm from the dying fall in 'gone from me' to the firm terminal syllable in 'la mia gioventù', Sereni substitutes two personally authenticated modes for what in Pound's poem are paired ironically alternating manners. Referring to Pound's 'Study in Aesthetics', which he also translated, Sereni notes 'that reciprocal exchange of ancient and modern'.[46]

---

[42] For English translations of these texts, see *The Selected Poetry and Prose of Vittorio Sereni*, pp. 296–99, 313–15, and 331–34.

[43] Sereni, *Poesie*, p. 119, and for 'Mille Miglia', p. 117.

[44] Ibid. p. 7.

[45] Francesco Petrarca, *Canzoniere*, ed. M. Santagata (Milan: Mondadori, 1996), p. 1401.

[46] 'Primo incontro con Ezra Pound', excerpted in Sereni, *La tentazione della prosa*, pp. 398–99. See my '"Una fitta di rimorso": Dante in Sereni', *Dante's Modern Afterlife: Reception and Response from Blake to Heaney*, ed. Nick Havely (London: Macmillan, 1998), pp. 185–208.

Yet his translation inhabits styles and modes Pound's poem was working to cast off.

At the heart of the 'Villanelle' is a contrast between the older writer, the speaker, and the younger couple who fail to keep their appointments with him:

> In their parts of the city
>> they are played on by diverse forces.
> How do I know?
>> Oh, I know well enough.
> For them there is something afoot.
>> As for me;
> I had over-prepared the event —

Here is Sereni's rendering of these lines:

> In preda a forze diverse
>> nei loro quartieri son mossi.
> Come faccio a saperlo?
>> Oh, fin troppo lo so.
> Per loro qualcosa è in cammino.
>> Come per me; con troppo
> Zelo avevo disposto l'evento —

The contrasting situation of the young couple ('For them') and the speaker ('As for me') is staged in these phrases. Sereni gives the passage a somewhat different emphasis. A colloquial rendering of 'As for me' might have been 'Per quanto mi riguardo'. 'Come per me' is closer to 'As it is for me' — shaping a similarity between the speaker and the younger couple for whom 'qualcosa è in cammino.' Pound's poem appears to be marking a separation: on the one hand, for them something is afoot; on the other, I had over-prepared the event. This contrast underlines the point that the older writer and the young couple have different priorities, and adds speculative weight to the question of why they don't come to visit him. Pound's lineation separates 'As for me' in a line on its own, helping to mark that contrastive movement.

The semi-colon in most texts of Pound's poem isolates the phrase so as to imply some similarity between the separated terms: the phrase could also just about be construed to mean 'For them something is afoot' — 'as it is for me'. The Library of America edition of Pound's *Poems and Translations* (2003) substitutes a colon for the semi-colon, as if to clear away this ambiguity, emphasizing that 'As for me' points forward to the 'I' in the next line, and thus underlines the contrast with the couple.[47] Sereni's version of the poem understands 'As for me' as 'Like for me': 'Come per me'. Let me emphasize that the sense Sereni translates is a possible construal of Pound's colloquial and eccentrically punctuated lines. However, the original is focused around

[47] See Ezra Pound, *Poems and Translations*, ed. Richard Sieburth (New York: Library of America, 2003), pp. 308–09.

the psychology of feeling excluded by the busy activity of the young, while Sereni's clings to a sense that, though the older person may be stylistically left behind, he's nevertheless just like the young in having 'qualcosa ... in cammino' ('something ... afoot'). This different emphasis chimes with a section towards the end of 'Il male d'Africa' [The African Sickness], from 1958, with its: 'Siamo noi, vuoi capirlo, la nuova / gioventù — quasi mi gridi in faccia — in credito / sull'anagrafe di almeno dieci anni ...' (It's us, don't you realize, we're the younger / generation — you almost shout in my face — / with at least ten years owed us on the civil register ...) .[48] They are a generation whose youth has been taken from them, by the Fascist regime in the decade of imperialist adventure and its consequences from 1935 to 1945. Despite his no longer being among the literary young in 1955, Sereni was inclined to see the conflicted relations between war and youth in different terms to those of Pound's 'Villanelle', as we can hear in the final lines of 'Appunti da un sogno' [Notes from a Dream], a prose poem added to the 1965 second edition of *Diario d'Algeria*: 'Quanti dispiaceri la gioventù (degli altri) ci darà d'ora in poi' [What disappointments the youth (of others) will give us from now on].[49]

Sereni notes of his work as a translator, and its relation to his own creative work: 'between my fairly external application, to the tiny extent that the "craft" allowed me, and the also emotive investment operated later upon other texts, there runs an analogical relation ... between "improvisation" and "future poem"'.[50] Similarly, in his 'Autoritratto', Sereni comments on how he could be brought to compose again by the mediation of translating.[51] An example of how such work issued in a future poem shows in a comparison of the improvisation that has gone into the 'Villanella' translation and 'Mille Miglia'. There, Sereni combines the bitterness and disappointment that may well come if your favourite Alfa Romeo driver fails to win, or if a love comes to nothing: 'Voci di dopo la corsa, voci amare: / si portano su un'onda di rimorso / a brani una futile passione' [Voices of after the race, bitter voices: / with them they bear on a wave of remorse / a futile passion in shreds].[52] The sense of frustration caused by Orlando's being 'impigliato a mezza strada' [ensnared at half distance] remains for Sereni as a more fundamentally irreparable lack, a need that no amount of later pleasure can erase.

In 'Cominciavi', he describes 'the crisis that caught you and others of your age after '45, back from the war and from the segregation (and of feeling yourself excluded from the Liberation, deprived of its struggle as if of an experience lacking in you, leaving you forever incomplete'.[53] Written

[48] Sereni, *Poesie*, p. 94.
[49] *The Selected Poetry and Prose of Vittorio Sereni*, pp. 112-13.
[50] Sereni, 'Premessa', *Il musicante di Saint-Merry*, p. vi.
[51] See Sereni, *La tentazione della prosa*, p. 110.
[52] Sereni, *Poesie*, p. 117.
[53] Sereni, *La tentazione della prosa*, p. 59.

five years earlier, 'Mille Miglia' represents an aftermath to that crisis of return. This is what Sereni found inspiring in the Leopardi fragment that describes Angelica as 'Tornata al patrio lito / dopo i casi e gli errori' [Returned to her native strand / after the events and errors] — as he implies in 'Un'idea per il Furioso', an essay drawn from his encyclopedia entry of 1957.[54] But after 'i casi e gli errori' on foreign shores for Sereni even the appearance of beauty seems too painful to endure, because it intensifies an inner lack: 'Folta di nuvole chiare / viene una bella sera e mi baci / avvinta a me con fresco di colline' [Thick with limpid clouds / a fine evening comes and kisses me / clasped to me with the freshness of hills]. The passing of crucial years and the absences that they contain detach the writer from subsequent fulfilment: 'Ma nulla senza amore è l'aria pura / l'amore è nulla senza la gioventù' [But without love the pure air is nothing, / love's nothing without youth].[55]

In the 'Premessa' for *Il musicante di Saint-Merry*, Sereni also noted that 'Translating has never been an exercise for me: sometimes, hard work, more often a pleasure. It has had, rather, some of the exercise's beneficial effect, things completed, mainly I'd say in a psychological sense. It's a work that makes me feel serene'.[56] 'Villanelle: The Psychological Hour' is by far the best and most substantial of the poems by Pound that Sereni translates. Why is it not included in the Einaudi collection of his translations? The translation of Pound, like Sereni's version of 'Ton œuvre' by Jean-Joseph Rabéarivelo (another version in *Gli immediati dintorni* but not *Il musicante di Saint-Merry*), appears too directly entangled with Sereni's own work and his creative situations.[57] He has read a little too much of himself into the other poet's inspiration. It's as if he has succumbed to the envy of another's occasion, rather than rising to the challenge of the other as a means of self-transcendence. This might explain why in the letter to Parronchi he brings together in the same phrase an implicit relation between 'the greatest love' and 'the less achieved'. It's as if for Sereni this translation, which was perfectly publishable in its original contexts and in *Gli immediati dintorni*, had a different status when it came to an ideal selection of his work as a translator.[58] Nevertheless, Sereni's 'Villanella' is a close approximation

---

[54] Vittorio Sereni, *Sentieri di gloria: Noti e ragionamenti sulla letteratura*, ed. G. Strazzeri (Milan: Mondadori, 1996), pp. 92–93.

[55] Sereni, *Poesie*, p. 117.

[56] Sereni, 'Premessa', *Il musicante di Saint-Merry*, p. viii.

[57] For Sereni's translation of 'Ton oeuvre', see *La tentazione della prosa*, pp. 32–33; for its citation in 'Un posto di vacanza', see *Poesie*, p. 224; and see the letter of 27 May 1952 in Vittorio Sereni, *Scritture private con Fortini e con Giudici* (Bocca di Magra: Edizioni Capannina, 1995), pp. 11–14. See also my 'The Music of Milan', *Times Literary Supplement*, no. 4868, 19 July 1996, p. 11.

[58] If this is why Sereni left out both poems, it qualifies P. V. Mengaldo's observation in his introduction to the second edition (2001) that 'Sereni's book of translations was selected and calibrated like one of his own books' (p. v). With the exception of *Frontiera*, Sereni's volumes of poetry are not choices from a larger output, but an organization of practically all the completed texts available.

of Pound's 'Villanelle', catching well, by means of elective affinities, the earlier poem's angle to the universe of London literary life in 1915. Its subtle differences from Pound's original can be identified and evaluated only by carefully considering the translator and translation's analogously different angles to the universe.

III

Sereni's prose memoir 'Ventisei' [Twenty-Six], which concerns a visit made to the scenes of his experience of military defeat and capture in western Sicily in July 1943, takes as its epigraph three lines from C. P. Cavafy's poem 'Na Meinei', rendered as follows in the Keeley and Sherrard translation that they call 'Comes to Rest': 'twenty-six years /your phantom's crossed over / now to remain in these lines'.[59] In 1956, when Scheiwiller published a collection of Cavafy translations in Milan, Sereni wrote an article on them that he included in his intermittent diary *Gli immediate dintorni*. The title of Sereni's piece is taken from the cover illustration to the volume he is discussing: '*The statue that has moved* painted by De Chirico — from 1921. It's reproduced on the cover of the Schiewiller Cavafy. Perhaps Cavafy would have wanted another light, another vibration. But his poetry lives entirely among statues that have moved, moved by the poetry itself. It deals with the likes of Enobarbus or Caesarion, or of adolescents "renowned for beauty"; or of simple shadows and glints from his own life — *and emotions of my relatives, emotions of the dead, of so little weight* — that thanks to repetitive fixing take on body and features once more'. Sereni then cites the poem's closing lines, and adds: 'Years or centuries, from your own or from the lives of others, it makes no difference for this carnal religion that, in the bodies' flourishing and decline, measures distances — and shortens them as if by magic through the upsurge of the senses, or at the resurgence of a desire.'[60] This is how Cavafy's poem works for Sereni at a point where it is only tacitly identified, if at all, with something from his own life.

'Per rimanere' in the Italian of Filippo Maria Pontani is the version Sereni used for his 1956 article, and the precise form of Cavafy's lines that came to mind when he revisited the place of his capture in July 1943.[61] Here is an English rendering of that Italian version:

> Maybe one at night,
> one-thirty.

[59] C. P. Cavafy, *Collected Poems*, trans. Edmund Keeley and Philip Sherrard (Princeton, NJ: Princeton University Press, 1975), p. 183.

[60] Vittorio Sereni, 'La statua che s'è mossa', *La tentazione della prosa*, ed. Giovanna Raboni (Milan: Mondadori, 1998), pp. 51-52. The translation is by myself with Ornella Trevisan.

[61] Constantino Kavafis, *Poesie*, ed. Filippo Maria Pontani (Milan: Mondadori, 1961), pp. 111 and 113.

> A tavern corner
> beyond the wood divide.
> In the empty haunt us two, alone.
> It's barely lit by the petrol lamp.
> And the barman, exhausted, slept.
>
> Not an eye on us. But, yes, enflamed
> desire so had us down below
> we grew blind to caution.
>
> Our clothes were half open,
> the few (July was burning).
>
> O blossoming of flesh
> through half-open clothes ... your phantom
> twenty-six years it has crossed and arrives
> now to remain in these lines.[62]

Two accidental coincidences of detail may have brought this particular text, and Sereni's own previous writing on it, back to mind. The first is that both the sexual encounter and Sereni's capture by the American 82nd Airborne Division took place in the early hours of a hot July night, while the second is that just as Cavafy's poem speaks of the twenty-six years that the visual phenomenon has traversed, so too, in 1969 twenty-six years have passed since the period of his deployment as part of the defence of Sicily between April and July 1943.[63] Now the lines come back to him with an added relevance, a newly resurging desire, that they may have already had in 1956, though he was not willing or able to make the connections at that mid-point in the twenty-six years which were to elapse before he was to articulate fully their significance in events, of shadows and glints, from his own experience.

The Italian translations Sereni had admired in 1956 are dedicated to Giuseppe Ungaretti, a poet who grew up in Alexandria, only leaving Egypt in 1912 — before which, in his final years there, he had regularly met Cavafy in the company of a group of young writers.[64] Ungaretti's influence on the formal resources of twentieth-century Italian poetry has been extensive and near ubiquitous. Pontani's translation, 'Per rimanere', is itself indebted in its cadences to the author of *L'allegria*, as can be sensed in the above translation's compacted lines. It begins with a speculative recollection of

---

[62] The translation is by myself with Ornella Trevisan. For the original, see C. P. Cavafy, *The Collected Poems*, trans. Evangelos Sachperoglou, pp. 111 and 113.

[63] For more details on these events, see my introduction to *The Selected Poetry and Prose of Vittorio Sereni*, ed. and trans. Peter Robinson and Marcus Perryman, with an introduction by Peter Robinson (Chicago: University of Chicago Press, 2006), pp. 1–3.

[64] See Giuseppe Ungaretti, 'Cavafy, ultimo Alessandrino', *Vita d'un uomo: Saggi e interventi*, ed. Mario Diacono and Luciano Rebay (Milan: Mondadori, 1974), pp. 666–67 and *Album Ungaretti*, ed. Paola Montefoschi (Milan: Mondadori, 1989), p. 45.

the time, sketching the scene in off-hand phrases, indicating the seclusion of the two people. Then it states their sexual excitement, using a casual style to make the occurrence appear as nothing unusual. The next two lines reveal the image of the exposed flesh and note that the season was collaborating in their physical intimacy. This image of the exposed bodies is what then travels the twenty-six years of his memory to be located and perpetuated (as in the European tradition of time-defeating poetry) here in Cavafy's poem.

Comparing this Italian translation with a French one, and with a number of English ones, I would suggest that 'the poetry' in so far as it is translatable, like a picture by Cézanne, is in the relations between the parts. This is not the only aspect of a poem that can be translated, but it is perhaps the one that can be rendered with least loss: 'rapide apparition de la chair nue — dont l'image / a traversé vingt-six années, et vient maintenant / se perpétuer dans cette poésie.'[65] [quick apparition of the naked flesh — whose image / has crossed twenty-six years, and comes now / to perpetuate itself in this poetry.] In this sense, and this alone, the poetry could be said to be not in the words, but in the relations between them; although, as with Cézanne's painting, the nature of these relationships has to be articulated in the terms of what surrounds them. Since the poetry is conveyed in the relations between the parts, it can be more thoroughly translated than we might at first imagine. What this also implies is that different translations can be more or less equally acceptable as ways of conveying these relationships, that paraphrasing translations don't necessarily fail to render these relationships, and therefore much of the poetry. This is a somewhat different argument to Auden's for why Cavafy may be more translatable — and it allows for his not being a solitary or unique case. Translators of poetry will have a sense of this if when rendering the lines of a short poem they feel that despite the difficulties produced by the different syntax structures of the two languages, it is incumbent upon them to try and render the order not of the words but of the sequenced revelation of sense units — implying thus that at least some of the poetry is in the ordering of this information release. To reproduce accurately this series, without any other aspects of a poem, as a prose crib might do, may well not give you a faithful translation, but without this structural shape, too much will be lost. It is, after all, like making sure that you print the stanzas of a poem in the right order, or that when anthologizing it you do not miss out any of the verses.

Towards the close of his memoir, Sereni dwells once more upon the significance of the closing lines from the Cavafy poem, which he had taken as his epigraph. Returning to the precise spot where he was captured, in the direction from which his captors arrived, he reflects:

65 C. P. Cavafy, *Poèmes*, trans. George Papoutsakis (Paris: Société d'édition 'Les Belles-lettres', 1958), p. 130.

> Presumably it was the same road, at least from a particular stretch, down which the enemy's vanguard had fallen upon us. Frightening to conceive of it, to put yourself for a second in *their* place. Precarious, characteristic of the strain of giving a name to certain states and moments. Later, I understood what it was, a tremor, a sustained vibration, Cavafy's lines come to my aid, rumbling far off, reinforcement for other reinforcements uncalled for. Twenty-six years ... your phantom ...
>
> But how many years is it, now I come to think of it? I wrench myself away from the rumble, count up: twenty-six exactly since I first set foot here.
>
> Twenty-six years.
>
> They're bending over us, these great afflicted trees.[66]

Earlier I questioned the benefit of military metaphors in Constantine's writing on poetry and translation, and yet here is something similar: 'reinforcements'. Yet Sereni is writing about an actual situation of military encounter and defeat. There were no reinforcements in the literal sense, for the entire situation of the Italian forces was a collapsing sham (Mussolini's government had fallen the day before Sereni's capture), and many of those around him would not have wanted real reinforcements anyway, for they hoped their relatives from New York would liberate them from the moribund Fascist regime. Sereni replaces that emptiness with the reinforcement, the support, in the singular, of lines from a lyrical poem made out of an erotic memory. Embodiments of enlivening experience, intimate feeling, a sexual life without shame, Cavafy's lines reappear once more at the close of this memoir-like prose evocation:

> But why at the moment in which, with the help of Cavafy's lines, peace was established, has there arisen, or better, has there returned to me — first in the form of a repressed cry and before that as a murmur, mumble, sustained vibration — the desire to write? How has the report of a journey transformed itself into the diagram of that wish? One thing only is clear: I am standing at the limit where I've always stopped myself whenever I put pen to paper. The point at which the true adventure, the true undertaking begins. From somewhere an anxiety rises resembling the one that urged me along the obliterated defensive system of twenty-six years ago so as to be everywhere, not in any specific place. And at the same time a repugnance. There stands before me a wood, the words, to travel through following a line that gradually forms as you walk, forwards (or back) towards the transparency, if that is the right word for the future.[67]

It didn't matter that the lines weren't by Sereni, and indeed it was better that way; it didn't matter that they were lines he remembered in Italian (he had written about them in *Gli immediate dintorni*); it didn't matter that

---

[66] Vittorio Sereni, 'Twenty-Six', *The Selected Poetry and Prose of Vittorio Sereni*, pp. 385–86.
[67] Ibid. p. 387.

they were in Greek originally (he had been stationed near Athens for most of the summer of 1942, and had seen the famishing effects of war on the local population); it didn't matter that they were by a Greek who had lived in Alexandria (he had known and learned from an Italian poet, Ungaretti, who grew up there); it didn't matter that they were lines which are not about war, which are frankly erotic, and homoerotic too. Sereni is crossing a number of frontiers not just in remembering those lines, but finding them useful.

To conclude, then, the profoundly liberating process in the theme of Sereni and translation is that not only can he accuse himself at one remove of wasting so much time in his version of Pound's 'Villanelle: The Psychological Hour', but he can also ease his psychological states by such imaginative acknowledgements. For Sereni even to acknowledge that translating was 'un lavoro rasserenante' [a work of making serene again] is likely to be yet another delicate self-accusation, like the recognition voiced through his father in 'Il muro' [The Wall]: 'Dice che è carità pelosa, di presagio / del mio prossimo ghiaccio, me lo dice come in gloria / rasser-enandosi rasserenandomi' [He says it's self-interested love, foreseeing / I'll soon be frozen, tells me as if in glory / reassuring himself, reassuring me].[68] For Sereni, translation was a way in which he sought, as he also puts it in 'Ventisei', to end the conflict in his name:

> In reality those few lines had played out the conflict in my name, it hardly mattered they weren't mine (they were mine, though, weren't they? more and better than if I'd been their author). Together they'd made me double between myself and the villa, myself and the man of the ruins — and established a reciprocity by which we found ourselves over and over again imploring forgiveness of each other for the time that had passed unopposed by us. This, if nothing else, was released by the voice come to my aid and not by chance.[69]

Sereni was allowed, by means of what he called in his 'Premessa' 'a silent but well-disposed and encouraging guest',[70] to resolve in his name and life the cruel dance that he and a majority of his generation had been led by dictatorially induced anxiety and defeat. Understandably, given the extent to which these states of disgrace in his life were the result of myth-driven nationalisms with imperial aspirations, of aggressively exaggerated differences between the 'homeland' and the 'foreign', it was identification with the work of poets in other languages, and appreciation of their uniquely specific angles to the universe, that had come to Sereni's aid.

[68] Sereni, *Poesie*, p. 180.
[69] Ibid. p. 386.
[70] Sereni, 'Premessa', *Il musicante di Saint-Merry*, p. viii.

CHAPTER 7

The Quick and the Dead

I

At the same moment Osip Mandestam described Acmeism as nostalgia for world culture, he declared, according to his widow, that 'he would disown neither the living nor the dead.'[1] A final aspect of translation that I consider here is that performed by moving imaginatively across the boundary line Edmund Waller described in his farewell poem: 'Leaving the old, both worlds at once they view, / That stand upon the threshold of the new.'[2] My chapter title's wording comes from the 1662 Anglican *Book of Common Prayer* version of the Apostles' Creed ('from thence he shall come to judge the quick and the dead'), a text translated from the Latin 'inde venturus est iudicare vivos et mortuos' — and the word 'the quick' (meaning 'the living') might itself now need to be translated, as can be seen from the *OED* entry for the first sense of the word. Translators have a nexus of responsibilities because they are entrusted with the conveying into other languages of qualities and values from other people's writings. They carry them into places where the quick and the dead are also judged, the places where books are bought, sold, read, and reviewed. Translations are themselves like reviews and critical writings: the more there are the less damage is done by the bad. It is not an impossible impulse in translating a poet that you wish to improve the impression given of an author you admire by retranslating a work misleadingly presented in an appropriative adaptation or a faulty translation. The reputations of the dead are as much in our hands as those of the living. If we don't continue to translate and read the great deceased from other cultures, they will, for us, die twice.

In one of his aphoristic notes on versions, Don Paterson deployed a Frost-like despairing council to free the translating poet from binding obligations

---

[1] Nadezhda Mandelstam, *Hope Against Hope: A Memoir*, trans. Max Hayward (London: Collins Harvill, 1989), p. 246.
[2] Edmund Waller, *The Poems*, 2 vols., ed. G. Thorn Drury (London: A. H. Bullen, 1901), ii, p. 144.

to the original, even implying that the 'version' effaces its source. A further reason why Paterson felt the need for release from such obligations may be because he experienced them as debilitating in their exorbitant demands. The eighth of his 'Fourteen Notes on the Version' is so significant it deserves to be offered in its entirety:

> There are no ghosts, no gods, nothing secretly lurking in the temple of the poem whose vengeful wrath we will incur through our failure to honour it. The author and critic might reasonably scream *travesty*, but they aren't in the poem either. Any faith in *anything* is misplaced, and masks an essentialist creed. A 'faithful' translation requires an original, a translation and an essence. A poem has no essence. (It has a spirit, but this is utterly subjective and unfixable.) Trust, on the other hand, requires only two terms. So while *faithful* is an impossible judgement, our versions might nonetheless be subjectively reckoned to be trustworthy. The original poem has a consensually agreed paraphrasable sense, and a consensually agreed unparaphrasable sense. We translate the former and imitate the latter.[3]

Persecutory anxiety may motivate the banishing of these 'wrathful' figures, and such anxiety equally appears to drive the flailing at essences and fidelities. The passage supposes that the source for translational judgments with an ethical implication must derive from a divinity-like figure. The author and critic are characterized by means of the verb '*scream*' as hysterically moralistic in their pursuit of the versioning poet. Yet the idea that 'faith in *anything*' is misplaced must itself be misplaced because Paterson goes on to speak about the subjective access to a spirit, for which there would have to be faith in subjectivity. There is also faith expressed, a little later, in the community of the *consensually* agreed paraphrasable sense: a consensus cannot be immune to the exclamations of authors and critics. Faith is equally implied in the idea of trust. The guiding assertions are equally doubtful. How does a scare-marked 'faithful' translation require those three things — a translation, an original, and an essence? I don't need to think that my wife has an essence to which I am faithful. The translator can attempt to be faithful to the original text. No essences are required. Since nothing can strictly be translated, let alone literally, a translation doesn't require a translation (whatever such a tautology might mean). It needs no more nor less than a secondary text that displays appreciable resemblances to its original. In this light, translations don't require or imply that the original has an essence. Translators, of all people, are unlikely to be holders of essentialist creeds. Nor does failing to hold beliefs in such essences exclude them from an ethical life.

Paterson's tenth note states that 'If, through naivety or over-ambition, both translation and version are attempted simultaneously, the result is foredoomed. Essentially, if we are not prepared to make a choice between

---

[3] Don Paterson, *Orpheus: A Version of Rilke's* Die Sonette an Orpheus (London: Faber & Faber, 2006), p. 79.

honouring the word or the spirit, we are likely to come away with nothing.'[4] Essentially? Since both translators and makers of versions are engaged in the same activity differently nuanced, it requires neither naivety nor over-ambition to attempt both simultaneously, for this is what cannot be avoided. The difference is that while translators have to do (and know they are doing) both, those making versions in Paterson's sense may pretend to have evaded questions about the original-derived reliability of their text. His reference to 'the word and the spirit' reveals once more his religiously inflected thinking, in this case St Paul in 2 Corinthians 3: 6, where the evangelist asserts that 'the letter killeth, but the spirit giveth life.' Writing of his attempt to render the spirit of Antonio Machado's poetry, Paterson admits in a parenthesis that 'Being true to a "spirit" rather than a literal meaning is, I acknowledge, a hopelessly subjective business — and one more reason to plead with the reader to forget the relation in which these poems stand to their originals, if he or she knows them.'[5] Intentional forgetting is not the easiest of reader expectations. Paterson knows that

> A poem derives much of its depth and complexity by developing the relationships between the vast entourage of semantic, acoustic and etymological friends, ghosts and ancestors that one word introduces to another. (In literal translation, the words often end up introducing one set of complete strangers to another; hence the result is usually just metred or unmetred prose — this kind of approach tends to limit its deviations from the original to the minimum number required to achieve a syntactic naturalism in the new language.)[6]

Like 'All that moves is ghost', another aphorism of Paterson's from *The Book of Shadows*,[7] this passage implies that there *are* spirits and ghosts in poems. Yet they're not the spirits of an author or a critic, but a selection from the haunted house of the dictionary, interred alive in the ground of texts, or as he puts it: 'Words are locked tombs in which the corpses still lie breathing.'[8] Paterson's similarly metaphorical rendering of words as if they were themselves human ('friends, ghosts and ancestors') is metaphorically suggestive, but not, perhaps, enough. After all, the words don't introduce themselves to each other. The auditory, semantic, and etymological intelligence of the writer combines them to activate some of these words' innumerable associations. It's because these associations have been brought out by a writer that the words can be described, remotely echoing *Julius Caesar* and Shakespeare, as 'friends, ghosts and ancestors'. Equally, the inexhaustible possibilities in a natural language mean that it is only when activated by a speaker or writer that particular links between them can show. What breathes in the mausoleum of the text is the living performance

---

[4] Ibid. p. 81.
[5] Don Paterson, *The Eye: A Version of Machado* (London: Faber & Faber, 1999), p. 56.
[6] Ibid. p. 57.
[7] Don Paterson, *The Book of Shadows* (London: Picador, 2004), p. 4.
[8] Ibid. p. 154.

of its writer. If you want to translate the 'spirit' of a poem, look for it in the humanly articulated words, those 'friends, ghosts and ancestors', which may be similarly approximated in the discovered collocations composed by someone in the second language.

T. S. Eliot reversed St Paul's assertion about the spirit and the letter in a footnote to 'Baudelaire in our Time', a review of translations by Arthur Symons: 'Of course Mr. Shaw and Mr. Wells are also much occupied with religion and *Erzatz-Religion*. But they are concerned with the spirit, not the letter. And the spirit killeth, but the letter giveth life.'[9] Alluding to St Paul, who was himself commenting on the interpretations of his epistle ('written not with ink, but with the Spirit of the living God' — 2 Corinthians 3: 3), Paterson suggests that because you cannot translate the words literally without loss you will have to interpret them and translate their spirit — which will give your version life, as contrasted with a dead-letter literal rendering. Eliot's reversal, in the context of a translation review, might be suggesting (aside from his religiously inflected quarrel with the cultural politics of Wells and Shaw) that in the world of letters it is the 'letter' that must be attended to most diligently. Yet perhaps not only can you not have the one without the other, but both will debilitate if believed in too much or alone. If, in making a translation, you want to render the spirit of the original, attempt a faithful rendering of the letter. That is where the spirit abides. You will nevertheless have to understand those words, and your translation will inevitably convey that understanding; but if you begin by assuming that you can't come to that understanding by creatively rendering the original's words in your translation, you are actively alienating yourself, your text, and its readers from the only trace of the very spirit that you may be claiming to render.

In humanly generated texts you cannot distinguish the spirit from the letter. Those particular words in that particular order, when experienced by a reader, are the work's spirit. Those words have been put in that way by an author whose name will be associated with the text through such conventions as title pages and copyright attributions. The words can only be understood, however we decide to understand them, if an intention to make meaning by employing words is assumed. The author, as a trace of intended acts, cannot be removed from the text. This is no less true if a particular word was added by an editor, or was suggested by a friend, or plucked from a hat, for that activity too is intended — as is the decision to publish the result. The author as a living legal entity has rights. The author as a dead historical entity (such as Machado or Rilke for Paterson) can still be a source of legal rights (by, for instance, banning translations of works in his or her will), and can be the target of such spiritual duties as literary estates, editors, and publishers feel are due. Translations are also literary texts, and a like unity of word and spirit must be true of them too. Those

[9] T. S. Eliot, 'Baudelaire in Our Time', *Essays Ancient & Modern* (London: Faber & Faber, 1936), p. 66n.

who wish to translate or version the spirit will attempt a translation of the letter. The text they achieve will not be or contain either the letter or the spirit of the unique original; the secondary text, the translation, will have a letter-spirit of its own. Questions of trust, fidelity, and reliability are to be debated by comparing and contrasting the character of the autonomous original with that of the related secondary text.

Nor is '*faithful*' an impossible judgment, requiring an intentionally etiolated and dismissed 'essence', while a subjective reckoning of trustworthiness is possible. Moral vocabularies support each other. What does it mean to have a faithful friend, or to have a husband who you believe is faithful to you? It means that you can trust them to behave in certain ways with regard to you and not in others. Fidelity and trust are also both qualities of behaviour that can be checked, ones that may surprise or disappoint. You can be misled or let down. It isn't enough to say that you subjectively reckon something to be trustworthy. It cannot be distinguished from a fool's paradise of delusion if inaccessible to testing. The secondary text must show it *is* trustworthy. Moral terms take their place in sentences with prepositions: faithful *to* someone or something, trustworthy *about* or *with regard to* some task or activity or responsibility. *Faithful* and *trustworthy* are both qualities that require some other thing towards which the qualities can be manifested. In practical life people and things have to earn a reputation for fidelity or trustworthiness. In writing, trust requires three terms: writer, text, and reader. In translations it needs six: writer, text, reader, translator, related text, and reader (bilingual or not).

Does it make a difference to this argument whether the poets whose works have been translated are living or dead? It certainly makes a difference if they are well known, like Rilke, or being rescued from relative obscurity, like Veronica Franco.[10] But how can it not but make a difference? Imagine you are working on translations of a poet you think is alive and you learn that this poet has suddenly died. This happened in 1983 while I was working on Vittorio Sereni's poetry. A friend who had read his obituary in the *Times* telephoned me with the news. Auden's elegy for Yeats imagines ways that the texts of authors change when they stop being part of a potentially continuing series: 'By mourning tongues / The death of the poet was kept from his poems' and 'he became his admirers'.[11] This could be equally applied to the work of the translator. The poet becomes his admirers, and there is no way this cannot happen, or reason why it shouldn't, while, though the poems don't appear to change (their author's death is kept from them), those reading the texts see them in the light of this definitively changed situation.

Yet, in another sense, whether the author is alive or dead makes little

---

[10] See Veronica Franco, *Poems and Selected Letters*, ed. and trans. Ann Rosalind Jones and Margaret F. Rosenthal (Chicago: University of Chicago Press, 1998).

[11] W. H. Auden, 'In Memory of W. B. Yeats', *Collected Poems*, ed. Edward Mendelson (New York: Vintage, 1991), p. 247, and see *Poetry, Poets, Readers*, pp. 29–58.

difference, because of the role played by intention in the attribution of meaning to verbal acts of any kind. Consider a situation such as mine just before the telephone rang on that day in February 1983: working on the translations I was imagining their author as a person to meet and discuss them with in a few months, when in fact this was not to be. The relation to the ramifications in life of your translation change, but the words you are translating don't change (they can't be revised by the author any more) and your imaginative attempt to dramatize them as human communication has to go on whether you can talk to the author about intended senses or not. What's more, poets will tell you that what they meant is what the words say: if you want to translate the spirit, translate the letter.[12] Without the attribution of will or human intending you cannot interpret or translate what a poem's words might mean, whether it is Horace's 'Ehev fugaces, Postume, Postume' you are reading, or some stanzas of your own written yesterday. Since this is true of the text that the translator is producing, it seems bizarre to suppose that while your own text can have the benefit of will and spirit, this necessary assumption cannot be extended to the words you are translating. What's more, you must make that assumption to translate them at all.

II

In the Translator's Preface to a selection from the poetry of his living younger contemporary Durs Grünbein, Michael Hofmann contrasts his task with that of Robert Lowell, whose Introduction to *Imitations* he describe as 'a sort of half-controversial Bible to me!'[13] 'But then', he writes, 'the poets Lowell translated were, with one or two exceptions, not his living contemporaries, and he was not offering the first or principal way into their work for an English readership.'[14] So Nabokov's wish 'that he would stop mutilating defenceless dead poets'[15] becomes for Hofmann an argument in support of their now defenceless dead imitator. Because most of his poets were not living contemporaries, and had already been multiply translated, they appear more available for mutilation than the living. It is easy to forget (though Hofmann doesn't quite) that among the poets Lowell rendered in his *Imitations* at least two were very much alive. Giuseppe Ungaretti was not to die for another eight years, and Eugenio Montale lived for a further twenty. In a piece on Lowell's Montale, Hofmann has described

[12] See my 'Translating Sereni: A Discussion', *Translation and Literature* vol. 12 no. 1, *Modernism and Translation*, guest ed. Adam Piette (Spring 2003), pp. 178–87.

[13] Durs Grünbein, *Ashes for Breakfast: Selected Poems*, trans. Michael Hofmann (London: Faber & Faber, 2005), p. xi.

[14] Ibid. p. xii.

[15] Vladimir Nabokov, *Selected Letters 1940–1977*, ed. Dimitri Nabokov and M. J. Bruccoli (San Diego, New York, London: Harcourt Brace Jovanovich, 1989), p. 387.

the American's versions of other poets as 'so electrified and distorted by feedback their own mothers wouldn't recognize them'.[16] This evocative phrasing imagines the poets, whether quick or dead, as alive and having changeling children foisted on them.

The lack of attentive relationship could also signal a risk of damage for the translator,[17] as Elizabeth Bishop may have been aware when expressing qualms about his versions in letters to Lowell and, more trenchantly, when in conversation with others — as Lloyd Schwarz remembered: 'Elizabeth's attitude about translations was quite rigid, and she considered *Imitations* a series of almost willful mistranslations. Not her idea of translating at all — though in practice she was more flexible'.[18] To Anne Stevenson on 8 January 1964, Bishop wrote:

> I don't think much of poetry translations and rarely attempt them, — just when I see a poem by someone I like that I think will go into English with less loss than usual. That means it isn't necessarily one of the poet's best poems. My translations are almost as literal as I can make them, — these from Brazilian poets are in the original meters, as far as English meters can correspond to Portuguese — which uses a different system. I wouldn't attempt the kind of 'imitation' Robert Lowell does, although he makes brilliant Lowell-poems that way, frequently.[19]

She then adds, with a different inflection to Lowell's description of George Kay's 'photographic' renditions of Italian poetry, that 'The most satisfactory translations of poetry, I think, are those Penguin Poets, with a straight prose text at the bottom of the page — at least those in languages I know something of seem quite good.'[20] Bishop doesn't attempt literal translations, but she does try to make them 'almost as literal as I can make them', and this attention to the detail from which she is working corresponds with her views on attention to the objects that she is rendering in her poetry, as can be seen from her concern about the detail of the goat's eyes in 'Crusoe in England' whose 'pupils, horizontal, narrowed up / and expressed nothing, or a little malice.'[21] Bishop's noted respect for facts in her own poetry corresponds with a respect for the fact, the made thing, of an original poem when attempting its translation. Such a concern, as with translation that

---

[16] Michael Hofmann, 'Montale's Eastbourne', *Behind the Lines: Pieces on Writing and Pictures* (London: Faber & Faber, 2001), p. 136.

[17] For a grimly comic poem about relations between the letter and the spirit, see Roy Fisher, 'Irreversible', *The Long and the Short of It: Poems 1955-2005* (Tarset: Bloodaxe Books, 2005), pp. 158-59. It begins: 'The *Atlantic Review* misspelled Kokoschka./ In three weeks he was dead.'

[18] Gary Fountain and Peter Brazeau (ed.), *Elizabeth Bishop: An Oral Biography* (Amherst: University of Massachusetts Press, 1994), p. 341.

[19] Elizabeth Bishop, *Poems, Prose, and Letters*, ed. Robert Giroux and Lloyd Schwarz (New York: Library of America, 2008), pp. 856-57.

[20] Ibid. p. 857.

[21] Ibid. p. 154.

stays in contact with its original, allows for the possibility of significant mistakes, a fact which Christopher Ricks noted of the 'eighty-watt bulb' that 'betrays us all' in 'Faustina, or Rock Roses'.[22] Translations are texts that rise to containing mistaken renderings from works in other languages. Versioning poets who leave the original behind can't get it wrong, and so can't get near it either.

Bishop's renderings of Carlos Drummond de Andrade were begun during the autumn of 1962, perhaps with the encouragement of Lowell, when both original author and translator were living in Brazil.[23] Writing to the poet on 27 June 1963, she invited his comments on a translation and described what she hoped to do for his poetry in her English:

> Here is a translation of one of your poems, and I hope you will have time to look at it. I began with this one because it seems to go into English fairly easily — I hope you'll take my word for it that it makes a very moving poem in English as well as in Portuguese. The translation is quite literal — except for very small liberties with punctuation, omitting 'ands' etc. — to keep the meter right. I've written in the margin some second choices, or spots where I may be wrong — but please tell me anything you don't like — or if you don't like any of it!

She reports that the magazine *Poetry (Chicago)* has asked for translations of Brazilian poetry, and requests permission to send the magazine some versions of his poems, then adds:

> I am working on A MESA now — it's much more difficult, naturally; but it's one of those I like best. I've also tried some of the shorter rhymed ones — they're almost impossible, of course, because of the rhymes — but I'd like to give the US reader an impression of the range of your poetry, if possible — and I'll write a note explaining the shortcomings of the translations.[24]

It is, unfortunately, not possible to tell from this letter which poem she is asking its poet to comment on, and her editors do not supply the information. But her approach to the living poet and submission of the work for appreciation, criticism, or commentary seems exemplary of how it may be done — on the principle that we should do unto others what we would have them do unto us, and, what's more, because in many cases we are the same people: the translators are poets, poets who have been or will be translated. Let me add that I see no reason why translators cannot imagine relationships with recently dead poets of a similar kind, even if

---

[22] Ibid. p. 55. For a discussion of Bishop's concern for fidelity to facts, her respect for the object, and Christopher Ricks's discussion of the issues, my see 'Matters of Fact and Value', *Poetry, Poets, Readers: Making Things Happen* (Oxford: Oxford University Press, 2002), pp. 102–03.

[23] See Brett C. Millier, *Elizabeth Bishop: Life and the Memory of It* (Berkeley and Los Angeles: University of California Press, 1993), p. 337.

[24] Bishop, *Poems, Prose, and Letters*, pp. 850–51.

they are no longer able to discuss the translations with them, and what goes for the recently dead might continue to be imaginatively true for our relations with the remote dead, as when, for instance, in translating Catullus's 'Vivamus, mea Lesbia' it helps to imagine the poet and his love as living people, to see them as surrounded by ill-wishers, ones who resent their vast wealth of kisses, growing like cunning investments ('basia mille, deinde centum'), which they will conceal with the equivalent of financial irregularities ('conturbabimus') so as to protect themselves from being victims of the envious reprisals their good fortune prompts. In rendering the famous line 'nox est perpetua una dormienda', you might imagine and try to perform the poet's grimly encouraging joke to his girl in which 'nox' implies a night of love (when you don't sleep because exchanging all those thousands of kisses), but also death, when a euphemistic 'sleep' is the only thing you can do. Imagining the action of a poem in such a way, translators are not involved in taxidermy, but in attempts to bring the dead back to life.[25]

Drummond de Andrade, alive when Bishop was working on his poems, has a contribution to the sub-genre of Robinson Crusoe poems, 'Infância', a work that can itself be compared with Bishop's own contribution, completed later, 'Crusoe in England', with its documented concern for correctness of detail:

> Meu pai montava a cavalo, ia para o campo.
> Minha mãe ficava sentada cosendo.
> Meu irmão pequeno dormia.
> Eu sozinho menino entre mangueiras
> lia a história de Robinson Crusoé,
> comprida história che não acaba mais.
>
> No meio-dia branco de luz uma voz que aprendeu
> a ninar nos longes da senzala — e nunca se esqueceu
> chamava para o café.
> Café preto que nem a preta velha
> café gostoso
> café bom.
>
> Minha mãe ficava sentada cosendo
> olhando para mim:
> — Psiu ... Não acorde o menino.
> Para o berço onde pousou um mosquito.
> E dava um suspiro ... que fundo!

[25] My comments are indebted to Guy Lee's notes on the poem in *The Poems of Catullus* (Oxford: Oxford University Press, 1990), p. 150. Lee's version (p. 7), attempting 'a little honesty' (p. xxv), unfortunately conveys little of his annotations' imaginative knowledge of the original. Ben Jonson's rendering effectively evokes the ill-wishers as 'houshold-spies', while Coleridge's renders more delicate Catullus's sexual urges and deletes the envious ill-wishers, preferring to confuse his girl so she'll keep on kissing him. See Julia Haig Gaisser (ed.), *Catullus in English* (Harmondsworth: Penguin Books, 2001), pp. 14 and 86.

Lá longe meu pai campeava
no mato sem fim da fazenda.

E eu não sabia que minha história
era mas bonita que a de Robinson Crusoé.[26]

Bishop's version, 'Infancy', retains the original's exact number of lines and orders the delivery of statement as close to the Portuguese as possible. Here she attempts what I commented on in the discussion of Cavafy's 'Na Meinei', namely rendering the 'poetry' in the relations between the parts which, since they reach the reader's understanding in this order, can be translated by retaining as closely as possible the sequence of the released detail. Even where it is possible to quibble slightly with her renditions, there is no sense that she is allowing herself freedoms to deviate from the course of the original. Errors or questionable interpretations are tributes to the principles of approximation and fidelity, supporting the notion that a translation is a text that rises to the level of containing mistakes (not one where such mistakes are considered irrelevant to the second-language felicity of the 'version'):

My father got on his horse and went into the field.
My mother stayed sitting and sewing.
My little brother slept.
A small boy alone under the mango trees,
I read the long story of Robinson Crusoe,
the long story that never comes to an end.

At noon, white with light, a voice that had learned
lullabies long ago in the slave-quarters — and never forgot —
called us for coffee.
Coffee blacker than the black old woman
delicious coffee
good coffee.

My mother stayed sitting and sewing
watching me:
Shh — don't wake the boy.
She stopped the cradle when a mosquito had lit
and gave a sigh ... how deep!
Away off there my father went riding
through the farm's endless wastes.

And I didn't know that my story
was prettier than that of Robinson Crusoe.[27]

It's possible that in the translation a stanza break between lines seventeen and eighteen has been, whether accidentally or not, suppressed. It could be that 'She stopped the cradle when a mosquito had lit / and gave a sigh ...

---

[26] Carlos Drummond de Andrade, *Cuore numeroso*, ed. Vincenzo Arsillo (Rome: Donzelli Editore, 2002), p. 14.
[27] Elizabeth Bishop, *The Complete Poems 1927-1979* (New York: Farrar, Straus & Giroux, 1983), p. 258.

how deep!' doesn't sufficiently convey what's happening, through a little filling out on the part of the translator. The mother can't be telling the young Carlos not to wake the baby, because he's sitting quietly reading *Robinson Crusoe*. 'Shh — don't wake the boy' is addressed 'Para o berço onde pousou um mosquito' ('Towards the cradle where a mosquito was poised.') The words are addressed to the mosquito. This can be understood in Bishop's version too; but by adding the phrase about the mother stopping the cradle she makes it more difficult to catch that sense. This part of the poem hears the tiny sounds of the mosquito, the mother's words, and profound sigh. What the sigh is about we have to intuit equally from original and translation — using the details of the father out riding on the farm, the servant woman, an ex-slave, and the similarities and differences with Defoe's book as our guides.

Bishop's use of comparative adjectives is working to collaborate in this interpretative activity. She may slightly over-characterize in the line 'Coffee blacker than the black old woman' — the Portuguese appears to say 'Coffee black like the old black woman' (though I appreciate the sensitivity with which Bishop deploys the odder adjective order, translating 'velha' as 'old woman' and qualifying that noun phrase with 'black'). There would be no saying that 'prettier' doesn't translate 'mais bonita', but 'more beautiful' might also be possible. Bishop's choice may be faintly too namby-pamby for the poem's final flourish. I express these doubts and qualms to indicate respect for Bishop's attempt faithfully to render the shape of Drummond de Andrade's original, to approach its spirit by translating its letter, to give it a convincing voice in English, and a voice with a delicate rhythmic cohesion. Bishop was aware how attempts to achieve these felicities could misfire, reporting on 1 March 1978 to Ashley Brown: 'A terrible translation of Drummond de Andrade in the last *American Poetry Review*. Well, everybody's doing it.'[28]

III

'Translation is resurrection', Henry Gifford said, 'but not of the body'.[29] At the close of his 'Afterword' to the Machado versions, Paterson appealingly comments on one of the benefits of making translations from other people's poetry when the writers are no longer with us:

> One of the best things about this job is having so many dead friends
> you can talk to, and I should acknowledge here the tutelary voices
> of Machado's own mentor Miguel de Unamuno, and my own hand
> in the dark, Emil Cioran. Because of the integrity and self-delighted

---

[28] Elizabeth Bishop, *One Art: The Selected Letters*, ed. Robert Giroux (London: Chatto & Windus, 1994), p. 620.
[29] Henry Gifford cited in Eric Griffiths and Matthew Reynolds (eds.), *Dante in English* (Harmondsworth: Penguin Books, 2005), p. 405.

purity of his enterprise, Alan Trueblood's solid literal translations have more poetry in them than most poems, and I apologize to him for those two or three occasions where I have, without acknowledgement, stolen lines of his because they seemed pretty much unimprovable.[30]

As in William Gass's relationship with Rilke, there is a risk of sentimentality in this: friendship is reciprocal or nothing. We can approach the dead through their artifacts, but strictly they can't respond to us. Yet it is part of the lifeblood in a culture and its relations with others that we humour such fictions of dialogue with the dead. In this light, something sad has happened to Paterson with regard to the translating 'job', for in his Machado (1999) he was willing to make gestures towards spiritual communication between the quick and the dead, but, as we have seen, in his Rilke (2007) he denies the presence of such figures: 'There are no ghosts, no gods, nothing secretly lurking in the temple of the poem whose vengeful wrath we will incur through our failure to honour it. The author and critic might reasonably scream *travesty*, but they aren't in the poem either.'[31] Rather, following out an implication from Paterson's recognition of consensually agreed meaning, I would suggest that we are all there, implicit in the words of the poem: author, critics, translators, and any reader who cares enough about a poem to want to know it as it is, to make its words echo within bodies and consciousnesses, for without that activation the poem is a dead letter. Its spirit has not been experienced. If Paterson reads Machado, Unamuno, and Cioran to maintain friendships with them, his readers may do the same with him if they so wish, just as I have been doing (and not only with Paterson), so as to benefit from the provocation of others' writings. Cioran being present in his texts, Rilke will be in his. It is part of readers' or translators' roles to make of this the most and the best we can.

John Dryden's version of the encounter between Dido and Aeneas in Book 6 of Virgil's epic is a key moment in the double translation of the quick and the dead:

> Not far from these *Phoenician Dido* stood;
> Fresh from her Wound, her Bosom bath'd in Blood.
> Whom, when the *Trojan* Heroe hardly knew,
> Obscure in Shades, and with a doubtful view,
> (Doubtful as he who runs thro' dusky Night,
> Or thinks he sees the Moon's uncertain Light:)
> With Tears he first approach'd the sullen Shade;
> And, as his Love inspir'd him, thus he said.[32]

Virgil renders the passage of the living Aeneas transported to the Underworld, in which he encounters the beloved woman, dead by her own hand, he had

---

[30] Paterson, *The Eye*, p. 60.
[31] Paterson, *Orpheus*, p. 79.
[32] *Virgil's Aeneid*, trans. John Dryden, ed. Fredrick M. Keener (Harmondsworth: Penguin Books, 1997), p. 164.

abandoned on the North African shore, which he had been required to do to fulfill his empire-founding destiny. There he attempts to engage her in the formal style of epic speech. Dryden continues to render Virgil in the elevated heroic couplets of his late seventeenth-century English:

> Unhappy Queen! then is the common breath
> Of Rumour true, in your reported Death,
> And I, alas, the Cause! By Heav'n, I vow,
> And all the Pow'rs that rule the Realms below,
> Unwilling I forsook your friendly State:
> Commanded by the Gods, and forc'd by Fate.

There follows a tercet explaining that they have also driven him to visit the underworld and so encounter Dido once more: 'Those Gods, that Fate, whose unresisted Might / Have sent me to these Regions, void of Light, / Thro' the vast Empire of eternal Night.' He goes on to tell her that he couldn't be expected to have imagined she would commit suicide:

> Nor dar'd I to presume, that, press'd with Grief,
> My Flight should urge you to this dire Relief.
> Stay, stay your Steps, and listen to my Vows:
> 'Tis the last Interview that Fate allows![33]

This is a wonderfully archaic use of the word 'interview' to mean both an occasion mutually to see each other, and through that occasion, to communicate. It's a use of the word that Thomas Hardy borrowed for the first published text of the encounter between himself and his recently deceased wife Emma Gifford in 'After a Journey': 'Hereto I come to interview a ghost'.[34] Hardy's Poems of 1912-1913 have been read as a sustained parallel between the writer's guiltily bereaved situation and the classical analogy of a lost love re-encountered after death in the underworld. In the Virgil, the dead Queen Dido doesn't respond to the living Aeneas. The rest of this frustrated 'interview' is given over to Dryden's rendering of her silent withdrawal:

> In vain he thus attempts her Mind to move,
> With Tears and Pray'rs, and late repenting Love.
> Disdainfully she look'd; then turning round,
> But fix'd her Eyes unmov'd upon the Ground.
> And, what he says, and swears, regards no more
> Than the deaf Rocks, when the loud Billows roar.
> But whirl'd away, to shun his hateful sight,
> Hid in the Forest, and the Shades of Night.

She returns to the dead Sicheus, 'Who answer'd all her Cares, and equal'd all her Love', at which Aeneas, 'the pitying Heroe', shed some 'pious Tears' and

---

[33] Ibid. pp. 164–65.
[34] See *The Complete Poetical Works of Thomas Hardy*, 5 vols., ed. Samuel Hynes (Oxford: Oxford University Press, 1982-1995), ii, p. 59n; and Donald Davie, 'Hardy's Virgilian Purples', *Agenda*, Thomas Hardy Special Issue, vol. 10 nos. 1-2 (Spring-Summer, 1972), pp. 138-56.

'follow'd with his eyes the flitting Shade.' The inability to communicate or make reassuring contact with the dead here is an analogy of the inability of the translation to resurrect the body of the original in Gifford's sense. In Dryden's translation, Virgil is as much a flitting shade as Dido, and the English poet's approach to his original is relevantly analogous to his hero's attempting to meet his lost love. However, we were better not to despair, for the impossibility of complete transparency of translation (which, if it were possible, would be like the sexual communication of the angels in Milton's Heaven) is, as I have been attempting to show, the very situation that occasions its gamut of expressive opportunities.

Translations of dead poets are kinds of frustrated interview in the underworld, meetings that in European poetry tend to be risky affairs in which relations between living and dead are by no means plain and simple. Dante's managing of the hand-over from Virgil to Beatrice as his guide out of Purgatory and on into Paradise alludes contrastively to the fatal relationship of Dido and Aeneas (as his allusion to *Aeneid* 4. 23 suggests), but reconfigured within the frame of Christian forgiveness (see *Purgatorio* 30, ll. 40-57). Here is Henry Carey's 1814 version of the living Dante's realization that the dead Virgil has disappeared without his being able to bid farewell to his inspiring forebear: 'But Virgil had bereaved us of himself, / Virgil, my best-lov'd father; Virgil, he / To whom I gave me up for safety'. Yet once more the editors of *Dante in English* detect a gulf between original and translation: 'the Italian is more lucid and plangent; a literal translation might run: "But Virgil had left us void of him, Virgil sweetest father, Virgil to whom for the sake of my well-being I gave myself", though "salvation" is another possibility for "well-being"'.[35] Well, run it might; but 'left us void of him' doesn't sound like English, never mind a more lucidly literal translation than Carey's, while Dante's 'dolcissimo' could equally be 'most tender', and a word that combines 'well-being' and 'salvation' would be 'health' — a translation that, as in the Italian original's 'salute', can have both physical and spiritual senses.

The literary textures of words and our choosing between them in making translations are not only haunted with the imagined presence of the dead poet and his translators, they recount multiplied imaginings of such haunting presences (ghosts and gods) as those of our inspiring predecessors and mistreated loves. Yet that this is an ordinary state of affairs in the echoing centuries of poetry is, as we have seen, exactly what at least one contemporary poet-translator has sometimes preferred to underplay. In Rilke's 'Orpheus. Euridike. Hermes', it is just such a non-recognition, the characters' failure to conduct an interview, that the poem dramatizes:

> Und als plötzlich jäh
> der Gott sie anhielt und mit Schmerz im ausruf

[35] Griffiths and Reynolds (eds.), *Dante in English*, p. 94.

die Worte sprach: Er hat sich umgewendet —,
begriff sie nicht und sagte leise: *Wer?*[36]

Such an approach to meeting stalled at a point of near approximation is manifested in the efforts of the faithful translators, ones like Leishmann for instance: 'And when, abruptly swift, / the god laid hold of her and, with an anguished / cry, uttered the words: He has turned round! — / she took in nothing, and said softly: Who?'[37] Even when we have to admit that the living cannot meet and be united with their dead predecessors and loves, even in the lines of classic poetry, it is the reluctance with which translators withdraw from the attempt at matching their texts to those of those predecessors that marks out the distinctiveness of *their* encounters.

IV

Yet perhaps the most intimate encounter with intractable distance possible when translating the quick or the dead is that of self-translation.[38] After all, you are yourself alive as you translate, though you are translating the results of a past creative moment, one that is likely to be, in effect, dead and gone. Self-translation has to address the complexes of human presence and absence in a poem, and to do so in a context where you might think the translator also holds all the cards, for she or he is also the originating author. This poet-translator is now acting a double role, and a role that is made possible by the fact that the translation cannot, strictly, be made simultaneously with the original, and is usually made at some distance of time. This makes the situation analogous to the question about who is deceiving whom in self-deception, namely: who is translating whom in self-translation? The relation of the original author to the translator in this unusual situation is instructive both for what human identity is like, and how identity in difference evolves. It also brings home the matter of the spirit and the letter, of what ghosts inhabit the 'cemetery of performance',[39] to borrow a phrase of Roy Fisher's, that is the completed poem. To bring such matters as close to home as possible, I take the liberty of briefly discussing one of my own pieces of self-translation (though let me acknowledge that I took advice from native speakers of the language into which the translation was made).

[36] Rainer Maria Rilke, *Die Gedichte* (Frankfurt am Main: Insel Verlag, 1986), p. 491.
[37] Rainer Maria Rilke, *Selected Poems*, trans. J. B. Leishmann (London: Hogarth Press, 1941), pp. 32-33. See Joseph Brodsky, 'Ninety Years After', *On Grief and Reason: Essays* (London: Hamish Hamilton, 1996), pp. 422-24.
[38] See, for example, Samuel Beckett, *Collected Poems 1930-1978* (London: John Calder, 1986), pp. 40-41, 50-51, and 58-63. Joseph Brodsky, *So Forth: Poems* (London: Hamish Hamilton, 1996) contains poems translated by the author alone, or in collaboration with others.
[39] Roy Fisher, 'The Poplars', *The Long and the Short of It: Poems 1955-2005* (Tarset: Bloodaxe, 2005), p. 39.

The original text, with the title 'Parma's Sky', was written on 5 October 1985 and left as a message for its implicit interlocutor. It is based in a situation of life, and is using poetry as a form of communication between two tacitly specified people, though the poem is also written with the aim of producing a publishable work (and a carbon copy was taken away by the thirty-two-year-old poet). Adding to the piquancy and challenge in making this translation was the fact that 'Aria di Parma', its title when first published three years later,[40] is an acrostic. This is another form with a venerable history going back to Biblical times and cultures, its Greek-derived word naming a text in which the initial letters, read vertically down or sometimes diagonally across the page, spell out a word — usually now a person's name. Though the first printing of 'Aria di Parma' concealed this further by beginning the lines with lower-case letters, I quote here the text from a later publication:

> Over shuttered frontages and nearly empty streets, the moon
> Rises into Parma's sky.
> Night of earliest October — unusually warm,
> Evidently tremulous with fugitive temptations —
> Lets friends talk and stray under cavernous church baroque
> Left unrestored, almost in ruins —
> At the tangled very end of confused, confusing youth.
>
> Trolley-bus cables divide that deep blue, all but black —
> Redouble the street-lamps' glare.
> Even though the torrent's dry and should be,
> Virtually every truth to tell, or compliment pay,
> Insinuates more torment in the name of clarity.
> Surely still it won't unravel, though the waning moon
> And dark have been surpassed by morning's obvious daylight —
> Now — on another couple's wedding day.

The acrostic message embedded in such a poem inevitably asks what the consensual meaning of the poem is that you are attempting to translate. It draws attention (as in translations of Eugenio Montale's poem 'Da un lago svizzero' such as Jonathan Galassi's 'From a Swiss Lake')[41] to the partly concealed, but by that token intended and present, communicative gesture in the writing of the poem — a gesture placing the poem between writer and encrypted dedicatee. To convey the sense of this poem but let the spelt-out name be lost would be to fail to render the communicative gesture, the seemingly difficult love poem, and so not to signal both its human and its poetic significance, while to stick to the initial letters of the lines would inevitably be to take the translated text away from the strict semantic shape of the original.

Still, the challenge in such an instance of impossibility could only come

[40] See Peter Robinson, *This Other Life* (Manchester: Carcanet Press, 1988), p. 65.
[41] See 'From a Swiss Lake', Eugenio Montale, *Collected Poems 1920-1954*, rev. ed. trans. Jonathan Galassi (New York: Farrar, Straus and Giroux, 2000), p. 401.

from accepting the need to retain the order of the initial letters, and then try to get the translation to approximate, as closely as possible, to what the original poem says, while effecting a rhythmical equivalent for it in the entirely different sonic economy of the language into which it is being translated. Here's how the Italian version of 'Aria di Parma', its title left in Italian, was eventually published, nineteen years after the original moment of composition:

> Oltre facciate con imposte e borghi quasi spopolati, la luna
> Risale nel cielo di Parma.
> Notte di primissimo ottobre — più calda del commune,
> Evidentemente tremula di tentazioni sfuggenti —
> Lascia amici a parlare e vagare sotto un barocco cavernoso di chiesa
> Lasciato senza restauro, quasi in rovina —
> All'aggrovigliata fine di una turbata, turbante giovinezza.
>
> Tutto quasi nero, cavi di filobus dividono quel blu profondo —
> Raddoppiando il riverbero dei lampioni.
> E anche se il torrente ha da esser secco e secco è,
> Verità da dire o complimento da fare, quasi tutto
> Insinua più tormento in nome della chiarezza.
> Sicuramente tuttavia non si scoglierà, benché la luna calante
> Alla mattina e il buio diventino la luce ovvia del giorno —
> Nozze di un'altra coppia, oggi pronta.[42]

The self who speaks the translation appears also to be rendering its communicative act into the culture that he, or his earlier manifestation, was not able to enter on 5 October 1985. The translation performs retroactively a literary version of the movement that the speaker wanted to make. It is, in this sense, an action, something happening between the two cultures; and yet, as importantly, the figure of the speaking poet in the original had ceased to exist by the time the translation was made. The quick figure that wrote the original was, metaphorically, dead, while the living translator (and his collaborators) needed to produce a fiction of his speaking trace, imaginatively located in the recent past and in another situation — another version of the ventriloquism inevitably involved in translating. He and his situation had to be brought back to life in order to make the translated poem communicate with others in the concealed dedicatee's culture. The Italian version of 'Aria di Parma' is a response to an earlier self, a self that is being brought over to a different life in time from that of its original. The freedom allowed in the Italian rendering above — and there are a few liberties taken in the interests of combining the variously meaningful threads — was calibrated (I hope you will feel) so as to reconstruct in the second language the expressive purpose and significance, the communicative occasion, in its oblique directness, of the original poem. Self-translation underlines a consideration that the translation of other

---

[42] Peter Robinson, *L'attaccapanni e altre poesie*, Italian versions by the author with Ornella Trevisan (Milan: Moretti & Vitali, 2004), pp. 50-51.

writers can either foster or stifle, namely respect for the nature of a writer's own inspirations and occasions. There is a great likelihood of self-damage in the conflicting pressures of creative composition. Self-translation involves us in reflecting upon how such damage could occur, and how it may be mitigated. The translation of 'Aria di Parma' also made the poem of that name available to the other couple, the Italian friends of the dedicatee, whose wedding day it had happened to be on October the 5th, 1985.

V

Simone Weil once proposed that the 'real way of writing is to write as we translate. When we translate a text written in some foreign language, we do not seek to add anything to it; on the contrary, we are scrupulously careful not to add anything to it. That is how we have to translate a text which is not written down.'[43] Translating the text of the world, the 'not written down', as it might be, we first have to imagine it as readable and interpretable. While this involves projection, unlimited projection is not reading or interpreting: it is having it your own way. Though Weil's statement asserts a non-exploitative relation to the world, it is not only impossible to avoid losing aspects of the original when translating, but impossible to avoid adding things — beginning with the entire sonic timbre of the second language. This is also true of translating the text of the world. Even imagining it as a text is adding to it, and translating it into a textual form requires the identification of salience, of detail that will accrue significance in its relations within the composed ensemble. Weil's observation can point towards an ethical stance both in translating and writing, but the activity cannot be simplified to vigilance about additions unprompted by the original from which we are working. It must lie in the scruple manifested regarding the text's relations to those inevitable losses and additions.

The good poet-translator, I have been suggesting throughout, is a writer who monitors and responds to inevitable changes in approaching the original in other terms. When asserting that 'we are scrupulously careful not to add anything to it', Weil urges the translator to avoid *egregious* additions, additions unprompted by the source object, though this should be perhaps enlarged to include the experience of the original in the process of translating. Thus, one of the promptings provided by the original is that experience of loss in rendering it, a loss that needs to be responded to in making the answering object, the translation or original poem. A way to rephrase what Weil appears to be advocating might be to suggest that what the poet can learn from translating is *a respect for his or her own occasions and imaginative materials*. The benefit for poetry of translating, or attempting to translate, with the guiding values that I have been exploring,

---

[43] *Simone Weil: An Anthology*, ed. Siân Miles (Harmondsworth: Penguin Books, 2005), p. 239.

is that it fosters a respectful approach to your own inspirations, losses and all, your own promptings; and it discourages the willfully omnipotent fantasy that because it's your own poetry you can do what you like to make it work, that supposed freedom of which Lowell wrote in his Introduction to *Imitations*.

Being scrupulously careful not to add when translating *is* impossible. The very act of rendering, as my book has been exploring, is to add and to take away, to undergo losses and to make relevant additions. This is as true of a poet's relation to an inspiration. As in the occasioned poem 'Aria di Parma', not all of the material circumstances of the situation could or would be, or should have been, included in the text. Much must equally be lost in the translation from life, while as we are attempting to render this situation or theme, there will be threads from the material that will be brought out by the collocations of words in the text, elements that are significantly interrelated in the text, as they could not be in the lived experience. The process of working on and revising the text will bring relations into it that can benefit the rendering. Nevertheless, there have to be facilitating limits — and this is where the two activities usefully coincide. The kind of translating that I have been advocating does not lose touch with the original: it is in a perpetual dialogue, preferably *en face* or *testo a fronte*, in which both texts can be seen at a glance and appreciated for what they are. Though this cannot be the case with original work, because the source material relatively rarely exists as an art object, nevertheless, the poet needs to project it as a potential work, maintaining a similar dialogue between work in progress and source.

In the process of composition such a dialogue is essential to the outcome of the poem, because a sense of respect for and fidelity to the materials is one of those guiding limits that can set a curb upon omnipotence, and create a constraint within which artistry enables its means. The constraints of the sonnet or the villanelle, of a metre or stanza form, or, equally, of the need to make an improvised form adhere dialogically to its theme at all points, these are as similarly useful as the obligation to approximate both the themes and the formal features of an original poem. Respect for the otherness of your own materials, for their independent existence as significant happenings, will occasion invention and focus its efforts. You have to learn how to receive gifts without spoiling them by your meddling, but you do have to learn how to receive them. Both in the translation of poetry and in writing poetry, the art of receiving gifts involves appreciating as faithfully as possible the nature of what you are being offered.

'The collecting of poetry from one's experience as one goes along' — Wallace Stevens wrote in an aphorism from *Adagia* — 'is not the same thing as merely writing poetry.'[44] Returning to Weil's injunction, it is only right to note that the experience or the material from which poetry might

---

[44] Wallace Stevens, *Collected Poetry and Prose*, ed. Frank Kermode and Joan Richardson (New York: Library of America, 1997), p. 901.

be collected is more ineffable in the case where the poet is translating from life, from his or her own materials. Paul Muldoon has combined the translation of poetry and the writing of poems in an the idea adapted from Octavio Paz:

> I want to go further than Lowell and propose (1) that the 'poetic translation' is itself an 'original poem,' (2) that the 'original poem' on which it's based is itself a 'translation' and (3) that both 'original poem' and 'poetic translation' are manifestations of some ur-poem.[45]

It will not be difficult to credit Muldoon's first proposal I hope, since, as we have seen, no translation can be the same as its original, and changes of linguistic and other sorts must occur for the original to be translated at all. The poetic text that is offered as the translation has every right to the status of an original poem, if we understand 'original' in the proper literary sense, namely, as not even beginning either to require or display total origination by its poet. This is, after all, what Muldoon implies by his second proposal, namely that original poems are themselves translations, both in being translations from the natural world (to borrow a title of Les Murray's),[46] and in being carried over from other texts and other language uses that the translator-poet has internalized and reproduced — as when Paul Celan echoed *Paradiso* 3, l. 81 ('di soglia in soglia') in his poem from *Mohn und Gedächtnis*, 'Chanson einer Dame im Schatten', with the translation 'von Schwelle zu Schwelle', then borrowed his own line for the title to his subsequent collection.[47] The original poem is thus a translation in two senses: it is a rendering and an understanding of some burden partly known to the poet, and reading it (which the poet must do as she or he writes it) is itself an act of rendering and translating, a talking through of this forming thing until it comes to be known and understood, a process which goes on beyond the end of the poem's writing into the afterlife of sporadic cohabitation that poetry readers take up with poems that either they wrote, or others did.

In an interview with Peter Orr, commenting on how inspiration came to him, Bernard Spencer describes his poetry's being collected from experience: 'I rather like what a Greek poet said (it was Seferis) that you meet poems like people and certain kinds of poems in different places. A certain kind you may run into in a railway station, you can expect them there, and other kinds in, shall we say, the bathroom.'[48] This interview, recorded on

45 Paul Muldoon, *The End of the Poem: Oxford Lectures on Poetry* (London: Faber & Faber, 2006), p. 195. See Octavio Paz, 'Translation: Literature and Letters', cited in ibid., p. 202.

46 See Les Murray, *Translations from the Natural World* (Manchester: Carcanet Press, 1993).

47 Paul Celan, *Die Gedichte: Kommentierte Gesamtausgabe in einem Band*, ed. Barbara Wiedermann (Frankfurt am Main: Suhrkamp, 2003), pp. 35 and 61.

48 'Bernard Spencer' in Peter Orr (ed.), *The Poet Speaks: Interviews with Contemporary Poets* (New York: Barnes & Noble, 1966), p. 237.

27 August 1962, shows the importance for Spencer not only of Seferis's example, but also of the magazine *Personal Landscape* where some eighteen years earlier he had published 'Mathaios Pascalis His Ideas about Poems', contributing to a series of statements on the art by its editors and others: 'Your *Ideas about poems*, gave me this <u>Idea about poems</u>, which I feel obliged to communicate, very confidentially, to you', Seferis wrote to Lawrence Durrell in January 1944.[49] Stevens's idea that poetry can be collected from experience is augmented with Seferis's notion that the works are already waiting to be gathered by a suitably attentive sensibility:

> Poems of the same kind meet usually in special places; they have their clubs. On this point I rely on my own experience which informs me that heroic poems meet in ships on a calm sea; poems about slumber in battlefields; poems about rapes in waterless islands; poems about death in green meadows at noon; poems about happiness on peaks of mountains; poems about self-indulgence on staircases (think of *Ash Wednesday*) and limericks in the bathroom.[50]

And to this Spencer further suggests that 'a lot of unrecognized poems, I think, are lived through every moment of your life. It depends on how alert or how undisturbed you are, or how excited and attentive you are at that very moment when the opportunity comes', and he describes the moments of excitement and attentiveness that make an event of life an occasion:

> But definitely it is a feeling as if some sort of signal has gone on and the fact that inside you, from that moment, is a so-far-unexplored area of feeling and emotion, which is almost disagreeable to hold on to. And the poet, for all reasons, must then work on this or let it hang about, preferably for some time before he starts working on it, and this will turn into a poem, with luck.[51]

Spencer follows Seferis in suggesting that an original poem is already there, like a text in another language, one that you don't know especially well, that you are attempting to understand and explore so as to be able to render it in your own language. Translating can in some cases be the only means you have for thoroughly reading a work, as original composition can be the one way you have of making sense of an experience. It will of course be your reading, and will be performed in a personal selection from the language, whether in the case of a translation or an original work. Spencer's experience of translating had begun with Greek poets, and a sustained collaboration on the first versions of Seferis to appear in English, *The King of Asine and Other Poems* (1948). He was also among the

---

[49] Cited in Roderick Beaton, *George Seferis Waiting for the Angel: A Biography* (New Haven and London: Yale University Press, 2003), p. 228.

[50] George Seferis, 'Ideas about Poems VII', 'Mathaios Pascalis His Ideas about Poems', *Personal Landscape: An Anthology of Exile*, ed. Robin Fedden et al. (London: Editions Poetry London, 1945), pp. 78-79.

[51] 'Bernard Spencer', *The Poet Speaks*, p. 237.

first British poets to render Montale, his versions probably done between September 1946 and August 1948.[52]

As we have seen, the exact reproduction of the poetry of the original is strictly impossible. However, since no translation can be such a reproduction, while this sets a limit to what translating can achieve, it doesn't set such a limit only to the translation of poetry but to the translation of anything, and to those translations from experience which are original poems. Once this is accepted, then it becomes possible to see how poetry, like everything else, is translatable, if that word is understood to mean a *remaking* in the other terms of a different structure of materials. Furthermore, it is only if it is recognized that exact reproduction is impossible (that a so-called word-for-word literal version is simply a competing way of remaking the original with a different arrangement of losses and gains) that ethical standards such as Weil's can be adjudged. It is because there is a significant gap between original and translation that such evaluative descriptions as those involved in adding or taking away, in fidelity or 'betrayal', can be attributed. Thus, as I have also noted, not only is the gap between poem and translation, poem and experience essential, it has to be preserved by keeping a sense of the original poem (an experience of a poem, after all) or other experience in view.

The version of poetic translation that I have been outlining and exploring in this book is an idea about a productive, a useful, a valuable idea of creativity itself, one that is linked to a conviction about the curbing will, and the deploying of energy for the realization of what lives beyond our selves. Spencer's poetry manifests such a stance to the world, as in 'On the Road', a poem written during the same period in which he probably made his Montale translations:

> Our roof was grapes and the broad hands of the vine
> as we two drank in the vine-chinky shade
> of harvest France:
> and wherever the white road led we could not care,
> it had brought us there
> to the arbour built on the valley side where time,
> if time any more existed, was that river
> of so profound a current, it at once
> both flowed and stayed.
>
> We two. And nothing in the whole world was lacking.
> It is later one realizes. I forget
> the exact year or what we said. But the place
> for a lifetime glows with noon. There are the rustic
> table and the benches set; beyond the river
> forests as soft as fallen clouds, and in
> our wine and eyes I remember other noons.

[52] Bernard Spencer, *Collected Poems*, ed. Roger Bowen (Oxford: Oxford University Press, 1981), pp. 103–7.

It is a lot to say, nothing was lacking;
river, sun, and leaves, and I am making
words to say 'grapes' and 'her skin'.[53]

This beautiful close deploys the quotation of words when in another linguistic culture. After all, they are 'sur la route' in a France at the time of the 'vendage', and it would be 'les grappes de raisins' hanging above their heads. Spencer is, as it were, translating from French life into English, and from lived life into language. 'On the Road' concludes by underlining this sense of composing as rendering from experience, exemplifying in its understated way Weil's comment that 'The real way of writing is to write as we translate'.[54] Spencer produces such a sense of adding nothing by first claiming that there was nothing that needed to be added, and then imitating that sense in the all but tautological reduction of what the poem needs to say in its conclusion so as to pay homage to that fleeting occasion.

Yet we also translate to overcome distances of time and space, the largest of which is doubtless death. Such distances are quietly caught in 'On the Road' by, for example, the change of pronominal relationship from the first person plurals of the first verse ('Our roof', 'we two', 'we did not care' and 'brought us there') to the first and third person singular relationship of the second where 'I am making / words to say ... "her skin"'. The togetherness of the first verse has already separated into the afterwards of the poet alone recalling them as distinct. This change acknowledging the distance between the moment of experience and that of writing may also imply the death in Rome from TB on 13 June 1947 of the woman, his first wife Nora Gibbs, with whom he had enjoyed the poised moment of plenitude, perhaps in late August 1946. Commenting on the poem for a radio programme in 1959, Spencer noted that it 'has a setting ... at a place along the River Loire. The theme is the possibility of entirely perfect and happy episodes in life, although the title implies that they do not usually last very long.'[55] This implication is shaped by the deftly hidden rhymes that hold in a poised suspension the syntactical unfolding of his two stanzas. In both cases, the terminal rhyme-word upon which the verse end-stops (the 'stayed' of the first also a beautifully understated compounding of relevant senses) is linked to a rapidly enjambed word — 'the vine-chinky shade /of harvest France' in verse 1, the 'and in / our wine and eyes' of verse 2. The interplay of what 'flowed' and 'stayed' is performed in these deft rhymes, ones that may be a homage to the similarly going and remaining close of Montale's 'La casa dei doganieri' where 'questa / mia sera' [this evening / of mine] rhymes with 'Ed io non so chi va e chi resta [and I don't know who goes and who's leaving].[56]

---

[53] Ibid. p. 82.
[54] *Simone Weil: An Anthology*, p. 239.
[55] 'Poems by Bernard Spencer', 30 July 1959 BBC Third Programme, cited in Spencer, *Collected Poems*, p. 141.
[56] Eugenio Montale, *Le occasioni*, ed. Dante Isella (Turin: Einaudi, 1996), p. 146.

'Ah! you phrase-makers!' Durrell recalled Spencer saying to him in his 1964 memoir, 'Your trouble is that you are insanely ambitious!'[57] Edward Lucie-Smith's admiration of Spencer's poems for their 'precision of imagery' chimes with Durrell's praise for the poet in his 'Alexandria': 'B. with his respect for the Object'.[58] These expressions imply that the style of Spencer's evocative lines is made from carefully calibrated adjective and noun pairings, ones shaped into syntactical units that draw a measured attention to the subjectivity implied by the act of evoking. Similarly, Lucie-Smith's 'truth of feeling'[59] is critical shorthand for a syntactical, rhythmical, formal and lexical approach to the writing of poetry: according to its tacit commitments, the poem may make no emotive claims other than those embedded in a style improvised from its sponsoring occasion, its circumstantial materials, the poetry collected from experience by listening to the promptings of a sensibility attentive to the significance implied there. Such an aesthetic will have none of the poetry attributed to experience by means of an elaborated diction and an authoritative rhythmic pulse prone to push on regardless of the sponsoring occasion or, if translating, of the original text.

Robert Lowell's poem 'The Art of the Possible' from his final collection, *Day by Day*, begins with a piece of quoted speech that catches a predicament that is not only its author's: '"Your profession of making what can't be done / the one thing you can do ..."'.[60] The responsibilities with which poets, translators, and poet-translator attempt this in their arts, and the needs to which they answer, come into play with distances, the distances of separation, such as those between the quick and the dead, and the strict impossibility of crossing over such boundaries, borders, and limits. Spencer's poem brings its commemorating poet as close as possible when he writes 'and I am making / words to say "grapes" and "her skin"'. His word 'making', though, doesn't perfectly chime with 'nothing was lacking' in the stanza's first line. Art and the impulse to make art arise when such limits are painfully encountered and acknowledged. The translator of poetry is engaged in the art of the impossible because exploring the edges of such shifting limits. Just so, the language frontier cannot be crossed in a translation, because then you would no longer be consciously rendering the poem in other words, but reading the original, which, though itself an interpretation, is not followed through in the composition of an equivalent text. Throughout this book the impossibility that I have been approaching like a horse shying at a fence is the limit without which there can be no

---

[57] Cited in Lawrence Durrell, 'Bernard Spencer', *London Magazine* vol. 3 no. 10 (Jan 1964), p. 44.

[58] Lawrence Durrell, *Collected Poems 1931–1974*, ed. James A. Brigham (London: Faber & Faber, 1980), p. 154.

[59] 'Bernard Spencer' headnote in Edward Lucie-Smith (ed.), *British Poetry since 1945* (Harmondsworth: Penguin Books, 1970), p. 108.

[60] Robert Lowell, *Collected Poems*, ed. Frank Bidart et al. (London: Faber & Faber, 2003), p. 746.

art. Translating poetry may be impossible, but, as the words quoted at the start of Lowell's poem imply, that is where imaginative activity sets up its stall ... or as an aphoristic phrase of George Santayana's goes: 'The Difficult is that which can be done immediately; the Impossible that which takes a little longer.'[61]

---

[61] George Santayana, cited in James Geary (ed.), *Geary's Guide to the World's Great Aphorists* (London: Bloomsbury, 2007), p. 347.

Bibliography

Alcides, Rafael, *Agradecido como un pero* (Havana: Editorial Letras Cubanas, 1983).

Alighieri, Dante, *La divina commedia*, ed. Natalino Sapegno, vol. 1: *Inferno*, 2nd edn. (Florence: 'La Nuova Italia' Editrice, 1968).

Andrade, Carlos Drummond de, *Cuore numeroso*, ed. Vincenzo Arsillo (Rome: Donzelli Editore, 2002).

Armitage, Simon, *Sir Gawain and the Green Knight* (London: Faber & Faber, 2007).

Arnold, Matthew, *The Complete Prose Works* vol. 1: *On the Classical Tradition*, ed. R. H. Super (Ann Arbor: University of Michigan Press, 1960).

Auden, W. H., *Forewords and Afterwords*, selected by Edward Mendelson (London: Faber & Faber, 1973).

— *The English Auden: Poems, Essays and Dramatic Writings 1927-1939*, ed. Edward Mendelson (London: Faber & Faber, 1977).

— *Collected Poems*, ed. Edward Mendelson, 2nd edn. (New York: Vintage, 1991).

Ayto, John, *Twentieth Century Words* (Oxford: Oxford University Press, 1999).

Barry, David, 'Faustian Pursuits: The Political-Cultural Dimension of Goethe's Weltliteratur and the Tragedy of Translation', *German Quarterly*, vol. 74, no. 2 (Spring 2001).

Bate, Jonathan, *Shakespeare and Ovid* (Oxford: Oxford University Press, 1993).

Beaton, Roderick, *George Seferis Waiting for the Angel: A Biography* (New Haven and London: Yale University Press, 2003).

Beckett, Samuel, *Collected Poems 1930-1978* (London: John Calder, 1986).

Benjamin, Walter, *Selected Writings* vol. 2 part 1, and vol. 3, ed. Howard Eiland and Michael W. Jennings, trans. Edmund Jephcott, Howard Eiland, et al. (Cambridge, MA, and London: Harvard University Press, 2002).

Biguenet, John, and Schulte, Rainers (ed.), *The Craft of Translation* (Chicago: University of Chicago Press, 1989).

Bishop, Elizabeth, *Complete Poems 1927-1979* (New York: Farrar, Straus and Giroux, 1983).

— *One Art: Selected Letters*, ed. R. Giroux (London: Chatto and Windus, 1994).

— *Edgar Allan Poe & the Juke-Box: Uncollected Poems, Drafts, and Fragments*, ed. Alice Quinn (New York: Farrar, Straus and Giroux, 2006).

— *Poems, Prose, and Letters*, ed. Robert Giroux and Lloyd Schwartz (New York: Library of America, 2008).

— and Lowell, Robert, *Words in the Air: The Complete Correspondence*, ed. Thomas Travisano and Saskia Hamilton (New York: Farrar, Straus and Giroux, 2008).

Blake, William, *The Marriage of Heaven and Hell*, ed. Geoffrey Keynes (Oxford: Oxford University Press, 1975).

Blanchot, Maurice, *La part du feu* (Paris: Gallimard, 1949).

Boyle, Nicolas, *Goethe: The Poet and the Age*, vol. 1: *The Poetry of Desire* (Oxford: Oxford University Press, 1991), p. 355.

Braddon, Mary Elizabeth, *Aurora Floyd*, ed. P. D. Edwards (Oxford: Oxford University Press, 1996).

Brodsky, Joseph, *On Grief and Reason: Essays* (London: Hamish Hamilton, 1996).

— *So Forth: Poems* (London: Hamish Hamilton, 1996).

Burnshaw, Stanley (ed.), *The Poem Itself* (1960), (Fayetteville: University of Arkansas Press, 1995).

Carpenter, Humphrey, *A Serious Character: The Life of Ezra Pound* (London: Faber and Faber, 1988).

Carson, Ciaran, *The Alexandrine Plan* (Oldcastle, Co. Meath: Gallery Press, 1998).

— *The Inferno of Dante Alighieri* (New York: New York Review Books, 2002).

Caselli, Daniela, and La Penna, Daniela (ed.), *Twentieth-Century Poetic Translation: Literary Cultures in Italian and English* (London: Continuum, 2008).

Cavafy, C. P., *Poèmes*, trans. George Papoutsakis (Paris: Société d'édition 'Les Belles-lettres', 1958).

— [as Kavafis, Constantino], *Poesie*, ed. Filippo Maria Pontani (Milan: Mondadori, 1961).

— *Collected Poems*, trans. Edmund Keeley and Philip Sherrard (Princeton, NJ: Princeton University Press, 1975).

— *The Collected Poems*, trans. Evangelos Sachperoglou, Greek text ed. Anthony Hirst, introduction by Peter Mackridge (Oxford: Oxford University Press, 2007).

Caws, Mary Ann, *Surprised by Translation* (Chicago: University of Chicago Press, 2006).

Celan, Paul, *Die Gedichte: Kommentierte Gesamtausgabe in einem Band* ed. Barbara Wiedermann (Frankfurt am Main: Suhrkamp, 2003).

Chapman, George, *Chapman's Homer*, 2 vols., ed. Allardyce Nicoll (London: Routledge & Kegan Paul, 1957).

Clement, Jennifer, *New and Selected Poems* (Exeter: Shearsman Books, 2008).

Cohn, Robert Greer, and Gilespie, Gerald (eds.), *Mallarmé in the Twentieth Century* (Madison and Teaneck, NJ: Fairleigh Dickinson University Press, 1998).

Cohn, Stephen, 'Rilke Where Art Thou?', *Agenda* vol. 42 nos. 2-3 (Spring 2007).

Coleridge, Samuel Taylor, *Poetical Works I: Poems (Reading Text)*, part 2, ed. J. C. C. Mays (Princeton, NJ: Princeton University Press, 2001).

Collingwood, R. G., *The Principles of Art* (Oxford: Oxford University Press, 1938).

Collo, Paolo (ed.), *The Raven, Ulalume, Annabel Lee di Edgar Allan Poe nella traduzione di Fernando Pessoa* (Turin: Einaudi, 1995).

Constantine, David, *Hölderlin* (Oxford: Oxford University Press, 1988).

— *A Living Language: Newcastle/Bloodaxe Poetry Lectures* (Tarset: Bloodaxe, 2004).

Cook, Elizabeth (ed.), *John Keats* (Oxford: Oxford University Press, 1990).

Cowden Clarke, Charles and Mary, *Recollections of Writers* (London, 1878).

Davidson, Donald, *Inquiries into Truth and Interpretation* (1984), 2nd edn. (Oxford: Oxford University Press, 2001).

— *Subjective, Intersubjective, Objective* (Oxford: Oxford University Press, 2001).

— *Truth and Predication* (Cambridge, MA: Harvard University Press, 2005).

— *Truth, Language, and History* (Oxford: Oxford University Press, 2005).

Davie, Donald, 'Hardy's Virgilian Purples', *Agenda*, Thomas Hardy Special Issue, vol. 10 nos. 1-2 (Spring-Summer 1972).

— *The Poet in the Imaginary Museum: Essays of Two Decades*, ed. Barry Alpert (Manchester: Carcanet Press, 1977).

Dentith, Simon, *Epic and Empire in Nineteenth-Century Britain* (Cambridge: Cambridge University Press, 2006).

Dodsworth, Martin, 'The God of Details', *Agenda* vol. 43 no. 1 (Autumn 2007).

Donne, John, *The Complete English Poems*, ed. A. J. Smith (Harmondsworth: Penguin Books, 1971).

Dougles, Keith, *The Complete Poems*, ed. Desmond Graham, 3rd edn. (Oxford: Oxford University Press, 1998).

Dowson, Ernest, *The Poems*, ed. Mark Longaker (Philadelphia: University of Pennsylvania Press, 1963).

Dryden, John (trans.), *Virgil's Aeneid*, ed. Fredrick M. Keener (Harmondsworth: Penguin Books, 1997).

Durrell, Lawrence, 'Bernard Spencer', *London Magazine* vol. 3 no. 10 (January 1964).

— *Collected Poems 1931-1974*, ed. James A. Brigham (London: Faber & Faber, 1980).

Eco, Umberto, *Mouse or Rat? Translation as Negotiation* (London: Weidenfeld & Nicholson, 2003).

Eliot, T. S., *On Poetry and Poets* (London: Faber & Faber, 1957).

— *Collected Poems 1909-1962* (London: Faber & Faber, 1963).

Empson, William, *Some Versions of Pastoral* (London: Chatto & Windus, 1935).

— *The Complete Poems*, ed. John Haffenden (Harmondsworth: Allen Lane, 2000).

Everett, Barbara, *Poets in Their Time: Essays on English Poetry from Donne to Larkin* (London: Faber & Faber, 1986).

Feden, Robin, et al. (eds.), *Personal Landscape: An Anthology of Exile* (London: Editions Poetry London, 1945).

Felstiner, John, *Paul Celan: Poet, Survivor, Jew* (New Haven and London: Yale University Press, 1995).

Fisher, Roy, *The Long and the Short of It: Poems 1955–2005* (Tarset: Bloodaxe, 2005).

Flint, F. S., *Otherworld: Cadences* (London: Poetry Bookshop, 1920).

Forrest-thomson, Veronica, *Poetic Artifice: A Theory of Twentieth-Century Poetry* (Manchester: Manchester University Press, 1978).

— *Selected Poems*, ed. Anthony Barnett (London: Invisible Books, 1999).

Forster, E. M., *Pharos and Pharillon* (Richmond, Surrey: Hogarth Press, 1923).

— 'The Complete Poetry of C.P. Cavafy', *Two Cheers for Democracy* (1951), Arbinger Edition, ed. Oliver Stallybrass (London: Edward Arnold, 1972).

Forster, Leonard, (ed. and trans.), *The Penguin Book of German Verse* (Harmondsworth: Penguin Books, 1957).

Franco, Veronica, *Poems and Selected Letters*, ed. and trans. Ann Rosalind Jones and Margaret F. Rosenthal (Chicago: University of Chicago Press, 1998).

Frost, Robert, *Collected Poems, Prose, & Plays*, ed. Richard Poirier and Mark Richardson (New York: Library of America, 1995).

— *The Collected Prose of Robert Frost*, ed. Mark Richardson (Cambridge, MA: Harvard University Press, 2008).

Gadamer Hans-georg, *Truth and Method*, trans. Garrett Braden and John Cumming (London: Sheed and Ward, 1975).

Gaisser, Julia Haig (ed.), *Catullus in English* (Harmondsworth: Penguin Books, 2001).

Gass, William H., *Reading Rilke: Reflections on the Problems of Translation* (New York: Basic Books, 1999).

Gautier, Théophile, *Émaux et Camées*, ed. Claudine Gothor-Mersch (Paris: Gallimard, 1981).

Gibson Jr., Roger F. (ed.), *The Cambridge Companion to Quine* (Cambridge: Cambridge University Press, 2004).

Glock, Hans-johann, *Quine and Davidson on Language, Thought and Reality* (Cambridge: Cambridge University Press, 2003).

Goehr, Lydia, 'Three Blind Mice: Goodman, McLuhan, and Adorno on the Art of Music and Listening in the Age of Global Transmission', *New German Critique* 104, vol. 35 no. 2 (Summer 2008).

Goethe, Johann Wolfgang von, *Wilhelm Meister*, trans. Thomas Carlyle (1824), 2 vols. (London: J. M. Dent, 1912).

— *Selected Verse*, ed. and trans. David Luke (Harmondsworth: Penguin Books, 1964).

— *West-östlicher Divan*, ed. Hans Albert Maier (Tübingen: Max Niemeyer, 1965).

Goodman, Nelson, *Languages of Art: An Approach to a Theory of Symbols* (1976; 2nd edn., Indianapolis, IN, and Cambridge: Hackett, 1988).

Griffiths, Eric, 'Blanks, misgivings, fallings from us', *The Salt Companion to Peter Robinson*, ed. Adam Piette and Katy Price (Cambridge and Perth: Salt Publications, 2007).

— and Reynolds, Matthew (eds.), *Dante in English* (Harmondsworth: Penguin Books, 2005).

Gross, John (ed.), *The Oxford Book of Aphorisms* (Oxford: Oxford University Press, 1983).

Grünbein, Durs, *Ashes for Breakfast: Selected Poems*, trans. Michael Hofmann (London: Faber & Faber, 2005).

Haffenden, John, *William Empson: Among the Mandarins* (Oxford: Oxford University Press, 2005).

Hahn, Lewis Edwin (ed.), *The Philosophy of Donald Davidson* (Chicago and La Salle, IL: Open Court, 1999).

Hamburger, Michael [anonymously], 'Poetic Moods', *Times Literary Language* no. 2807, 16 December 1955.

— (trans.), *An Unofficial Rilke: Poems 1912-1926* (London: Anvil Press, 1981).

Hamilton, Ian, 'Four Conversations', *London Magazine* vol. 4 no. 8, November 1964.

Hardy, Thomas, *The Collected Letters*, 7 vols., ed. Richard L. Purdy and Michael Millgate (Oxford: Oxford University Press, 1978–87).

— *The Complete Poetical Works of Thomas Hardy*, ed. Samuel Hynes, 5 vols. (Oxford: Oxford University Press, 1982–95).

Hass, Robert, Introduction, *The Selected Poetry of Rainer Maria Rilke*, trans. Stephen Mitchell (London: Picador, 1982).

Haughton, Hugh, '"The Importance of Elsewhere": Mahon and Translation', *The Poetry of Derek Mahon*, ed. Elmer Kennedy-Andrews (Gerrards Cross: Colin Smyth, 2002).

— *The Poetry of Derek Mahon* (Oxford: Oxford University Press, 2007).

Hazlitt, William, *The Complete Works of William Hazlitt*, 21 vols., ed. P. P. Howe (London and Toronto: J. M. Dent, 1930).

Heaney, Seamus, *North* (London: Faber & Faber, 1975).

— *Beowulf: A New Translation* (New York: Norton, 2000).

Hill, Geoffrey, *Collected Critical Writings*, ed. Kenneth Hayes (Oxford: Oxford University Press, 2008).

Hofmann, Michael, *Behind the Lines: Pieces on Writing and Pictures* (London: Faber & Faber, 2001).

— and Lasdun, James (ed.), *After Ovid: New Metamorphoses* (London: Faber & Faber, 1994).

Hölderlin, Friedrich, *Selected Poems*, trans. David Constantine, 2nd expanded edn. (Newcastle upon Tyne: Bloodaxe Books, 1996).

— *Selected Poems and Fragments*, trans. Michael Hamburger, ed. Jeremy Adler (Harmondsworth: Penguin Books, 1998).

Hughes, Ted, *Tales from Ovid: Twenty-Four Passages from the* Metamorphoses (London: Faber & Faber, 1997).

— *Selected Translations*, ed. Daniel Weissbort (London: Faber & Faber, 2006).

Hunt, Leigh, *Lord Byron and Some of His Contemporaries* (London, 1828).

James, John, *Collected Poems* (Great Wilbraham: Salt Publications, 2002).

Jiménez, Juan Ramón, and Machado, Antonio, *Selected Poems*, trans. J. B. Trend and J. L. Gili, and Charles Tomlinson and Henry Gifford (Harmondworth: Penguin Books, 1974).

Johnson, Samuel, *The Complete English Poems*, ed. J. D. Fleeman (Harmondsworth: Penguin Books, 1971).

Keats, John, *The Letters of John Keats* ed. Maurice Buxton Forman, 4th edn. (London: Oxford University Press, 1952).

— *The Collected Poems*, ed. Miriam Allott (London: Longmans, 1970).

— *The Complete Poems*, ed. John Barnard, 3rd edn. (Harmondsworth: Penguin Books, 1988).

Kehew, Robert (ed.), *Lark in the Morning: The Verses of the Troubadours*, trans. Ezra Pound, W. D. Snodgrass, and Robert Kehew (Chicago: University of Chicago Press, 2005).

Kinsley, James (ed.), *The Poems and Fables of John Dryden* (Oxford: Oxford University Press, 1970).

Kirk, Ludwig (ed.), *Donald Davidson* (Cambridge: Cambridge University Press, 2003).

Kraus, Karl, *Half-Truths and One & One-and-a-Half Truths: Selected Aphorisms*, ed. and trans. Harry Zohn (Manchester: Carcanet Press, 1986).

— *Dicta and Contradicta,* trans. Jonathan McVity (Urbana and Chicago: Illinois University Press, 2001).

Larkin, Philip, *The Whitsun Weddings* (London: Faber & Faber, 1964).

— *Required Writing: Miscellaneous Pieces 1955–1982* (London: Faber & Faber, 1983).

— *Selected Letters of Philip Larkin 1940–1985*, ed. Anthony Thwaite (London: Faber & Faber, 1992).

— *Further Requirements: Interviews, Broadcasts, Statements and Books Reviews*, ed. Anthony Thwaite (London: Faber & Faber, 2001).

Lee, Guy (ed. and trans.), *The Poems of Catullus* (Oxford: Oxford University Press, 1990).

Leopardi, Giacomo, *Canti*, ed. John Humphreys Whitfield, rev. ed. (Manchester: Mancheser University Press, 1978).

Liddell, Robert, *C. P. Cavafy* (London: Duckworth, 2000).

Lisboa, Eugénio, and Taylor, L. C., *A Centenary Pessoa* (Manchester: Carcanet Press, 1995).

Lloyd, Rosemary, *Mallarmé: The Poet and His Circle* (Ithaca, NY, and London: Cornell University Press, 1999).

Longville, Tim (ed.), *For John Riley* (Leeds and Wirksworth: Grosseteste, 1979).

Lowell, Robert, *Imitations* (London: Faber and Faber, 1962).

— *Collected Poems*, ed. Frank Bidart et al. (London: Faber & Faber, 2003).

— *The Letters of Robert Lowell*, ed. Saskia Hamilton (London: Faber and Faber, 2005).

Lucie-smith, Edward (ed.), *British Poetry since 1945* (Harmondsworth: Penguin Books, 1970).

Macarthy, Patricia (ed.), *Agenda, Translation as Metamorphosis* vol. 40 no. 4 (Autumn-Winter 2004).

Macinnes, Mairi, *The Girl I Left Behind Me: Poems of a Lifetime* (Nottingham: Shoestring Press, 2007).

Mahon, Derek, *Collected Poems* (Oldcastle, Co. Meath: Gallery Press, 1999).

— *Adaptations* (Oldcastle, Co. Meath: Gallery Press, 2006).

Mallarmé, Stéphane, *Oeuvres complètes*, ed. Henri Mondor and G. Jean-Aubry (Paris: Gallimard, 1945).

— *Mallarmé*, ed. Anthony Hartley (Harmondsworth: Penguin Books, 1965).

— *Mallarmé: The Poems*, ed. Keith Bosley (Harmondsworth: Penguin Books, 1977).

— *Collected Poems*, trans. Henry Weinfield (Berkeley and Los Angeles: University of California Press, 1995).

— *Collected Poems and Other Verse*, trans. E. H. and A. M. Blackmore, introduced by Elizabeth McCombie (Oxford: Oxford University Press, 2006).

Mandelstam, Nadezhda, *Hope Against Hope: A Memoir*, trans. Max Hayward (London: Collins Harvill, 1989).

Mandelstam, Osip, *Selected Essays*, trans. Sidney Monas (Austin: University of Texas Press, 1977).

McGuinness, Patrick, *The Canals of Mars* (Manchester: Carcanet Press, 2004).

Mead, Matthew, *The Autumn-Born in Autumn: Selected Poems* (London: Anvil Press, 2008).

Mead, Ruth and Matthew, *Word for Word: Selected Translations from German Poets* (London: Anvil Press, 2009).

Millier, Brett C., *Elizabeth Bishop: Life and the Memory of It* (Berkeley and Los Angeles: University of California Press, 1993).

Montale, Eugenio, *Tutte le poesie*, ed. Giorgio Zampa (Milan: Mondadori, 1984).

— *Il secondo mestiere: Prose 1920-1979*, 2 vols., ed. Giorgio Zampa (Milan: Mondadori, 1996).

— *Le occasioni*, ed. Dante Isella (Turin: Einaudi, 1996).

Montefoschi, Paola (ed), *Album Ungaretti* (Milan: Mondadori, 1989).

Moody, A. David, *Ezra Pound: Poet. A Portrait of the Man and his Work: I. The Young Genius 1885-1920* (Oxford: Oxford University Press, 2007).

Morgan, Edwin, *The New Divan* (Manchester: Carcanet Press, 1977).

Motion, Andrew, *Keats* (London: Faber & Faber, 1997).

Muldoon, Paul, *Quoof* (London: Faber & Faber, 1983).

— *The Annals of Chile* (London: Faber & Faber, 1994).

— *The End of the Poem: Oxford Lectures on Poetry* (London: Faber & Faber, 2006).

Mulhall, Stephen, *Wittgenstein's Private Language: Grammar, Nonsense, and Imagination in* Philosophical Investigations, §§ 243-315 (Oxford: Oxford University Press, 2007).

Nabokov, Vladimir, *The Annotated Lolita*, ed. A. Appel Jr. (New York: Vintage, 1970).

— *Strong Opinions* (New York: Vintage, 1973).

— *Selected Letters 1940-1977*, ed. Dimitri Nabokov and M. J. Bruccoli (San Diego, New York, London: Harcourt Brace Jovanovich, 1989).

Nicholl, Charles, *Someone Else: Arthur Rimbaud in Africa 1880-1891* (London: Jonathan Cape, 1997).

— *The Lodger: Shakespeare on Silver Street* (Harmondsworth: Penguin Books, 2008).

Ní Chuilleanáin, Eiléan, *Selected Poems*, ed. Peter Fallon (Oldcastle, Co. Meath: Gallery Press and London: Faber & Faber, 2008).

Ní Dhomhnaill, Nuala, *Pharaoh's Daughter* (Oldcastle, Co. Meath: Gallery Books, 1990).

Nietzsche, Friedrich, *On the Genealogy of Morals,* trans. Douglas Smith (Oxford: Oxford University Press, 1996).

O'donoghue, Bernard, *Sir Gawain and the Green Knight* (Harmondsworth: Penguin Books, 2006).

Orr, Peter (ed.), *The Poet Speaks: Interviews with Contemporary Poets* (New York: Barnes and Noble, 1966).

Parks, Tim, *Translating Style: The English Modernists and Their Italian Translators* (London: Cassell, 1998).

Pasolini, Pier Paolo, *La meglio gioventú,* ed. Antonia Arveda (Rome: Salerno Editrice, 1998).

Paterson, Don, *Nil Nil* (London: Faber & Faber, 1993).

— *The Eye: A Version of Machado* (London: Faber & Faber, 1999).

— *Landing Light* (London: Faber & Faber, 2003).

— *The Book of Shadows* (London: Picador, 2004).

— *Orpheus: A Version of Rilke's* Die Sonette an Orpheus (London: Faber & Faber, 2006).

Perloff, Marjorie, *Wittgenstein's Ladder: Poetic Language and the Strangeness of the Ordinary* (Chicago: University of Chicago Press, 1996).

— *Differentials: Poetry, Poetics, Pedagogy* (Tuscaloosa: University of Alabama Press, 2004).

— *The Vienna Paradox: A Memoir* (New York: New Directions, 2004).

Perse, St.-John, *Anabasis,* trans. T. S. Eliot (London: Faber & Faber, 1959).

— *Oeuvres complètes* (Paris: Gallimard, 1972).

Pessoa, Fernando, *Selected Poems,* trans. Jonathan Griffin, 2nd ed. (Harmondsworth: Penguin Books, 1982).

Petrarca, Francesco, *Canzoniere,* ed. Marco Santagata (Milan: Mondadori, 1996).

Poe, Edgar Allan, *The Complete Poems,* ed. Thomas Ollive Mabbott (Urbana and Chicago: University of Illinois Press, 2000).

Poole, Adrian and Maule, Jeremy (ed.), *The Oxford Book of Classical Verse in Translation* (Oxford: Oxford University Press, 1995).

Pope, Alexander, *The Odyssey of Homer,* ed. Maynard Mack (London: Methuen, 1967).

Pound, Ezra, *The Translations of Ezra Pound,* ed. Hugh Kenner (London: Faber & Faber, 1953).

— *ABC of Reading* (London: Faber & Faber, 1961).

— *Collected Shorter Poems* (London: Faber & Faber, 1968).

— *Personae: The Shorter Poems,* rev. ed. L. Baechler and A. Walton Litz (New York: New Directions, 1990).

— *Poems and Translations,* ed. Richard Sieburth (New York: The Library of America, 2003).

Pozzi, Antonia, *Breath: Poems and Letters,* ed. and trans. Lawrence Venuti (Middletown, CT: Wesleyan University Press, 2002).

Prater, Donald, *A Ringing Glass: The Life of Rainer Maria Rilke* (Oxford: Oxford University Press, 1986).

Pushkin, Alexandr, *Eugene Onegin: A Novel in Verse,* trans. Vladimir Nabokov, vol. 1: *Introduction and Translation* (Princeton, NJ: Princeton University Press, rev. ed. 1975).

— [as Pushkin, Alexander], *Eugene Onegin*, trans. Charles Johnston, introduction by John Bayley (Harmondsworth: Penguin Books, 1979).

Queneau, Raymond, *Esercizi di stile*, trans. Umberto Eco (Turin: Einaudi, 1986).

Quine, W. V., *Word and Object* (Cambridge, MA: MIT Press, 1960).

— *Theories and Things* (Cambridge, MA: Harvard University Press, 1981).

Ransom, John Crowe, *Selected Poems*, 2nd edn. (New York: Knopf, 1991).

Rees, William (trans.), *French Poetry 1820-1950* (Harmondsworth: Penguin Books, 1990).

Reeves, Gareth, *Listening In* (Manchester: Carcanet Press, 1993).

Ricks, Christopher, *The Force of Poetry* (Oxford: Oxford University Press, 1984).

— *Essays in Appreciation* (Oxford: Oxford University Press, 1996).

Rilke, Rainer Maria, *Sonnets to Orpheus*, trans. J. B. Leishman (London: Hogarth Press, 1936).

— *Selected Poems*, trans. J. B. Leishmann (London: Hogarth Press, 1941).

— *Die Gedichte* (Frankfurt am Main: Insel Verlag, 1986).

Rimbaud, Arthur, *Selected Verse Poems of Arthur Rimbaud*, trans. Norman Cameron (London: The Hogarth Press, 1942).

— *Oeuvres complètes*, ed. Antoine Adam (Paris: Gallimard, 1972).

Reid, Christopher, *For and After* (London: Faber & Faber, 2003).

Robb, Graham, *Rimbaud* (London: Picador, 2000).

Robinson, Peter, *This Other Life* (Manchester: Carcanet Press, 1988).

— 'Philip Larkin: Here and There', *Review of English Literature* (Kyoto) vol. 59 (March 1990).

— *In the Circumstances: About Poetry and Poets* (Oxford: Oxford University Press, 1992).

— 'The Music of Milan', *Times Literary Supplement* no. 4868, 19 July 1996.

— '"Una fitta di rimorso": Dante in Sereni', *Dante's Modern Afterlife: Reception and Response from Blake to Heaney*, ed. Nick Havely (Basingstoke: Macmillan, 1998).

— *Poetry, Poets, Readers: Making Things Happen* (Oxford: Oxford University Press, 2002).

— *The Great Friend and Other Translated Poems* (Tonbridge, Kent: Worple Press, 2002).

— *Selected Poems 1976-2001* (Manchester: Carcanet, 2003).

— 'Translating Sereni: A Discussion', *Translation and Literature* vol. 12 no. 1: *Modernism and Translation*, guest ed. Adam Piette (Spring 2003).

— *L'attaccapanni e altre poesie*, Italian versions by the author with Ornella Trevisan (Milan: Moretti & Vitali, 2004).

— *Twentieth Century Poetry: Selves and Situations* (Oxford: Oxford University Press, 2005).

— 'C. Hatakeyama and W. E.', *Versions of Empson*, ed. Matthew Bevis (Oxford: Oxford University Press, 2007).

Roche Jr., Thomas P. (ed.), *Petrarch in English* (Harmondsworth: Penguin Books, 2005).

Rouse, W. H. D. (ed.), *Shakespeare's Ovid, Being Arthur Golding's Translation of the Metamorphoses* (London: Centaur Press, 1961).

Scarry, Elaine, *The Body in Pain: The Making and Unmaking of the World* (New York: Oxford University Press, 1985).

Seferis, George, 'The King of Asini', trans. Lawrence Durrell, Bernard Spencer, and Nanos Valaoritis, *Personal Landscape* vol. 2 no. 3 (1944).

— *The King of Asine and Other Poems*, trans. Bernard Spencer, Nanos Valaoritis, and Lawrence Durrell (London: John Lehmann, 1948).

— *A Levant Journal*, trans. Roderick Beaton (Jerusalem: Ibis Editions, 2007).

Senn, Fritz, *Joyce's Dislocutions: Essays on Reading as Translation*, ed. John Paul Riquelme (Baltimore and London: Johns Hopkins University Press, 1984).

Sereni, Vittorio, *Il musicante di Saint-Merry* (1981), 2nd edn., Introduction by P. V. Mendaldo (Turin: Einaudi, 2001).

— *Gli immediati dintorni*, primi e secondi (Milan: Il Saggiatore, 1983).

— *Poesie*, ed. Dante Isella (Milan: Mondadori, 1995).

— *Scritture private con Fortini e con Giudici* (Bocca di Magra: Edizioni Capannina, 1995).

— *Sentieri di gloria: Noti e ragionamenti sulla letteratura*, ed. G. Strazzeri (Milan: Mondadori, 1996).

— *La tentazione della prosa*, ed. Giovanna Raboni (Milan: Mondadori, 1998).

— *Un tacito mistero: Il carteggio Vittorio Sereni-Alessandro Parronchi (1941-1982)*, ed. Barbara Colli and Giovanna Raboni (Milan: Feltrinelli, 2004).

— *The Selected Poetry and Prose of Vittorio Sereni*, ed. and trans. Peter Robinson and Marcus Perryman (Chicago: University of Chicago Press, 2006).

Seth, Vikram, *The Golden Gate* (London: Faber & Faber, 1986).

Shakespeare, William, *The Complete Works*, ed. Stanley Wells and Gary Taylor (Oxford: Oxford University Press, 1988).

— *The Complete Sonnets and Poems*, ed. Colin Burrow (Oxford: Oxford University Press, 2002).

Shapcott, Jo, *Phrase Book* (Oxford: Oxford University Press, 1992).

Spark, Muriel, *The Prime of Miss Jean Brodie* (Harmondsworth: Penguin Books, 1965).

Spencer, Bernard, *Collected Poems*, ed. Roger Bowen (Oxford: Oxford University Press, 1981).

Steiner, George, *After Babel: Aspects of Language and Translation* (Oxford: Oxford University Press, 1975).

Stern, J. P., *Lichtenberg: A Doctrine of Scattered Occasions Reconstructed from His Aphorisms and Reflections* (London: Thames and Hudson, 1963).

Sterne, Laurence, *A Sentimental Journey*, ed. Graham Petrie (Harmondsworth: Penguin Books, 1967).

Stevens, Wallace, *Collected Poetry and Prose*, ed. Frank Kermode and Joan Richardson (New York: Library of America, 1997).

Thwaite, Anthony (ed.), *Larkin at Sixty* (London: Faber & Faber, 1982).

Tomlinson, Charles (ed.), *The Oxford Book of Verse in English Translation* (Oxford: Oxford University Press, 1980).

— *Poetry and Metamorphosis* (Cambridge: Cambridge University Press, 1983).

Tonks, Rosemary, *Notes on Cafés and Bedrooms* (London: Putnam, 1963).

— *Iliad of Broken Sentences* (London: Bodley Head, 1967).

Tranter, John, *Borrowed Voices* (Nottingham: Shoestring Press, 2002).

Ungaretti, Giuseppe, *Vita d'un uomo: Saggi e interventi*, ed. Mario Diacono and Luciano Rebay (Milan: Mondadori, 1974).

Vallejo, César, *Twenty Poems*, trans. John Knoepfle, James Wright, and Robert Bly (Madison, MN: Sixties Press, 1962).

— *Poemas Humanos /Human Poems*, trans. Clayton Eshleman (London: Jonathan Cape, 1969).

— *Complete Later Poems 1923-1938*, trans. Valentino Gianuzzi and Michael Smith (Exeter: Shearsman Books, 2005).

— *'Spain, Take This Chalice from Me' and Other Poems*, trans. Margaret Sayers Peden, ed. Ilan Stavans (Harmondsworth: Penguin Books, 2008).

Valéry, Paul, *Oeuvres*, vol. 1, ed. Jean Hytier (Paris: Gallimard, 1957).

Vendler, Helen, *The Art of Shakespeare's Sonnets* (Cambridge, MA: Harvard University Press, 1997).

— *Coming of Age as a Poet: Milton, Keats, Eliot, Plath* (Cambridge, MA: Harvard University Press, 2003)

Venuti, Lawrence, *The Scandals of Translation: Towards an Ethics of Difference* (London: Routledge, 1998).

— (ed.), *The Translations Studies Reader* (London: Routledge, 2000).

— *The Translator's Invisibility: A History of Translation*, 2nd edn. (London: Routledge, 2008).

Waller, Edmund, *The Poems*, 2 vols., ed. G. Thorn Drury (London: A. H. Bullen, 1901).

Warner, Simon, 'Raising the Consciousness? Revisiting Allen Ginsberg's Trip in 1965', *Centre of the Creative Universe: Liverpool and the Avant-garde*, ed. Christoph Grunenberg and Robert Knifton (Liverpool: Liverpool University Press, 2007).

Weil, Simone, *Simone Weil: An Anthology*, ed. Siân Miles (Harmondsworth: Penguin Books, 2005).

Weissbort, Daniel (ed.), *Translating Poetry: The Double Labyrinth* (Basingstoke: Macmillan, 1989).

— and Eysteinsson, Astradure (eds.), *Translation — Theory and Practice: A Historical Reader* (Oxford: Oxford University Press, 2006).

Wilde, Oscar, *The Soul of Man under Socialism and Selected Critical Prose*, ed. Linda Dowling (Harmondsworth: Penguin Books, 2001).

Williams, Bernard, *The Sense of the Past: Essays in the History of Philosophy*, ed. Myles Burneat (Princeton and Oxford: Princeton University Press, 2006).

Wilmer, Clive, *Of Earthly Paradise* (Manchester: Carcanet Press, 1992).

— 'The Translator's Apology', *Agenda, Sheet Music* vol. 42 no. 2 (Autumn 2006).

Wittgenstein, Ludwig, *Tractatus Logico-Philosophicus* (1922), trans. C. K. Ogden (London: Routledge, 1995).

— *Lectures and Conversations on Aesthetics, Psychology and Religious Belief*, ed. Cyril Barrett (Oxford, Blackwell, 1966).

— *Culture and Value: A Selection from the Posthumous Remains*, rev. 2nd edn., ed. G. H. von Wright et al., trans. Peter Winch (Oxford: Blackwell, 1998).

— *Philosophical Investigations*, trans. G. E. M. Anscombe, 3rd edn. (Oxford: Blackwell, 2001).

Wollheim, Richard, *Art and Its Objects*, 2nd edn. (Cambridge: Cambridge University Press, 1980).

Wood, Michael, 'Start Thinking', *London Review of Books* vol. 24 no. 5, 7 March 2002.

Wordsworth, William, *Poetical Works*, ed. Thomas Hutchinson, rev, ed. Ernest de Selincourt (Oxford: Oxford University Press, 1969).

— *Poems, in Two Volumes, and Other Poems, 1800-1807*, ed. Jared Curtis (Ithaca, NY: Cornell University Press, 1983).

— *Selected Poems*, ed. Damian Walford Davies (London: Everyman's Library, 1994).

Yeats, W. B., *The Variorum Edition of the Poems of W. B. Yeats*, ed. Peter Allt and R. K. Alspach (New York: Macmillan, 1971).

— *The Collected Poems*, 2nd edn., ed. Richard J. Finneran (Basingstoke: Macmillan, 1991).

Index